Table Laid for First Course of a Formal Dinner

THE
INTERNATIONAL
COOK BOOK

Totally Different and Complete with Suggested
Menus, rules for Proper Table Service, an
abundance of Practical Recipes for every need,
Famous International Recipes, all Home Tested,
Cookery Technique and Complete Indexing

Compiled and written by

MARGARET WEIMER HEYWOOD

in co-operation with

WORLD'S FAMOUS CHEFS

ILLUSTRATED IN COLORS

Conceived and Published by

MERCHANDISERS INC.

BOSTON, MASS.

1929

Printed and Bound in the U.S.A. by
KINGSPORT PRESS, INC., KINGSPORT, TENNESSEE

Dedicated to

THE HOMEMAKERS OF THE WORLD

*that its use may prove of real benefit in
the development of better food
and service and may create a
broader conception of
Table Hospitality*

THE AUTHORS

NEVER before has a cook book gone so far in securing its contents as has The International Cook Book. The greatest compilation of recipes ever assembled is in this book.

The co-author and compiler of The International Cook Book is Mrs. Margaret Weimer Heywood. Mrs. Heywood finished her Home Economics training at The Stout Institute, Menomonie, Wisconsin, in 1916, and has a B.S. degree from Columbia Teachers College. Since that time she has been doing home economics work throughout the entire United States, meeting thousands of women and gaining the knowledge of just what these women of today need and want in a cook book.

Upon invitation, chefs from the leading hotels of the world have sent their favorite and most famous recipes to The International Cook Book. The women of America will now be able to prepare for their own tables dishes that are totally different, for they need only refer to this book to enable them to prepare courses that are in good taste and from most any country they may desire.

And too, the chefs of the largest and best ocean liners, whose menus are greatly praised and talked of by travelers to all ports of the world, are giving their choicest and most desired recipes to The International Cook Book, in order that the women of this country may use them in their daily meals.

MARGARET WEIMER HEYWOOD

in co-operation with the following

WORLD'S FAMOUS CHEFS

Chef ANTHONY ROTA	*The Mayflower*, Washington, D. C.
Chef ERNEST E. AMIET	*Palmer House*, Chicago, Ill.
Chef ANGLADE	*Royal Hotel*, Deauville, France
Chef LOUIS BALTERA	*Château Frontenac*, Quebec, Canada
Chef JAN C. BORN	*S.S. Rotterdam*, Holland-America Line
Chef F. BOSCHEN	*S.S. Berlin*, North German Lloyd Line
Chef S. BORRA	*Hotel Tiberias*, Tiberias, Palestine

Chef ALESSANDRO CEDRINI . . . *S.S. Conte Grande*, Lloyd Sabaudo Line
Chef ENRICO COMOGLIO . . . . *Grand Hotel*, Venice, Italy
Chef EUGENE CORDIER . . . . *S.S. Rochambeau*, French Line
Chef GUSTAVE COUTANT . *Restaurant des Ambassadeurs*, Deauville, France
Chef E. G. DASTUGUES . . . . . . *Turnberry Hotel*, Ayrshire, Scotland
Chef GEORGE DHOYER . . . . . . *S.S. Statendam*, Holland-America Line
Chef HARRY DUKE . . . . . *S.S. President Madison*, American Mail Line
Chef LOUIS DUPEROUX . . . . *Adelphi Hotel*, Liverpool, England
Chef A. ECKERT . . . . *Hotel Bellevue*, Dresden, Germany
Chef GASTON FERRAND . . . . *Hotel du Golf*, Deauville, France
Chef A. FRANCHI . . . . *Château Laurier*, Ottawa, Canada
Chef PAUL GERMAIN . . . . *S.S. Belgenland*, Red Star Line
Chef GUILLAUME GUILLOU . . . . *Australia Hotel*, Sydney, Australia
Chef MAX GUTTERA . . . . *Grand Hotel Elefant*, Graz, Austria
Chef WILLIAM HAAG . . . . . *The Macdonald Hotel*, Edmonton, Canada
Chef DAVID DE HAAY . . . . . *S.S. Volendam*, Holland-America Line
Chef WILLIAM H. HASEL . . . . *S.S. Adriatic*, White Star Line
Chef KYUTARO HISATOMI . . . . *The Nara Hotel*, Nara, Japan
Chef ERNEST HUNZIKER . . . . . *S.S. Leviathan*, United States Lines
Chef A. JAMMES . . . . *Central Hotel*, Glasgow, Scotland
Chef KERN . . *S.S. Empress of Australia*, Canadian Pacific Railway Co.
Chef EDGARD KINA . . . . . . *Royal Hawaiian Hotel*, Honolulu, Hawaii
Chef KINJIRO KOJIMA . . . . . . *Fujiya Hotel*, Miyanoshita, Japan
Chef JEAN KRITICOS . . . . . . *Hotel Grande-Bretagne*, Athens, Greece
Chef JACQUES LINDAUER . . . . . . *S.S. Île de France*, French Line
Chef GASTON MAGRIN . . . . *S.S. France*, French Line
Chef A. MALLE . . . . . *Pera Palace Hotel*, Constantinople, Turkey
Chef BAPTISTE MONNIER . . . . . *Grand Nouvel Hotel*, Lyon, France
Chef PIERRE MOREAU . . . . . *Hotel Normandy*, Deauville, France
Chef JOHN MCGUIRE . . . *Newfoundland Hotel*, St. John's, Newfoundland
Chef ALBERTO MORA . . . . *Hotel Vittoria*, Venice, Italy
Chef DON FRANCISCO MORENO . . . . *Hotel Imperial*, Guadalajara, Mexico
Chef NEWHOUSE . . . . *Gleneagles Hotel*, Perthshire, Scotland
Chef HENRI ODIAU . . . . *Banff Springs Hotel*, Banff, Canada
Chef JACOB PIES . . . . *Coblenzer Hof Hotel*, Coblenz, Germany
Chef JOHN PEARSE . . . . *S.S. Majestic*, White Star Line
Chef JOSEPH ROELLI . . . . *Midland Hotel*, Manchester, England
Chef ROGET . . . . *Hotel Imperial*, Boulogne-sur-Mer, France
Chef ADOLPHE ROUQUIER . . . . *Hotel Negresco*, Nice, France
Chef A. SALKOWSKI . . . . . *S.S. Bremen*, North German Lloyd Line
Chef CARLO SCARABELLI . . . . *Jasper Park Lodge*, Jasper, Canada
Chef KARL SCHNEIDER . . . . *S.S. New York*, Hamburg-American Line
Chef W. SCHULZE . . . . *Hotel Atlantic*, Hamburg, Germany
Chef SIMON *S.S. Empress of France*, Canadian Pacific Railway Company
Chef A. TURC . . . . *Hotel Excelsior*, Rome, Italy
Chef MAURICE VANE . . . . . *The Fort Garry Hotel*, Winnipeg, Canada
Chef KARL VETTER . . . . *Hotel Tyrol*, Innsbruck, Austria
Chef S. WEIL . . . . *New Grand Hotel*, Yokohama, Japan
Chef JOHN ZAPPA . . . . *Hotel Excelsior*, Belgrade, Jugoslavia

MARGARET WEIMER HEYWOOD

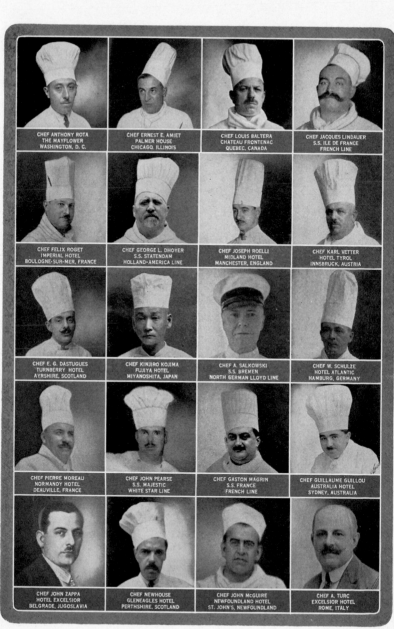

CHEF ANTHONY ROTA
THE MAYFLOWER
WASHINGTON, D. C.

CHEF ERNEST E. AMIET
PALMER HOUSE
CHICAGO, ILLINOIS

CHEF LOUIS BALTERA
CHATEAU FRONTENAC
QUEBEC, CANADA

CHEF JACQUES LINDAUER
S.S. ILE DE FRANCE
FRENCH LINE

CHEF FELIX ROGET
IMPERIAL HOTEL
BOULOGNE-SUR-MER, FRANCE

CHEF GEORGE L. DHOYER
S.S. STATENDAM
HOLLAND-AMERICA LINE

CHEF JOSEPH ROELLI
MIDLAND HOTEL
MANCHESTER, ENGLAND

CHEF KARL VETTER
HOTEL TYROL
INNSBRUCK, AUSTRIA

CHEF E. G. DASTUGUES
TURNBERRY HOTEL
AYRSHIRE, SCOTLAND

CHEF KINJIRO KOJIMA
FUJIYA HOTEL
MIYANOSHITA, JAPAN

CHEF A. SALKOWSKI
S.S. BREMEN
NORTH GERMAN LLOYD LINE

CHEF W. SCHULZE
HOTEL ATLANTIC
HAMBURG, GERMANY

CHEF PIERRE MOREAU
NORMANDY HOTEL
DEAUVILLE, FRANCE

CHEF JOHN PEARSE
S.S. MAJESTIC
WHITE STAR LINE

CHEF GASTON MAGRIN
S.S. FRANCE
FRENCH LINE

CHEF GUILLAUME GUILLOU
AUSTRALIA HOTEL
SYDNEY, AUSTRALIA

CHEF JOHN ZAPPA
HOTEL EXCELSIOR
BELGRADE, JUGOSLAVIA

CHEF NEWHOUSE
GLENEAGLES HOTEL
PERTHSHIRE, SCOTLAND

CHEF JOHN McGUIRE
NEWFOUNDLAND HOTEL
ST. JOHN'S, NEWFOUNDLAND

CHEF A. TURC
EXCELSIOR HOTEL
ROME, ITALY

CHEF M. KERN
S.S. EMPRESS OF AUSTRALIA
CANADIAN PACIFIC RAILWAY CO.

CHEF ERNEST HUNZIKER
S.S. LEVIATHAN
UNITED STATES LINES

CHEF ALBERTO MORA
HOTEL VITTORIA
VENICE, ITALY

CHEF F. BOSCHEN
S.S. BERLIN
NORTH GERMAN LLOYD LINE

CHEF ALESSANDRO CEDRINI
S.S. "CONTE GRANDE"
LLOYD SABAUDO LINE

CHEF RICHARD SIMON
S.S. EMPRESS OF FRANCE
CANADIAN PACIFIC RAILWAY CO.

CHEF KARL SCHNEIDER
S.S. NEW YORK
HAMBURG-AMERICAN LINE

CHEF DAVID Y. DE HAAY
S.S. VOLENDAM
HOLLAND-AMERICA LINE

CHEF JACOB PIES
COBLENZER HOF HOTEL
COBLENZ, GERMANY

CHEF GASTON FERRAND
HOTEL DU GOLF
DEAUVILLE, FRANCE

CHEF HENRI ODIAU
BANFF SPRINGS HOTEL
BANFF CANADA

CHEF MAX GUTTERA
GRAND HOTEL ELEFANT
GRAZ, AUSTRIA

CHEF JAN C. BORN
S.S. ROTTERDAM
HOLLAND-AMERICA LINE

CHEF A. FRANCHI
CHATEAU LAURIER
OTTAWA, CANADA

CHEF ENRICO COMOGLIO
GRAND HOTEL
VENICE, ITALY

CHEF DON FRANCISCO MORENO
HOTEL IMPERIAL
GUADALAJARA, MEXICO

CHEF CARLO SCARABELLI
JASPER PARK LODGE
JASPER, CANADA

CHEF ANGLADE
ROYAL HOTEL
DEAUVILLE, FRANCE

CHEF EUGENE CORDIER
S.S. ROCHAMBEAU
FRENCH LINE

CHEF A. MALLE
PERA PALACE HOTEL
CONSTANTINOPLE, TURKEY

CHEF PAUL GERMAIN
S.S. BELGENLAND
RED STAR LINE

CHEF JEAN KRITICOS
HOTEL GRANDE BRETAGNE
ATHENS, GREECE

CHEF WILLIAM HAAG
HE MACDONALD HOTEL
EDMONTON, CANADA

CHEF A. ECKERT
HOTEL BELLEVUE
DRESDEN, GERMANY

CHEF A. JAMMES
CENTRAL HOTEL
GLASGOW, SCOTLAND

CHEF MAURICE VANE
THE FORT GARRY HOTEL
WINNIPEG, CANADA

CHEF HARRY DUKE
S.S. PRESIDENT MADISON
AMERICAN MAIL LINE

CHEF ADOLPHE ROUQUIER
HOTEL NEGRESCO
NICE, FRANCE

CHEF LOUIS DUPEROUX
ADELPHI HOTEL
LIVERPOOL, ENGLAND

CHEF GUSTAVE COUTANT
RESTAURANT DES AMBʼSSADEURS
DEAUVILLE, FRANCE

CHEF EDGARD KINA
ROYAL HAWAIIAN HOTEL
HONOLULU, HAWAIIAN ISLANDS

CHEF WILLIAM H. HASEL
S.S. ADRIATIC
WHITE STAR LINE

CHEF BAPTISTE MONNIER
GRAND NOUVEL HOTEL
LYON, FRANCE

CHEF KYUTARO HISATOMI
THE NARA HOTEL
NARA, JAPAN

CHEF S. BORRA
HOTEL TIBERIAS
TIBERIAS, PALESTINE

CHEF S. WEIL
NEW GRAND HOTEL
YOKOHAMA, JAPAN

CONTENTS

SECTION THREE

SECTION FOUR

SECTION FIVE

ILLUSTRATIONS

INTRODUCTION

THE International Cook Book has been published as an authoritative reference book, with the hope that it will prove an inspiration and help to all women interested in better foods and better service.

The International Cook Book has been compiled and completed, after many years' experience in research, study, testing, and proving the world's requirements, that it may justly be accredited The World's Most Practical Cook Book.

You will find this book the world's most complete treatment of Food and Service divided into the four following sections.

SECTION ONE — *Menus and Table Service*

What foods shall we serve together? This is a question that is more frequently asked than almost anything else. It is a known fact that good food is often spoiled by having it served in combination with something else that does not blend with it either in color or flavor. In Section One we discuss food so as to give help in planning and serving attractive meals to the family. Each menu has been carefully taken into consideration by itself, and the combination of food suggested with directions given will be of help to even the uninitiated. Suggested menus for all occasions are given.

Good food is frequently ruined by amateurish table service. Realizing that Service is as important to the meal as the food itself, complete information is given as to how to serve properly for all occasions — the arrangement of the silver, the tablecloth, and napkins, the dishes, glasses, and the decorations. All recipes for dishes suggested in Menus will be found in Section Two. See Index for pages.

SECTION TWO — *Recipes*. SECTION THREE — *International Recipes*

In the planning and writing of The International Cook Book, only recipes are given which can easily be applied to home use.

xiii

The whole world holds a wealth of cookery knowledge, but not many of us are aware that outside of our small realm food is served that is "different." It is our purpose to help housewives incorporate this colorful palatable food into their menus that has inspired us to compile The International Cook Book. We have gathered from the leading chefs of the world the best that they have to offer and have translated their recipes so that they may easily be used in the home kitchen. Every recipe, both foreign and domestic, has been Home Tested.

To plan three meals for the family day after day may indeed be the monotonous course that is sometimes spoken of when we have not a great source of information to draw from, but with recipes handed to us here from countries of the world, there is no reason why the planning of the food for the family should not be interesting and educational. With these international recipes it should be an easy and enjoyable task to plan for the family meals that are nutritious, interesting, palatable, and colorful. The real homemaker is a cook at heart, and a good cook is an artist at heart. Combined with these recipes are foods that will blend so beautifully in color and flavor that each meal served with the help of The International Cook Book will be truly a picture.

Section Four — *Cookery Technique*

Vitally interesting subjects such as — How to Buy Food, Measurements in Cookery, Methods of Cookery, Proper Temperatures for Cooking, Weights and Measures, Food Equivalents, and Calories and Value are discussed in this section.

Section Five — *Indexing*

Without a complete and simplified index, no cook book can be successful. In The International Cook Book this feature is particularly emphasized, and its index has been so compiled that its readers may find anything in the book instantly.

Illustrations

In the book you will find full-page illustrations, in actual colors, showing the different cuts of meat with each part marked by name, to assist the homemakers who now have difficulty when marketing in knowing whether or not they are buying the right kind of meats.

Other illustrations display correct table service and some attractively prepared dishes.

Thus in The International Cook Book, one will find not only an abundance of real practical recipes for every need, but suggested menus — proper table service — famous international recipes, allowing and encouraging the homemakers to prepare surprise and totally different meals — all subjects of cookery technique — and complete indexing.

The International Cook Book will prove a real education to the homemaker, whether she is a bride unaccustomed to cookery, or an experienced cook.

                    THE PUBLISHERS

SECTION I
Menus and Table Service

CHAPTER I

Breakfasts

BREAKFAST is the beginning of every day. The quality
of the meal served affects our disposition for the whole
day more often than we realize. How it is served, where
it is served, and what is served has a decided influence on us
mortals.

The value of breakfast is considerable. Now and again we
meet someone who does not like to eat breakfast. This may be
the truth, or perhaps it is just one of the many rules the human
race has made for itself because of the diet schedules that are
now in vogue. Whether or not one likes to eat breakfast, it is
an essential meal, and if attractively served, one which will
appeal to anyone. From a dietetic point of view it is altogether
fitting and proper to begin the day with a good meal.

Breakfast may be served in the dining room, but many homes
have succumbed to the popularity of the breakfast room or
breakfast nook. Wherever it is served, this meal should be
attractive. Not only must the food be of good quality, but the
appointments of the room and table should be given careful
consideration. Have the place where you are to serve breakfast
light, bright, clean, and cheerful.

If possible, build a breakfast room or convert some room into
a breakfast room. Furnish this room so that it will have individuality and will be colorful. Window hangings, table linen,
dishes, and pictures should be harmonious and cheerful.

If the regular dining room is used to serve breakfast, this meal
may be distinguished from other meals by reserving for its use
special linen and, whenever possible, special table appointments.
Today we consider the breakfast admirable if it is a bit unusual,
gay, and attractive. Breakfast linen should be colorful. The
square cloth with the bright border of stripes, conventional
design, or flowers is recommended. Napkins should match, of
course. The table decoration should be simple, unassuming, and
good to look at. Flowers or fruit are suitable for the breakfast
centerpiece. Seasonal table decorations may be used, such as

partridge berries, bitter sweet, bayberries, or bouquets from the fruit trees in the spring.

Lay the table carefully whether for family or for guests. It is just as important to consider the family, and care should be taken each time the table is laid. For breakfast, simplicity is the keynote for a well-set table. A plate is laid for each person. The knife is placed to the right of the plate and the fork to the left. Next to the knife is placed a dessert spoon for cereal and next to the cereal spoon the fruit spoon. The coffee spoon is placed on the saucer with the cup. The bread and butter plate is put to the left of the breakfast plate at the tip of the fork. The bread and butter spreader is placed on the bread and butter plate. The water glass is put to the right of the plate near the tip of the knife and the napkin carefully folded is placed to the left of the fork.

The silver used for breakfast should be carefully kept and should always be clean and polished. The cups and saucers should be grouped at the right of the hostess so that she may serve the coffee. The coffee service, which includes coffee pot, sugar, and creamer, is placed in front of the hostess. The salt and pepper shakers are placed in pairs at opposite sides of the table.

The family breakfast is of greatest importance, of course, for it is the one that we have to consider every day.

Suggested Menus for the Family Breakfast follow:

Menu 1

Orange juice
Oatmeal with cream and sugar
Four-minute eggs

Toast   Butter   Strawberry jam
               Coffee   Milk

Menu 2

Stewed prunes
Broiled bacon

Bran muffins   Butter   Ginger marmalade
               Coffee   Milk

Menu 3

Half grapefruit
Dry cereal with sugar and cream
Plain omelet

Graham toast   Butter   Apple jelly
            Coffee   Milk

Menu 4

Sliced oranges
Buckwheat pancakes with maple syrup
Country sausage
Coffee   Milk

Menu 5

Baked apple

Scrambled eggs   Broiled bacon
Corn muffins   Butter   Currant and raspberry jelly
            Coffee   Milk

Dry or cooked cereal served with sugar and cream is optional as a breakfast food. Where there are growing children in the family, cereal is an essential part of the breakfast menu, but in planning a breakfast for adults the cereal may be omitted.

Fruit, such as sliced peaches, strawberries or fresh berries of any kind, may be served with a dry cereal, sugar, and cream as a first course for breakfast, in which case the regular fruit course is omitted. Prunes, dates, or raisins may be added to a cooked cereal, and again the regular fruit course may be omitted.

When any one of the foregoing breakfast menus is to be served, the fruit course is already on the table when the family is called.

Jams and jellies help to decorate the most matter-of-fact breakfast. When they are served for breakfast they are put on the table with the fruit course. They are most attractive in silver or glass jelly or compote dishes. The jelly spoon is put into the dish rather than beside it on the table. Both jams and jellies serve two purposes. As a toast or hot-bread accompaniment they are delicious, and they lend beauty to the table because of their sparkle and color. Butter, either in balls or squares, is placed on the individual bread and butter plate. A tiny sprig of parsley on each piece of butter makes it more attractive.

Toast may be made at the table or may be served from the kitchen on a bread plate, carefully covered with a napkin to keep it from getting cold. Hot breads are served on a bread plate similarly covered with a napkin. Pancakes may be served in a covered dish from the kitchen or, when an electric pancake griddle is available, they may be baked at the table, assuring their crispness. Waffles, too, are better if cooked on an electric waffle iron at the table.

You will find that the most jaded appetite will respond to a breakfast that is carefully planned, well cooked, and attractively served.

The Sunday Morning Breakfast is a meal of decided individuality. It is one of the meals that we try to make just a little bit different. Menus follow:

Menu 1

Fresh strawberries with sugar and cream
Broiled chicken

Popovers   Butter   Grape jelly

Coffee   Milk

Menu 2

Orange juice
Broiled ham slices

Waffles   Maple syrup

Coffee   Milk

Menu 3

Half grapefruit
Broiled bacon

French toast   Maple syrup or confectioners' sugar
Coffee   Milk

Menu 4

Diced fresh pineapple
Dropped eggs on toast   Broiled bacon
Doughnuts
Coffee   Milk

Menu 5

Iced cantaloupe
Broiled lamb chop with water-cress garnish
Whole wheat muffins   Butter   Apricot conserve
Coffee   Milk

A special container for syrup is advisable. This may be of silver, glass, or china. A silver container that harmonizes with the flat silver and coffee service is the very best. A sugar shaker for the confectioners' sugar used on waffles, pancakes, or French toast may be of glass or china, but one of silver that harmonizes with the salts and peppers is the most desirable. Salt and pepper shakers, when placed on the breakfast table, are placed in pairs on either side of the table within easy reach of the guests. The sugar shaker is kept near the hostess, so that she can put the sugar on the waffles or the French toast as she serves them. French toast is served from the kitchen in a covered silver dish or on a silver platter covered with a napkin.

Garnishes enhance the beauty of any food. With the Sunday morning hot meats use either parsley or water cress, with radish roses or slices of tomato as a garnish. The popularity of the Sunday Morning Breakfast may be increased if, during the warm weather, this meal is served either on the porch or in the garden; and on a rainy day nothing can be more delightful than the Sunday Morning Breakfast served by an open fire in the living room. The open-fire breakfast is also recommended during the cold winter months, when the cheer of the fire extends itself to the meal.

The hour for Sunday Morning Breakfast is usually later than the regular breakfast of the week, and for this reason it may be more hearty. Frequently the Sunday Morning Breakfast is the most substantial meal of the day, being followed later by a light supper or an afternoon tea. A little thought and careful planning, a little special service, different china and linen from that which is used during the week, will make the Sunday Morning Breakfast delightful and an occasion that is looked forward to by all. A centerpiece of fruit or flowers appropriate to the season of the year adds charm to the appearance of the table.

What can be more cordial than the Breakfast Party? There is a hospitality about food that is generally underrated. It is a delightful custom to begin the day with a gathering around the breakfast table of friends and family, and one which is fast gaining favor.

The table is laid with the same care and thought that is given the regular breakfast table, with perhaps an added touch by using more elaborate linen and china, a little different from that usually used.

The menu may be symbolic of the occasion. It may consist of favorite dishes of the guest of honor, if it be a birthday party; it may be a Patriotic Breakfast or a May-day Breakfast; it may be an Easter Morning Breakfast or a Christmas Breakfast; or better still, it may just be the menu for a Breakfast Party for congenial friends who want to start the day right. The following menus are suggested:

Menu 1

Iced balls of watermelon and cantaloupe
Fried chicken
Waffles with maple syrup

| Cinnamon pinwheels | Strawberry jam |
| Coffee | Milk |

Menu 2

Chilled honeydew melon
Breakfast grill

| Popovers | Jelly doughnut |
| Coffee | Milk |

Menu 3

Orange juice, or strawberries with hull, served with confectioners' sugar
Calves' liver with bacon

Corn muffins	Butter
Plum conserve	Molasses cookies
Coffee	Milk

Menu 4

Breakfast figs with cream
Fried fillet of sole with lemon and tomato garnish
Potato chips
Blueberry muffins
Coffee   Milk

Menu 5

Half grapefruit with maraschino cherry
Grilled ham

Egg pancakes   Butter   Maple syrup

Coffee   Milk

The watermelon and cantaloupe balls suggested in the first menu should be served very cold. The combination of color stimulates the appetite and lends beauty to the table. They are also a delicious first course for any meal. Luscious red strawberries, carefully washed, chilled, and served with the hulls as a first course for breakfast, are ornamental as well as palatable. For a spring breakfast these are perhaps the most perfect first course.

The fried chicken, fried to a crisp brown and garnished with parsley, is good to look at and to eat. Cinnamon pinwheels, jelly doughnuts, and molasses cookies give an added touch to the menu.

A group of congenial friends gathered around the breakfast table, served with a tempting array of well-prepared food, appreciate the festiveness of the occasion and will help establish the custom of the Breakfast Party.

Whether we are serving the Family Breakfast, the Sunday Morning Breakfast, or the Breakfast Party, the underlying principles never vary. The attractive appearance of the table, the fitness of the service, and the goodness of the food have been considered. The same consideration is given the breakfast table for the family as is given the breakfast table for the party. The butter, either balls or cubes, and the first course are on the table when the guests are called; the coffee is served by the hostess at the table. Garnishes, such as paprika, parsley, slices of lemon, water cress, and slices of tomato should be used freely. Food that is attractive is always palatable, and the high coloring of the garnishes gives the final touch of beauty. A dash of paprika and a sprig of parsley will glorify and change the appearance of even a dropped egg on toast.

For Wedding Breakfasts we suggest the following menus:

Menu 1

Iced balls of cassava and honeydew melon garnished with fresh
strawberries

Chicken patties   Potato balls with parsley
Sweetbread and almond salad   Potato chips
Grilled tomatoes with garnish of water cress
Vegetable aspic ring
Dainty Parker House rolls   Mint jelly   Red currant jelly
Strawberry ice cream   Lemon sherbet
Marmalade tarts   Assorted cakes
Salted nuts   Coffee   Bonbons

Menu 2

Strawberries with hulls served with confectioners' sugar
Chicken salad   French fried potatoes
Lobster Newburgh   Potato puffs
Asparagus loaf in aspic   Anchovy rolls
Clover leaf rolls   Grape fudge   Strawberry jam
Lady fingers   Rosettes   Angel cake
Pistachio ice cream   Raspberry ice
Salted nuts   Coffee   Mint patties

The service for the Wedding Breakfast differs from our regular
breakfast service in that it is more elaborate. The linen is of the
finest. Lace cloths are frequently used as a table cover. The
floral centerpiece is delicate. Roses and lilies of the valley are
most frequently used. The service is formal. The buffet wedding
breakfast is the most popular form of service. The table should
be covered with a lace or fine linen cloth. The flowers are put
in the center of the table. Silver candlesticks with candles are
arranged around the floral centerpiece. The coffee urn is placed
at one end of the table. If two urns are used they are placed
at either end of the table and the cups are arranged around the
urns. Sugar and cream in silver containers are placed on a small
tray so that they can be easily served with the coffee. The plates
and napkins are arranged in piles on the table. The silver, which
is shining, is arranged in rows, — forks, fruit spoons, coffee
spoons, and dessert spoons. The food is arranged on platters
and dishes and placed on the table attractively and within
easy reach.

CHAPTER II

Luncheons

FOR second consideration in planning the meals for the day we have luncheons. In this meal flexibility of menu is essential.

We have the Family Luncheon, which is served in homes to every member of the family, or we have the luncheon which is served to only the children and the mother when the father does not come home. We have the Bridge or Party Luncheon and the Formal Luncheon, which has gained such favor in recent years that it is now one of our most popular forms of entertainment. Whether the luncheon to be served is of the family type or whether it belongs to the Formal or Party class, the menu must be given careful consideration.

Luncheon is usually served in the dining room. A fine linen luncheon cloth, either hemstitched or embroidered, with napkins to match, may be used as a table cover. Or the luncheon set of either linen or lace with the individual square for each guest is also popular. The setting of the luncheon table is simple. Lay the cloth or the doilies on the table first, and for a centerpiece use a bowl of fruit or a bowl of flowers. The centerpiece for the luncheon table may be seasonal, in that fresh flowers from the garden may be used during the summer months and berries in the fall, with Christmas decorations during the holiday season. The table is laid by giving each person a service plate, a knife, fork, salad fork, and teaspoon. The knife is placed at the right of the service plate and the teaspoon next to the knife. The salad fork is placed at the left of the service plate and the luncheon fork at the left of the salad fork. The napkin carefully folded is at the left of the luncheon fork. At the tip of the fork we put the bread and butter plate with the bread and butter spreader on it. Goblets of crystal or colored glass are popular for the luncheon table. The goblet is placed at the tip of the knife. The service plate is on the table, and the first course may be on it before the guests or family are called. Salt and pepper shakers are put on the table when it is laid. If the salts and peppers are individual, they are placed at the right of each service. If only two pairs of salt and pepper shakers are used for the luncheon table, they are placed at opposite ends of the table.

Colored glass may be used instead of china in serving the luncheon to family or guests. This colored glass may harmonize with the menu so that a very definite color scheme is carried out.

In some families every member of the family comes home to luncheon, and in other families only the mother and the children are at home. In either case the family luncheon menu must be carefully planned and considered. It is of vital importance that the children be trained in correct table service and form good food habits. During the winter months or on a damp, dreary, rainy day at any time during the year, nothing is more acceptable for a luncheon dish than a bowl of soup. This is of equal nutritive value for children and adults. Left-over vegetables, cut fine or chopped, mixed with a thin white sauce and seasoned, will make a delicious luncheon soup. Garnish with finely cut parsley and a dash of paprika and serve with either a hot wafer or a hot cheese biscuit. A soup of this sort can be served either in a cup as a first course or in a bowl as the main dish, supplemented with a salad and a hot bread and followed by a dessert. Left-over meat or fish may be combined with vegetables and hard-cooked eggs, mixed with medium thick white sauce and served in timbales or in pattie shells as a main dish for luncheon, around which you may build an attractive menu with the addition of relishes, salads, hot breads, and dessert.

During the warm months, similar combinations, using meat or fish with a vegetable, egg, and celery, and mixed with salad dressing, may be served on a lettuce leaf as a salad for your main dish for a family luncheon. Precede the salad with a consommé or fruit cup. Serve a hot bread with the salad and complete the meal with a good but simple dessert.

It is understood that the ingenious housewife utilizes left overs attractively, and it takes a more clever planner and cook to serve a meal attractively when utilizing left overs than it does to begin with fresh material.

The following family luncheon menus are popular and can be adapted to groups of both grown-ups and children.

Menus for Family Luncheon:

Menu 1

Cream of asparagus soup

Fruit salad   Hot cheese biscuit

Coffee

Menu 2

Tomato with cottage cheese salad   Blueberry muffin

Apple cake

Coffee

Menu 3

Lamb chop   Sautéed pineapple

Grilled sweet potato   New peas

Melba toast

Strawberry shortcake

Coffee

Menu 4

Cheese soufflé   Lettuce and tomato salad

Toasted English muffin   Blackberry jam

Prune whip with cream

Coffee

Menu 5

Consommé   Wafers

Open club sandwich

Hot gingerbread with hard sauce

Coffee

A good fruit salad, made from either fresh fruit or canned, served with a hot biscuit after a soup course, will take the place of a main dish and a dessert, provided that the salad is substantial, palatable, and attractive. It is of vital importance in serving the luncheon for the family or guests that the food be prepared carefully so that hot things are hot and cold things are cold. Paprika, spices, and crisp fresh parsley will add to the attractive appearance of any luncheon menu. The family luncheon is one of our most informal meals and for this reason one of our most popular.

Bridge Luncheons or Party Luncheons of any sort are more popular today than formerly. The Luncheon Party may be served at small tables of four guests each, or in the dining room at a large table, in which case the guests later may play bridge in the living room at the small tables. In any event the tables are laid carefully. If the small card tables are used, luncheon cloths with napkins to match are the best sort of table cover, but for the large dining table the lace luncheon cloths or luncheon sets with the individual squares for each person are most popular. The table decoration for the small tables may be a single rose in a bud vase, and for the large table a bowl or basket of flowers attractively arranged is best. The centerpiece should be beautiful, but simple and low enough so that the guests can easily see over it.

A service plate is laid for each guest and the silver placed carefully, with the knife and spoon to the right of the service plate and the salad fork and luncheon fork to the left. The goblet, bread and butter plate, with bread and butter spreader and the napkin, are placed as for the family luncheon. Crystal or colored glass may be used. The Luncheon Party may be an Announcement Party, a Birthday Party, a Farewell Party, or in celebration of some patriotic occasion, as a George Washington Luncheon; or it may be a Valentine Party. Whatever it is, the Luncheon Party is carefully thought out and planned. The table is laid with the occasion in mind, and often a color scheme is used, the colors being emphasized by table decorations and foods.

The first course for the Luncheon Party may be on the service plate when the guests are called to the table. The party menus suggested can be used to advantage at any season of the year.

Menu 1

Fruit cocktail
Lobster salad with garnish of stuffed eggs and tomato
French fried potato balls
Hot biscuit   Butter   Gooseberry jam
Cheese and crackers
Coffee

Menu 2

Half grapefruit

Broiled chicken Potato chips Peas in timbales

Popovers Butter Apple jelly

Tomato aspic salad   Wafers

Ice-cream sandwich with butterscotch sauce

Coffee

Menu 3

Cream of pea soup Cheese wafers

Club sandwich (three decker)

Assorted relishes

Strawberry shortcake

Coffee

Menu 4

Cream of tomato soup

Sandwich loaf with garnishes of cucumber, tomato, radishes, celery,
stuffed eggs, olives and pickles, lettuce and parsley

Individual butterscotch pie

Coffee

Menu 5

Consommé Wafers

Lamb chop grill

Mint jelly   Watermelon pickle

Romaine salad Muffins Butter

Individual lemon meringue pie

Coffee

The fruit cocktail or fruit cup may be the first course of any luncheon. This is best if the fruits used are cut not too fine and served very cold. Fresh strawberries, raspberries, blackberries, cherries, green grapes, or other fruit will tend to add color and flavor to the cocktail. Maraschino cherries and the highly colored bottled grapes, either green or red, will add color to the cocktail in seasons of the year when fresh fruits are not available. The fruit cocktail should be served in regular fruit cocktail glasses. These may be of colored glass or crystal. The crystal ones may have a silver rim, thereby enhancing their beauty. The large bowl of the fruit cocktail should be filled with shaved ice. This cocktail course may be on the table when the guests are called.

Jams, jellies, and relishes add zest to the luncheon menu. The relish dishes, with divisions for jellies, jams, pickles, and radishes, make the service more attractive. Whole figs, stuffed prunes, and cucumber rings are relish suggestions that are delicious.

Salads, such as lobster and chicken, are particularly nice if garnished with halves of chilled tomato and stuffed egg. Caviar, stuffed olives, onions, or nut meats may be used in the filling for the egg.

Hot breads for the company luncheon are just as popular as the hot breads for the family luncheon. They are served on a silver plate carefully covered with a napkin.

For the Bridge Luncheon the sandwich loaf with its attractive garnish of eggs and vegetables may be made large enough to be brought to the table whole and served by the hostess at the table; or if the guests are served at small tables the sandwich loaf may be made into small individual loaves serving four guests each, and one guest at each table will act as hostess and serve the loaf at her table.

For the Formal Luncheon the following menus may be used:

Menu 1

Slices of honeydew melon with chopped candied ginger
Chicken broth   Wafers
Hearts of celery
Fried chicken   Potato balls
Asparagus on toast Melba toast
Assorted relishes
Hearts of artichoke salad
Cheese puffs
Strawberry mousse Dainty angel food cakes
Coffee Bonbons

Menu 2

Half grapefruit

Tomato bouillon   Finger rolls

Curled celery and olives

Broiled salmon   Parsley potatoes

Peas   Dinner rolls

Blackberry jelly   Mint jelly

Endive and water-cress salad   Cucumber slices

Russian loaf

Coffee   Bonbons

The table cover for the formal luncheon is usually lace, — either a large lace cloth or a long runner of lace with individual lace mats for each guest. The silver is polished to a shining brightness and carefully placed on the table with the knife and spoon at the right of the service plate and the salad fork and luncheon fork at the left of the service plate. The coffee spoon is placed on the saucer with the coffee cup. The goblet, which may be either crystal or colored glass, is placed at the right of the service plate near the tip of the knife, and the bread and butter plate with the bread and butter spreader on it is placed at the left of the service plate near the tip of the fork. The napkin, carefully folded, is placed at the left of the fork. The salt and pepper shakers, if individual, are placed at the right of each service, or if two pairs are used they are placed at opposite ends of the table. The bouillon or soup spoon is placed at the right of the teaspoon. The centerpiece for a formal luncheon is usually of flowers, which may be placed in a low silver bowl or basket and should be beautifully arranged. The colors should harmonize with the general color scheme of the luncheon.

The first course for the luncheon may be either cocktail or soup. The cocktail iced, or the soup hot, are on the table when the guests are called. The water is poured before the guests are called. The main course for the formal luncheon is served from the kitchen. The plate is placed before each guest as the service plate is removed. The salad is served as a separate course and the coffee is served with the dessert.

For the Bridge or Party Luncheon, coffee may be served from the buffet with the main luncheon course, or the hostess may serve the coffee at the table, having the silver service placed before her with the cups at her right. The coffee spoon is placed on the saucer with the cup. After the hostess has filled the cup with coffee the maid takes the cup and saucer and places it at the right of each guest. The maid then serves the guest with sugar and cream.

The serving of coffee with the main course for the Bridge or Party Luncheon is optional. If coffee is served with the main course, it is left on the table and again served with the dessert. If coffee has not been served with the main course, it is put on the table and served with the dessert. In this case the coffee may be served by the hostess as suggested previously, or it may be served from the buffet by the maid or from the kitchen.

There is little formality about the Bridge or Party Luncheon. It is usually a gathering of congenial friends or family who appreciate being together.

CHAPTER III

Dinners

DINNER is served. Whether this announcement is made by the hostess herself, the maid, or the butler, the call is a welcome one.

Family dinners are probably our most important consideration. We find that although other meals may be enjoyed by the entire family, it is more often dinner that brings us all together.

The table for the family dinner should be laid as attractively as possible. A complete table covering is desirable. This may be of lace or linen, preferably linen, with napkins to match. The family dinner table has a complete service laid for each member of the family. This may or may not have a service plate. Whether or not a service plate is used the knife is placed on the right and the salad fork on the left, with a distance between large enough to accommodate a dinner plate without crowding. A teaspoon, if one is to be used, is placed next to the knife and the dinner fork next to the salad fork. It is customary and desirable not to consider dessert in laying the table, but to bring the fork or spoon needed for the dessert to the table when the dessert is served. Bread and butter plates need not be put on the table for the dinner unless it is a family custom to serve bread and butter with the meal. It is better to serve rolls or biscuits with the dinner, and these may be placed on the regular dinner plate. The dinner rolls or biscuits may be served without butter or they may be buttered in the kitchen and brought to the table on a silver bread plate or basket, being covered carefully with a napkin to keep them warm. The goblet is placed at the right, at the tip of the knife, and the napkin, which should match the table cover, is placed at the left of the fork. Salt and pepper shakers, if two pairs are used, are placed at either end of the table. If individual salt and pepper shakers are used, they are placed at the right of each service. Like every other meal, the centerpiece is, of course, considered in laying the table. This should be flowers whenever possible, with the

35

flowers low enough so that the members of the family can easily see over them. A low bowl of silver or crystal is suggested as a holder for the table decoration. During spring and summer months fresh flowers from the garden may be used. The blossoms of fruit trees in the early spring or some of the late fall berries of brilliant color are excellent table decorations.

Candles will add to the festivity of the family meal. The candlesticks should be of silver or crystal, and should be kept highly polished and clean. If silver candlesticks are used, they should harmonize with the silver service and with the bowl which holds the flowers. The color of the candles depends on the preference of the hostess. They may be colored to harmonize with the flowers on the table or they may be of a contrasting color. They may be white. Either cream or ivory are the very best. Some people still associate the using of candles with a party. Today, however, the importance of the family is especially emphasized. We appreciate that nothing is too good for our own people, and the family dinner has come to be an outstanding occasion of every day. Because of this and because the candlelight is soft and restful, we have come to associate the use of candles with the family meal.

Menus for the family dinner may be as simple or as elaborate as the occasion warrants. The simplest meal should be attractive and nutritious. A first course may be served. If it is, it may be either a fruit cup, a simple canapé, or a light soup. With any of the menus following, the first course may be added or the meals may be served as they are given.

Menu 1

Roast leg of lamb   Browned potatoes

Peas with garnish of baby carrots

Mint jelly   Mustard pickle   Wafers

Tomato aspic salad

Apple pie   Cheese

Coffee

Menu 2

Roast beef with Yorkshire pudding
Buttered carrots   Riced potatoes
Turned lettuce salad
Rolls
Individual chocolate cream tart   Coffee

Menu 3

Baked pork chop with browned potato   Baked onion
Baked apples stuffed with raisins
Cole slaw   Baking powder biscuits
Lemon Soufflé   Coffee

Menu 4

Tomato bouillon
Steak   Baked potatoes
Fresh vegetable salad
Vanilla ice cream   Butterscotch sauce
Sponge cake   Coffee

Menu 5

Veal pie with biscuit top   Harvard beets
Water-cress salad
Steamed molasses pudding   Foamy hard sauce
Coffee

It is customary in family dinners to bring the food to the table and have the host or hostess serve. When a roast is used, it is well to place it in the center of the platter with the potatoes and vegetables arranged around it. Every cook is at heart an artist, and the ingenious cook can paint a beautiful picture with food. For example, in Menu 1, with the lamb roast as a center and the browned potatoes around it, with peas mounded at one end of the platter garnished with slices of carrot, and the whole garnished with parsley, we get a beautiful picture. Mint jelly is associated with lamb, and not only does it blend in well with the rest of the menu, but it helps to add to the attractiveness of the table. The mint jelly may be served from compote or jelly dishes. These are either silver or glass. Salad for the family dinner may be served as a separate course or may be on the table when the guests are called. The salad should be crisp and beautiful. Contrasting colors in food enhances its beauty. The tomato aspic salad served on a crisp bed of lettuce leaves and garnished with parsley is good to look at. The salad which is moulded individually may be heart shape, or any other form may be used. Mint jelly and the aspic salad have contrasting colors and are desirable for that reason.

When pie, such as the apple pie spoken of, is used for a dessert, it may be served in the kitchen or may be brought to the table for the hostess to serve to the family. Cheese or ice cream may be served with the pie. The top crust of an apple pie is particularly good if the cheese has been worked into the crust, using the regular cheese straw recipe.

Coffee for the family dinner is served by the hostess at the table. The coffee service, which is preferably of silver, is placed before the hostess and the cups and saucers are placed at the right. A coffee spoon is placed on each saucer as the coffee is served. The spoon or fork used for dessert is served with the dessert.

There is a sociability about food which we all recognize today, and the formal dinner party is rapidly gaining favor. A formal dinner should not be attempted without maid service. The service for a formal dinner differs from the family service in that a service plate is essential. It is placed on the table after the cloth has been laid. The cloth for a formal dinner should be of finest linen and may have a monogram with monogrammed napkins to match. Flowers placed in a silver or crystal basket or bowl form the centerpiece. Roses are perhaps the best table decoration for a formal dinner. Candles are used. The color of the candles is left to the discretion of the hostess. They may be either white, ivory, or cream, or they may harmonize in color with the flowers used. The salt and pepper shakers, if individual, are placed at the right of the service plate. If they are not individual, they are arranged in pairs at opposite ends of the table. Silver dishes with nuts and candies are placed on the table when the table is laid. Bread and butter plates are eliminated for the formal dinner. If rolls are served, they may be placed either on the dinner plate or on the table. The dinner knife is placed at the right of the service plate; the fish knife, if one is used, is placed at the right of the dinner knife. The soup spoon, cocktail spoon, or oyster fork are placed, when they are used, at the right of the dinner knife, or of the fish knife when it is used. The first thing used is placed at the extreme right of the dinner knife. The salad fork is placed at the left of the service plate, the dinner fork at the left of the salad fork, and the fish fork at the left of the dinner fork. The service plate need not match the regular dinner china. It may be of an entirely different pattern. The service plate is usually ornate, with a colored design either in the center or in the border. The dinner napkin, folded oblong or square with the monogram visible, is placed either on the service plate or at the left of the fish fork. The first course for a formal dinner, whether it is a fruit cocktail, an oyster cocktail, or strawberries served with the hull, may be on the table when the guests are called, or it may be brought in by the maid after the guests are seated. The water has been poured. The goblet for a formal dinner is crystal. Colored glass may be used for family dinners, but for the formal dinner it is not recommended. The candles of course are lighted. Soup, or the second course, is served by the maid. The cocktail is removed from the right and the soup is placed from the left onto the service plate. Celery and olives are served with the soup. These are served in silver dishes on a bed of shaved ice. Cheese wafers, cut in heart shape and served on a silver bread plate, are served with the soup. The fish course, if it is included in the menu, is served from the kitchen. The main course for the formal dinner is served from the kitchen on the dinner plate. The service plate is removed before the dinner plate is placed before the guest. A relish dish, the most popular one with divisions, with spiced cantelope, watermelon rind, an assortment of jellies and pickles, adds zest to the dinner menu, and beauty too. Light dinner rolls, small in size, may be served with the main course on a silver bread plate. Have the rolls carefully covered with a napkin to keep them warm.

The salad course is served separately at the formal dinner. The service of the salad course varies with the salad. We may have an individual salad prepared in the kitchen and each serving placed before the guest as the main course is removed, or the salad plates may be placed before each guest as the main course is removed and the salad served as a whole. If it is an aspic salad in ring mould, it is passed by the maid to each guest and the guest serves himself. Or the aspic mould may be placed before the hostess and she may serve each guest, giving the maid each plate to place before the guests. If this service is used, the table is cleared of the main course before the salad is brought in. Small, crisp wafers are served with the salad. The salad plate may harmonize or match the dinner china or it may be of crystal matching the goblets.

The dessert is served, when an ice or ice cream, in sherbet glasses of crystal on crystal plates. The sherbet glass and plate should match the goblet. Cake or cookies served with the dessert may be served on each plate individually, or may be brought to the table in a silver basket or dish and served by the maid.

Coffee for the formal dinner may be served with the dessert course. It is served from the kitchen or the buffet by the maid. After-dinner coffee may be served in the living room. During cold months or on a dreary rainy night, after-dinner coffee may be served around an open fire in the living room, or during warm weather it may be served on the porch. The silver after-dinner coffee service is preferable. The after-dinner coffee spoons are placed on the saucer with the cup. Bonbons and nuts are served with the dessert. The following menus may be used:

Menu 1

Grapefruit cocktail (cherry garnish)

Mock turtle soup   Cheese wafers

Celery   Olives   Radishes

Broiled chicken   Parsley potatoes

String beans   Pocket rolls

Currant jelly

Cucumber and green grape aspic   Wafers

Orange sherbet   Butterscotch whistles

Salted nuts   Coffee   Bonbons

An Attractive Family Dinner Table

Menu 2
Sardellan canapé

Consommé   Wafers
Celery   Pickles
Crown roast of pork with dressing   Browned potatoes
Cauliflower with garnish of browned crumbs and asparagus tips
Jellied apples
Endive salad   Cheese sticks
Cherry tart   Whipped cream
Salted almonds   Coffee   Peppermint Creams

Menu 3
Strawberries with hulls   Confectioners' sugar
Essence of celery soup   Melba toast
Ripe olives
Grilled ham   Sautéed pineapple
Au gratin potatoes
Spinach ring with garnish of hard-cooked eggs
Tomato and cucumber salad   Anchovy roll
Rhubarb tart   Whipped cream
Coffee   Mint patties

Menu 4
Fresh shrimp cocktail
Jellied consommé   Cheese crescent
Olives   Radishes
Roast fillet of beef   French fried potatoes
Lima beans   Grilled tomatoes
Lettuce and artichoke hearts salad   Wafer
Frozen cream puffs   Coffee

Menu 5
Oyster cocktail
Clear asparagus soup   Wafers
Curled celery   Olives
Roast chicken with garnish of sautéed orange and apple rings
Dressing
Chestnut purée   Baked squash en casserole
Potato rolls
Chinese cabbage   Tomato slices
Macaroon mousse   Lady fingers
Coffee   Cinnamon cream patties

Holiday dinners are always important. The Thanksgiving dinner, the Christmas dinner, and the New Year's dinner have a very definite place in our lives. The service for the holiday dinner is formal and the table is laid accordingly. The table decorations are planned for the occasion. For a Thanksgiving dinner they may be a basket of fruit. For Christmas, tiny Christmas trees or other holiday decorations. Menus planned for the holiday are seasonal. The following are suggested:

NEW YEAR'S DINNER

Caviar canapé
Cream of mushroom soup   Wafers
Olives   Hearts of celery
Crown roast of lamb   Dressing
Baked potato   Green peas   Baby carrots
Mint ice
Currant jelly
Pineapple cream cheese and anchovy salad   Wafers
Prune pie   Ice cream
Salted nuts   Coffee   Bonbons

EASTER DINNER

Smoked salmon canapé
Chicken bouillon   Bread sticks
Ripe olives   Stuffed olives
Baked ham   Candied sweet potato
Broccoli   Hollandaise sauce
Stuffed baked onions
Apple jelly   Watermelon pickle
Parker House rolls
Ice cream   Fresh strawberry sauce
Angel cakes   Coffee   Bonbons

JULY FOURTH DINNER

Jellied tomato consommé   Wafers
Broiled salmon   New peas
Potato chips   Clover leaf rolls
Green grape and pineapple salad   Cheese puffs
Strawberry shortcake   Coffee

THANKSGIVING DINNER

Orange basket   Mint garnish

Clam broth   Melba toast

Stuffed celery   Cucumber rings   Olives

Roast turkey   Sage dressing

Mashed potato   Giblet gravy

Mashed turnip   Boiled onions

Cranberry ice

Stuffed green pepper salad   Saltines

Hot mince pie   Hot pumpkin pie

Assorted cheese   Toasted crackers

Coffee

Nuts   Raisins   Bonbons

CHRISTMAS DINNER

Oyster cocktail

Tomato consommé   Toast points

Roast goose   Apple dressing

Mashed sweet potato   Carrot rings

Cooked celery hearts

Pineapple ice

Orange and onion salad   Salad wafers

Plum pudding   Hard sauce

Salted nuts   Coffee   Bonbons

CHAPTER IV

Suppers

THERE are still many families where supper is served every day. In some families we have breakfast, luncheon, and dinner, with the heavy meal the last in the day. In others, particularly when every member comes home at noon and when there are small children to be considered, the heavy meal is served at noon and a simple supper at night. When such is the case the supper is much the same as a luncheon. The table is laid with a linen cloth, either all white or with a colored border, and the napkins match. Gaily colored dishes add to the attractiveness of the table. For the centerpiece we prefer cut flowers, arranged in a low bowl of silver or glass. Candlelight is appreciated. The candles are arranged in silver candlesticks around the centerpiece.

A plate is laid for each person, with the knife placed at the right of the plate and the fork at the left. A teaspoon is placed at the right of the knife and the folded napkin is placed at the left of the fork. The goblet, which may be crystal or colored glass, is placed at the right of the plate near the tip of the knife. The bread and butter plate is placed at the left of the plate near the tip of the fork, and the bread and butter spreader is placed on the bread and butter plate.

The service is informal. The head of the family may serve the guests; the food may be passed family style from guest to guest, or it may be served to each one by the maid. The coffee is served at the table by the hostess. The coffee service, which matches the china or is of silver, is placed in front of the hostess and the cups are arranged at her right. Coffee may be served with the supper and the dessert, or it may be served with the dessert only.

Simplicity is the keynote in planning supper menus. Cheese, macaroni, spaghetti, or the egg combinations are excellent for supper dishes. Cold assorted meats or omelets as suggested in the following menus are appropriate for the family supper:

Menu 1

Assorted cold plate   Potato salad
Tongue (sliced)   Tomato and cucumber slices   Stuffed eggs
Hot muffins   Peach jam   Butter
Cheese cake   Coffee

Menu 2

Macaroni mousse   Hot biscuit
Fresh mushroom sauce   Butter
Hearts of lettuce salad   Chow-chow
Grape jelly
Danish apple cake   Coffee

Menu 3

American chop suey   Hot cheese biscuit
Butter
Rice   Pickled peaches
Hot gingerbread with whipped cream   Coffee

Menu 4

Spanish omelette   Bran muffins
Raspberry jam
Fruit salad with cream dressing
Coffee   Molasses cookies

Menu 5

Asparagus shortcake with broiled bacon
Graham bread   Butter
Stuffed prune salad
Coffee or Cocoa

When the cold plate is served, the cold meat is arranged on the platter with the stuffed eggs, and the vegetables take the place of a garnish as well as a food. If the platter is large enough, it is advisable to arrange the potato salad or similar salad with the meats and garnishes. Sprigs of parsley and a dash of paprika complete the picture.

The charm of the unusual in planning menus for the Sunday-night supper has helped give this meal its place of importance in the diet and has helped evolve menus that are different. Sometimes women assume that after a heavy Sunday dinner it is not necessary to plan for a supper. However, the Sunday-night supper custom is here to stay. We make an occasion of this meal, whether we are serving it to the family or to guests. Chafing-dish combinations, toasted sandwiches, waffles, or pancakes each have a decided place of importance when planning the menu. The Sunday-night supper may be served in the living room, around an open fire during the cold months, or on the porch or in the garden during the warm weather. The service is informal. Reception plates with cups to match may be used. The table may be set in the room where the supper is to be served or the food may be brought into the room on a tea cart. If the cart is used, all of the food is arranged on it, ready to serve. If the table is set, the food is arranged on it in buffet style. The plates and napkins are arranged in piles. The silver is laid in rows and the cups are placed around the coffee urn at one end of the table. The guests may serve themselves or a waitress or the hostess may serve. It is important to be sure that hot things are hot and cold things cold. The five menus following are excellent for Sunday-night supper use:

Menu 1

Creamed minced ham with mushrooms on toast
Lettuce salad sandwiches   Relishes and jelly
Brandy snaps   Coffee

Menu 2

Sandwich loaf with garnishes (lettuce, tomato, pickles, olives, stuffed eggs, hearts of celery)
Fancy cakes   Coffee

Menu 3

Lobster Newburgh on toast points
Vegetable aspic in mould
Rosettes with fresh raspberries (whipped cream)   Coffee

Menu 4

Frozen vegetable salad   Ham sandwiches
        Gingersnaps   Coffee

Menu 5

Jellied chicken   Potato chips
    Nut bread   Butter
Spiced cantaloupe   Sliced pickles
    Chocolate cake   Coffee

The creamed minced ham with mushrooms, or the Newburgh, may be served from an electric grill or chafing dish. The sandwich loaf is a meal in itself. It is easily served and most satisfying. The dessert for Sunday-night supper should be simple, and whenever possible should be such that it may be served without change of plate. Fancy small cakes, brandy snaps, or cookies may easily be served from a large silver cake basket, and may be brought into the room with the other things for the meal. Candlelight lends a charm that nothing else does.

The after-the-theatre supper is deserving of consideration, and the menus to be recommended are:

Menu 1

Assorted canapés
Celery   Olives   Pickles
Hot apple pie with welsh rarebit sauce
            Coffee

Menu 2

Chicken à la King in timbales   Toasted English muffins
        Cream cheese   Bar-le-Duc
    Fresh black cherries   Coffee

Menu 3

Club sandwich with tuna fish
Radishes   Small pickles
    Brownies   Coffee

Menu 4

| Waffles | Country sausage |
| Maple syrup | Coffee |

Menu 5

Shrimp wiggle on toast

| Sliced tomatoes | Cucumber rings |
| Sponge cake | Coffee |

The assorted canapés may be prepared ahead and the kind so planned and made that the platter of canapés will strangely resemble a plate of assorted French pastries. The hot apple pie with the rarebit sauce is not only different, but is delicious. Toasted sandwiches, chafing-dish combinations, or grilled assortments are frequently used for the after-the-theatre party. If the weather is cold, the table laid near the open fire is delightful. The table is very simply laid. A luncheon cloth of linen that completely covers the table is best. Napkins should match the cloth. A centerpiece of flowers may be used, but is not essential. Grills and chafing dishes are so often used on the table for these menus that the centerpiece may be omitted. Candles lend a soft light and should be used. A plate is laid for each person, a knife at the right of the plate and a fork at the left. A teaspoon is laid at the right of the knife. The goblet is placed at the right of the plate near the tip of the knife. Coffee is usually served by the hostess or by the waitress from the buffet, or the silver coffee service may be placed on the table in front of the hostess with the cups placed at her right. A coffee spoon is placed on each saucer. If a chafing dish or grill is used, it is placed on the table and the hostess or one of the guests may do the serving. The dessert may be on the table or it may be served after the first-course plates have been removed.

On a stormy night nothing can surpass the fireside supper. This, of necessity, should be a simple meal, since it is served without a dining table. For a fireside supper a nest of tables is a decided asset. A salad and hot biscuit, a simple dessert and beverage, is sufficient for this meal. After a holiday meal or a late Sunday dinner, hot chocolate served in chocolate cups and topped with whipped cream and served with nut bread and butter sandwiches is satisfying and sufficient. An open fire furnishes the perfect setting for such a meal. The following are suggested menus:

Menu 1

Red beet and onion salad

Hot pigs in clover
Mustard

Vanities

Coffee

Menu 2

Nut bread and butter sandwiches   Chilled orange sections
Hot chocolate with whipped cream

Menu 3

Sliced chicken sandwiches

Stuffed celery

Ripe olives

Marmalade tarts

Coffee

Menu 4

Swiss cheese and ham sandwich (rye bread)
Mustard pickle

Doughnuts

Coffee

Menu 5

Frozen fruit salad

Pop-overs

Coffee

The Buffet Supper may be used for an occasion or the Sunday-night supper may be served buffet style. The table for a Buffet Supper is laid carefully. The favorite covering is fine linen or an all lace cloth. The plates and napkins are arranged in piles. The silver is arranged in rows, — forks, knives when necessary, teaspoons, and coffee spoons. The coffee urn is at one end of the table with cups and saucers around it. The food is attractively arranged on platters and in dishes and is then put on the table so that it will show up attractively. The rolls for a Buffet Supper may be buttered in the kitchen and served on a silver bread plate, carefully covered with a napkin to keep them warm. Candlelight is of first consideration in serving the Buffet Supper. A low centerpiece of flowers adds beauty to the appearance of the table.

BUFFET SUPPER

Menu 1

Moulded shrimp and crab meat salad   Cold boiled ham

Lattice potatoes

Stuffed celery   Ripe olives   Spiced cantaloupe

Clover-leaf rolls

Apricot ice   German crisps

Salted nuts   Coffee   Bonbons

Menu 2

Chicken à la King in timbale cases

Aspic ring with vegetables

Parker House rolls

Apple jelly   Cucumber Rings   Ripe olives

Fresh strawberries   Cream and sugar

Angel food cake   Coffee

Bonbons   Salted nuts

Menu 3

Cold sliced turkey   Lobster salad

Potato chips

Cranberry ice   Frozen cream puffs   Stuffed olives

Curled celery   Mint patties   Mint jelly

Hot biscuit   Butter   Coffee

Salted nuts

Suppers, whether family or otherwise, are informal meals. They should be colorful. Linen, china, and the food served will aid in bringing color to this meal. Although the service is informal, the table appointments for suppers should be given careful consideration. It is important that the coffee service should harmonize with the flat silver and that the linen be fine and beautiful. Colored glass may be used. When salads are served on a glass plate, the glass of the salad plate should match or harmonize with the color of the goblet. Colored-glass and pottery supper sets are attractive additions in laying the supper table, but when they are used they should always harmonize in color. There is a sociability about supper that makes it an attractive and important meal.

CHAPTER V

Afternoon Teas

THREE meals a day. This is assumed to be the regular allotment for each individual, and yet we have a fourth meal which is deserving of special consideration. Afternoon tea has come into its own. A friendly cup of tea with friends or family is fast becoming a custom. There is a social aspect about the cup of tea with the simple sandwich, cookie, or light cake that deserves recognition. It makes and establishes friendships. The friendly cup often helps to clear away the cobwebs and to take away that tired feeling. It gives renewed strength and cheers one on to finish the day's work well. Tea during the cold weather may be hot, or on a warm day it may be a chilled fruit punch, iced tea, or coffee. If a fruit punch is served and the color is clear and bright, a sprig of mint tucked into the top of the ice cubes will improve its flavor and appearance. The friendly cup of tea demands no service. A napkin and a plate with cup to match and a teaspoon are all that are really essential. Tea may be carried to the living room on a tray, to be served near an open fire, or it may be brought in on a tea cart, or it may be carried to the porch. If crisp toast or hot breads are used, they should be served on a silver, glass, or china plate covered with a napkin to keep them warm. The following may easily be served:

Menu 1

Cinnamon toast   Tea

Menu 2

Orange tea biscuit   Tea

Menu 3

Tea biscuit filled with lobster salad   Tea

Menu 4

Lettuce sandwich   Iced tea or punch

Menu 5

Brown bread sandwiches with cream cheese filling Tea

51

The Bridge Tea is just as important as the Bridge Luncheon and may be made just as attractive and interesting a meal. It may be served buffet style or may be served to the guests at small tables. If the small table service is used, each table is carefully covered with a fine linen cloth and each guest is given the silver necessary for the refreshments. A fork is placed at the left of each service and a knife and spoon at the right. The napkin is placed at the left of the fork. A rose, a jonquil, or some single flower placed in a bud vase is used as a centerpiece. The refreshments are usually served from the kitchen and are brought to the table on plates with each service complete. Salads, creamed combinations in timbales, or club sandwiches garnished with paprika and parsley, furnish an alluring repast. The jellies and relishes are passed by the hostess or the maid to the guests. The dessert is simple, and is brought to each guest as the main dish is removed. Coffee or tea is served from the kitchen. The cup and saucer is placed at the right of the plate and the coffee spoon is on the saucer with the cup. Cream and sugar are passed to each guest with the coffee. Colored glass may be used in serving the Bridge Tea but crystal is preferable. If the buffet service is used, the table may be laid in the dining room, in the garden, on the porch, or in the living room. In such case the table is covered with a lace or fine linen cloth with a centerpiece of flowers. Candles in silver candlesticks are grouped around the centerpiece; plates and napkins are placed in piles with the silver in rows. The food is so arranged that it presents a beautiful picture and is easily accessible to the guests. At the Buffet Bridge Tea a waitress may serve, or if it is informal, the guests may serve themselves. Coffee is served from an urn at one end of the table. The cups and saucers are grouped around the urn with the coffee spoon on the saucer with the cup. This tea is a congenial meal and popular, because it brings to a close a delightful party.

Menu 1

Fresh pineapple and green grape salad with Normandy dressing
Hearts of celery   Potato biscuit
French pastry   Coffee

Menu 2

Chicken aspic salad   Assorted hot breads
Watermelon pickle   Radishes   Mint jelly
Chocolate roll   Coffee

Menu 3

Watermelon and cream cheese salad   Toasted mushroom sandwich
Olives
Lemon ice   Sponge drops
Coffee

The High Tea or Tea Party is a favorite with many. The occasion may be an anniversary or it may be a holiday. It is a delightful way of introducing the guest of honor to one's friends, or it is a charming way of welcoming a newcomer to her home. The table is laid buffet style. A lace or fine linen cloth, one covering the table completely, is best. The centerpiece may be roses, lilies of the valley, daisies, bachelor buttons, or a bouquet of garden flowers. It should be low and attractive. Candles in silver candlesticks are arranged around the centerpiece. The napkins and plates are placed in piles and the silver in rows. The coffee urn is placed at the end or in the center of one side of the table. The coffee is served here. If coffee and tea are both served, two services are used, — one at either side or either end of the table. The cups are placed around the service. Two invited guests are asked to pour the tea and coffee. The refreshments for a high tea resemble those of a wedding breakfast and the service is very similar. The following menus are suggested:

Menu 1

Lobster salad   Creamed mushrooms on rosettes
Hot Parker House rolls   Potato puff
Stuffed celery   Cucumber rings   Ripe olives
Mint jelly   Apple jelly
Strawberry ice cream
Gold cookies   Macaroons
Tea   Coffee
Salted pecans   Bonbons

Menu 2

Tea biscuits filled with lobster salad and chicken salad
Assorted rolled sandwiches
Fresh fruit salad
Sweet gherkins   Celery hearts   Stuffed olives
Macaroon ice cream
Angel cake   Sunshine cake
Coffee   Tea
Salted nuts   Mint patties

Menu 3

Tuna fish salad   Hot biscuit
Pickled peaches   Radish roses
Strawberries   Cream and sugar
Small cakes   Coffee

Menu 4

Assorted sandwiches
Pickles   Cranberry jelly   Olives
Butterscotch tarts   Coffee

Tea parties are often planned as an entertainment for a special occasion. A Valentine Tea, a Hallowe'en Tea, or a New Year's Tea are examples. When the party is planned for a special occasion, the refreshments are symbolic of the occasion and the centerpiece and table decorations are such that they harmonize with the food and also suggest the event.

CHAPTER VI

Food for the Child

THE correct feeding of children is of vital importance. It deserves all of the time, space, and energy that is devoted to it. To feed children well is a real achievement. The cultivation of violent likes and dislikes in food is a problem that confronts mothers today. These preferences usually result from the child's observation of similar preferences in the adults around him, and they should not be encouraged. Children under five years of age are given a diet especially planned and usually especially prepared every day. Milk is perhaps the most important food, bread, vegetables, and fruit follow. Meat is first introduced into the diet by meat juices. Gradually bacon and chops are added. A child's breakfast should vary just as an adult's does. Fruit, which includes orange juice, prunes, or any stewed fruit, is always recommended. Cereal is a valuable food for the child, and may well be served twice a day. Cereal, eggs, bread, toast, or perhaps a muffin, with milk, complete a breakfast for the child. Dinner may consist of a vegetable plate or bacon and chops combined with good vegetables. After five years of age the diet of the child gradually increases, and at the age of ten the child is probably eating the same food as the grown-ups. Supper usually consists of sandwiches and cocoa, cereals, or cream soups. These soups are of value, particularly if there is a meat stock or vegetable used as the base. Desserts for children should be simple. Gelatine, custard, prune whip, bread and butter pudding, and ice cream are some of the desserts recommended. The gelatine may be colored pink, making it pretty to look at and of more interest. Menus for the child follow:

Menu 1

Orange juice

Oatmeal   Top milk and sugar

Dropped egg on toast

Milk

Menu 2
Stewed prunes

Cereal   Top milk and sugar
Buttered toast   Milk

Menu 3
Cooked cereal with dates, top milk or cream
Scrambled eggs   Buttered toast
Milk or cocoa

Menu 4
Apple sauce

Cereal   Top milk and sugar
Whole wheat toast   Jelly
Cocoa

Menu 5
Dry cereal, sliced ripe bananas with top milk and sugar
Graham toast   Cocoa

CHILD'S DINNER
Menu 1
Lamb chop

Baked potato   Spinach
Floating Island   Milk

Menu 2
Cream of carrot soup   Lettuce sandwiches
Fruit gelatine   Sugar cookies
Cocoa

Menu 3
Vegetable plate   Bread and butter sandwiches
(string beans, mashed potato, summer squash, carrots)
Irish moss pudding   Milk

Menu 4
Tomato omelet   Baked potato
Sliced oranges   Sponge cake
Milk

Menu 5
Creamed chicken

Rice   Peas
Vanilla ice cream   Milk

CHILD'S HOME LUNCH
Menu 1
Cream of celery soup   Lettuce sandwich
    Cream tapioca pudding   Cocoa

Menu 2
Minced lamb on toast   Sliced tomato
    Floating island   Cocoa

Menu 3
Vegetable soup with noodles Graham bread and butter sandwiches
    Bread pudding   Milk

Menu 4
Eggs à la goldenrod
Stewed peaches   Vanilla wafer
                Milk

Menu 5
Fish chowder
Bread and butter sandwich   Lettuce and tomato salad
    Rhubarb sauce   Lady fingers
                Cocoa

SCHOOL LUNCH
Menu 1
Egg sandwiches   Whole tomato
    Oatmeal cookies   Cocoa

Menu 2
Chicken sandwiches   Orange
    Molasses cookies   Cocoa

Menu 3
Whole wheat sandwich (cream cheese and dates)
Cup cake   Apple
                Cocoa

Menu 4
Peanut butter sandwiches   Jelly sandwich
    Strawberries with the hull   Milk

Menu 5
Chopped roast beef sandwiches
Filled cookies   Cherries
                Cocoa

Cocoa and milk are carried in a thermos bottle with the school lunch. Creamed soups may sometimes be added to these menus, and when they are they may also be carried in a thermos bottle.

The children's party is a real event in their lives. Usually it is a birthday party, and the desire on the part of the child to entertain should be encouraged. Charm of manner, which is appreciated later in life, may be developed and cultivated when the child is very young. Menus for the party are suggested. These may be varied easily, according to the age of the child.

Menu 1

Creamed chicken on toast
Lettuce sandwiches   Tomato sandwiches
Vanilla ice cream   Angel cake
Milk or cocoa

Menu 2

Fruit salad in orange basket
Sliced chicken sandwich   Jelly sandwich
Bavarian cream (pink)
Milk or cocoa

Menu 3

Gelatine salad
Cream cheese and jelly sandwich   Milk
Chocolate ice cream   Cup cakes

Menu 4

Pear and strawberry salad
Chopped meat sandwich   Jam sandwich
Floating Island   Cocoa

Menu 5

Fruit cup
Broiled lamb chop   Mashed potatoes
Buttered peas
Strawberry ice cream   Sponge cake
Milk or cocoa

CHAPTER VII

Picnic Parties

LET'S have a picnic. Who does not welcome this announcement, no matter what age? A lunch or supper served under a shady tree in the woods overlooking a river or lake, or on some beach, has a charm that is undeniable. In planning a picnic party several things must be considered. Is all of the food for the picnic prepared at home and carried to the picnic place, or is much of it cooked around an open fire? If raw materials are carried to the picnic grounds, there is not much difficulty in packing the picnic lunch. Arrange the kit with the utensils and dishes so that they can be transported easily, and pack the cooked foods in one basket and the raw material in another. Nothing is more delightful than a picnic party when the coffee, steak, corn, and potatoes are cooked in the open over the coals. When the picnic party is such that all of the food is cooked in the home and transported to the grounds, the task is more difficult. Food must be selected which can stand several hours without deterioration. Sandwiches are of course the mainstay of the picnic lunch. Next comes the potato salad, stuffed eggs, fruit, and a cake that will pack easily. We try when possible to select a menu and wrap it so that cold foods can be kept cold and hot ones hot. Thermos bottles, vacuum packs, and small ice chests are all helpful in the preparation of a modern picnic. Do try these menus:

Menu 1

Ham and celery sandwich
Cream cheese and olive sandwich
Sardine and horseradish sandwich

Potato salad	Stuffed eggs
Pickles	Whole tomatoes
Apples	Bananas
Date bars	Coffee

Ginger ale

Menu 2

Chicken sandwich
Dried beef and cream cheese sandwich
Nut bread sandwich
Potato chips   Hard-cooked eggs
Olives   Pickles
Oranges   Cup cakes
Coffee

Menu 3

Steak and onion sandwiches
(steak broiled over fire)
Green bean salad   Roast corn
Doughnuts   Cheese
Coffee

Menu 4

Potato salad with cucumber
Frankfurters   Rolls
Mustard   Dill pickles
Black cherries   Chocolate cookies
Coffee

Menu 5

Meat loaf   Baked beans
Brown bread sandwiches   Pickles
Watermelon   Jelly doughnuts
Coffee

CHAPTER VIII

The Unexpected Guest

THE most appreciative of all is the guest who was n't expected, but who was served a good meal. In these days of automobiles we never know when friends will call, — and how hospitable it is to ask them to stay and dine! The emergency shelf can be relied on for supplies. Canned fruits, vegetables, meats, and other foods will help serve a meal that is tempting and nourishing. These foods may best be used for salads or desserts. A luncheon of vegetable salad served with cold sliced tongue and baking-powder biscuit needs only the coffee and a hot gingerbread to complete it. Toasted sandwiches and eggs in bacon nests are real sensations.

The home with a cupboard of jellies, jams, and preserves need never worry about the unexpected. These additions to even the simplest menu are worthy of the appreciation they receive.

The cookie jar will help with dessert, or the quick cakes are also good. Shortcakes come into their own in an emergency. Easily made, they are always joyfully received.

Menus for every meal follow:

FOR UNEXPECTED GUESTS

BREAKFAST

Menu 1

Breakfast figs
Eggs in bacon nests

Muffins   Butter   Blackberry jam
Coffee

Menu 2

Canned grapefruit
Dry cereal, sugar and cream   Dropped egg on toast
Doughnuts   Coffee

61

Menu 3

Grape juice

French toast

Maple syrup

Coffee

Menu 4

Chilled grapefruit juice

Date muffin

Broiled bacon

Peach jam

Butter

Coffee

Menu 5

Canned red raspberries

Plain omelet

Toast

Grape jelly

Butter

Coffee

DINNER

Menu 1

Macaroni and cheese   Cold sliced tongue
    Mustard pickle   Apple jelly
            Butterscotch rolls
Stewed pears   Brownies
            Coffee

Menu 2

Salmon loaf — egg sauce
    Baked potato   Buttered peas
Lettuce   Roquefort dressing
    Hot rolls   Plum jam
    Caramel layer cake   Coffee

Menu 3

Ham and potato casserole
Asparagus tips   Currant jelly
        Lettuce with Russian dressing
    Gingerbread   Whipped cream
            Coffee

Menu 4

Baked beans   Brown bread
Cabbage, pineapple, marshmallow salad
Baked apple   Whipped cream
Coffee

Menu 5

Cold sliced meat
Creamed potatoes   Buttered peas
Lettuce and tomato salad
Date torte   Whipped cream
Coffee

SUPPERS

Menu 1

Toasted bacon and tomato sandwich
Fruit salad
Peanut cookies   Coffee

Menu 2

Bean rarebit on toast   Broiled bacon
Cole slaw
Canned peaches   Whipped cream
Sand tarts   Coffee

Menu 3

Grapefruit and strawberry salad
Toasted cheese sandwiches   Coffee

Menu 4

Creamed dried beef on toast
Buttered toast   Apricot conserve
Fresh raspberries with cream and sugar
Coffee

Menu 5

Egg and tomato salad
Bran muffin   Butter
Cream cheese   Blackberry jam
Coffee

TEA

Menu 1

Buttered toast   Tea   Strawberry jam

Menu 2

Cinnamon pinwheels   Tea

Menu 3

Lettuce sandwich   Sugar cookies
                Tea

Menu 4

Mincemeat cookies   Tea

Menu 5

Cream cheese and marmalade sandwiches
Tea

LUNCHEON

Menu 1

Tuna fish salad
Graham muffin   Butter
                Grape fudge
        Apricot slices   Coffee

Menu 2

Creamed crab meat and peas on toast
Waldorf salad   Baking-powder biscuit
        Orange marmalade   Butter
                Coffee

Menu 3

Minced lamb on toast
Pineapple salad   Buttered toast
    Bishop bread   Coffee

Menu 4

Scrambled eggs
Hot biscuit
Fruit salad

Broiled bacon
Butter
Coffee

Menu 5

Vegetable hash
Cheese biscuit
Molasses cookies

Grapefruit salad
Apple jelly
Coffee

CHAPTER IX

Attractive Utilization of Left Overs

IT is not always the unusual meal that is most deserving of praise. The home maker, who prides herself on the skill with which she plans and prepares food for her family, has no doubt learned the secret of using left overs successfully. To prepare a meal with fresh food material is not too difficult, but to serve a meal that is attractive and nutritive without fresh material is an art. A bowl of piping hot cream soup — just the right consistency — made from two, three, or four left-over vegetables, chopped fine and combined with a well-seasoned cream sauce, is a delicious luncheon for child or adult. Hot biscuit or toast served with this soup is all that is needed for a main course. Islands of small crackers topped with whipped cream and garnished with paprika and chopped parsley will make the soup most acceptable. Salads, sandwiches, baked casseroles, or creamed combinations on toast, will also give the ingenious cook an opportunity to prove her skill. Fruit — fresh, stewed, or canned — left from a previous meal lends itself easily to desserts of gelatine or shortcake nature, while sour milk and cream will help in making muffins, cookies, and gingerbread. Ends or small pieces of ham chopped or ground fine can be used temptingly in many ways. Ham omelet is always delicious, or minced ham on toast can be served. Ham timbales, or biscuit, or escalloped combinations, are some other good ways of utilizing the meat. Vegetables may well be served as vegetable hash, combining with it a fresh green salad and hot bread. Salads are always excellent. Left-over vegetables, cut into small pieces and marinated with a French dressing, can be made into an interesting salad by adding some celery cut fine, then arranging it on a bed of lettuce leaves with perhaps a slice of tomato or stuffed egg to finish the product. Such a salad is hearty, and with cold meat and hot muffins will tempt any appetite. Shepherd's pie, and casserole dishes of meat and vegetables with crusty biscuit top, offer other solutions. These menus that follow can be easily prepared and served:

Menu 1

Ham omelet
Cooked vegetable salad   Baking-powder biscuit
Butter
Apple sauce   Sour cream cookies
Coffee

Menu 2

Finnan haddie au gratin
Water-cress salad   French dressing
Whole wheat toast   Butter
Fruit gelatine   Whipped cream
Ginger snaps   Coffee

Menu 3

Shepherd's pie   Pickled beets
Date muffins   Butter
Apricot whip   Custard sauce
Coffee

Menu 4

Corned beef hash with dropped egg
Turned salad   Hot biscuit
Prune pie   Coffee

Menu 5

Meat pie with vegetables and biscuit top
Cucumber salad
Chocolate bread pudding   Hard sauce
Coffee

Seventy-Five Palatable and Attractive Left-Over Suggestions

SOUPS

1 Cream of Celery Soup
2 Cream of Spinach Soup
3 Cream of Lettuce Soup
4 Cream of Squash Soup

FISH

5 Jellied Tuna Fish
6 Tuna Fish Casserole
7 Macaroni and Salmon Croquettes
8 Salmon Loaf
9 Fish Cakes
10 Fish Chowder
11 Shrimp Wiggle

MEATS

12 Ham Flakes with Noodles
13 Ham Mousse
14 Ham Timbales
15 Minced Ham on Toast
16 Veal and Ham Pie
17 Mushrooms and Veal Timbales
18 Corned Beef Hash
19 American Chop Suey
20 Meat Pie
21 Shepherd's Pie
22 Beefsteak Roll
23 Hash
24 Creamed Chicken
25 Chicken Pie
26 Chicken à la King
27 Chicken Timbales
28 Spaghetti with Chicken Livers
29 Meat Stuffed Tomatoes
30 A Luncheon Dish

VEGETABLES AND EGGS

31 Creole Omelet
32 Bacon, Egg, and Onion Sandwich
33 Baked Eggs and Cheese
34 Potatoes Scalloped with Eggs
35 Spaghetti au Gratin
36 Spaghetti Loaf
37 Cheese Soufflé
38 Blushing Bunny
39 Bean Rarebit
40 Macaroni Mousse
41 Pea Timbales
42 Stuffed Cabbage Roll
43 Mushroom Dream
44 Vegetable Hash
45 Vegetable Chowder
46 Carrot and Nut Loaf
47 Toasted Cheese Sandwich
48 Scalloped Cauliflower
49 Vegetable Loaf
50 Rice Suprême
51 Chili Concarne
52 Fried Corn Meal Mush

SALADS

53 Fish and Potato Salad
54 Vegetable Salad
55 Veal Salad
56 Jellied Carrot Salad
57 Macaroni Salad

58 Mexican Salad
59 Potato Salad
60 Frozen Vegetable Salad
61 Fruit Salad Aspic

66 Rice Griddle Cakes
67 Pineapple Waffles
68 Sour Milk Waffles
69 Bread Dressing

BREADS

62 Rice Muffins
63 Sour Milk Muffins
64 Sour Milk Baking Powder
　　Biscuits
65 Bread Crumb Griddle
　　Cakes

DESSERTS

70 Chocolate Bread Pudding
71 Mince Meat Cookies
72 Brown Betty
73 Bread Pudding
74 Ginger Bread
75 Danish Apple Cake

CHAPTER X

Invalid Cookery

DIETETICS is the science of food. A complete understanding of this science makes it possible for us to select the proper kind of diet. To work out a satisfactory diet we must know the correct classification of food. Foods are classified as follows: carbohydrates, proteins, fats, minerals, water, and vitamines. At all times food has a tremendous influence upon the body, and during illness special care must be taken to select food that will nourish the patient and at the same time correct his condition. The food selected must stimulate the appetite and appeal to the eye. Some foods, ordinarily digestible, will become indigestible if they are repugnant to the patient.

All eating is very much influenced by the setting of the food. Therefore one of the important phases in feeding the sick is the appearance of the tray. This should be of the correct size, covered by a spotless tray cloth which just laps over the edge of the tray. On every tray there must be cold water in a moderately sized tumbler of the sort that will not tip over easily, a dainty, spotless napkin, and small salt and pepper shakers. For the tray select the daintiest china, and if possible change the china for each meal. It is often a good idea to devise a color scheme. Bright flowers on the tray always have a pleasing effect. Such devices lend a cheerful note, tempt the appetite, keep the patient interested, and help him to shake off nervousness or depression. The breakfast tray is perhaps the most important, for nervous patients are apt to be depressed early in the morning.

Arrange the separate articles on the tray with the patient's convenience in mind. Do not fill the dishes too full. As a rule, hot things should be hot and cold things cold. But in this respect, too, the individual taste must be consulted. It is a well-known fact that the temperature of the food has a marked influence on digestion. Under certain conditions extremes of heat and cold retard digestion and make the patient expend more energy than is wise in the absorption of the food. It is not wise to overindulge the invalid, but in planning the diet of the patient one should study the values and classifications of foods in relation to the patient and his condition.

Uncover the first dish the patient is to eat, and if necessary cut the meat. Always place a bell on the tray for the patient's convenience.

There is a wide range of diet to choose from, and as a rule the physician will make recommendations. The diet may be liquid, either with milk or without; or it may be a soft, solid diet, depending upon the individual and the kind of illness. After consulting the physician in regard to the food to be given to the patient, carry out his instructions carefully. However, the rules above regarding the appearance of the tray should be carried out, regardless of the kind of diet recommended.

Oftentimes convalescing patients or invalids not seriously ill may be given the regular family diet. But if special foods are required to tempt the appetite, some of the following menus may be of value:

BREAKFAST

Menu 1
Orange juice
Farina with sugar and cream
Dropped egg on toast   Coffee

Menu 2
Iced canteloupe
Broiled bacon   Blueberry muffin
Coffee

Menu 3
Stewed prunes
Soft cooked egg   Whole wheat muffin
Coffee

Menu 4
Strawberries with sugar and cream
Scrambled eggs   Toast
Coffee

Menu 5

Orange sections
Oatmeal with sugar and cream
Toast   Strawberry jam
Coffee

DINNER

Menu 1

Cream of tomato soup
Broiled lamb chop   Buttered peas
Baked potato   Water-cress salad
French dressing
Graham bread   Butter
Prune whip   Custard sauce

Menu 2

Fruit cup
Roast chicken   Summer squash
Mashed potato
Lettuce and tomato salad   French dressing
Cranberry jelly
Vanilla ice cream   Sponge drops

Menu 3

Chicken broth
Broiled tenderloin steak   Buttered carrots
Potatoes with parsley sauce
Endive salad   French dressing
Melba toast
Fruit gelatine with whipped cream

Menu 4

Half grapefruit
Broiled liver and bacon   Spinach
Creamed potatoes   Buttered beets
Apricot ice   Sugar wafer

An Invalid's Tray that will Appeal

Menu 5

Celery soup with croutons
Broiled fillet of sole   Baked potato
Escalloped tomatoes   Currant jelly
Whole wheat bread   Butter
Strawberry shortcake

SUPPER

Menu 1

Beef broth with rice
Omelet   Buttered toast
Fresh strawberries with sugar and cream   Tea

Menu 2

Vegetable salad   Assorted sandwiches
Caramel custard   Iced tea

Menu 3

Fruit salad   Baking-powder biscuit
Cookies   Milk

Menu 4

Creamed chicken on toast
Sliced peaches   Angel food cake
Milk

Menu 5

Club sandwich
Stewed rhubarb   Molasses cookies
Cocoa

SECTION II
Recipes

CHAPTER XI

Beverages

Percolated Coffee

TO make percolated coffee, measure one tablespoon of ground coffee to each cup of water, allowing one extra tablespoon of coffee for the pot. The water for percolated coffee may be either boiling or cold. Cold is preferable. After the coffee begins to percolate allow it to percolate from five to eight minutes, depending on the strength desired. Serve immediately.

Drip Coffee

Drip coffee is made by allowing one tablespoon of ground coffee for each cup of water and one extra tablespoon for the pot. Put the coffee in the container for it and pour the boiling water through the coffee. If extra strength is desired, the liquid may be poured through a second time, but once is all that is necessary. Keep the coffee pot over a low flame while coffee is dripping.

Iced Coffee

Fill a tumbler with cracked ice. Pour hot coffee over the ice.

Iced Coffee with Cream Float

Fill tumbler with cracked ice. Pour hot coffee over the ice. Add two tablespoons heavy cream. Top with one tablespoon of whipped cream.

Tea

Allow one-half teaspoon of tea per cup. Scald teapot with boiling water. Put tea leaves in the bottom of the teapot. Add boiling water. Let stand five minutes. Serve.

Iced Tea

Fill a tumbler with cracked ice. Pour hot tea over the ice Add a slice of lemon before serving.

Tea Punch

¼ cup cloves (whole)   ½ cup tea
            1½ cups water (boiling)

Let stand one-half hour. Strain, then add:

1 cup orange juice   ¾ cup lemon juice
1 cup peach juice   3 quarts water

Serve cold with ice. Garnish with mint leaves.

Tea and Fruit Punch

1 cup boiling water   2 tablespoons sugar
1 teaspoon tea   3 tablespoons lemon juice
            1 cup pineapple syrup

Pour boiling water over the tea and let stand five minutes.
Strain. Add sugar, lemon juice, and syrup. Serve in small
glasses with crushed ice. Garnish with maraschino cherry.

Cocoa

½ cup cocoa   ⅛ teaspoon salt
1½ cups water   ½ cup sugar

Mix thoroughly. Bring to the boiling point. Simmer five
minutes. Add two quarts of scalded milk and one teaspoon
vanilla. Beat with rotary egg beater. Serve hot. Top with
whipped cream.

Chocolate Syrup

2 squares bitter chocolate   ½ cup milk
1 cup sugar   1 tablespoon butter
¼ teaspoon salt   1 teaspoon vanilla

Mix the ingredients. Cook slowly until chocolate melts. Let
simmer ten minutes. Pour into jar. This may be used for milk
shake, chocolate float, or chocolate sauce. Will keep indefinitely.

Chocolate

2 squares chocolate	½ cup sugar
¼ teaspoon salt	1 cup milk

Heat until chocolate melts. Cook until mixture begins to thicken. Add one quart of scalded milk and beat with egg beater until smooth. Serve with marshmallow or whipped cream float. More sugar may be added to taste.

Chocolate Milk Shake

1 glass milk   1 tablespoon vanilla ice cream
¼ cup chocolate syrup

Combine milk and chocolate sauce, add ice cream and shake well. Serve at once.

Chocolate Float

¼ cup chocolate syrup   1 cup milk
¼ teaspoon vanilla

Shake thoroughly. Pour into glass filled with crushed ice. Top with one tablespoon of whipped cream. Garnish with chocolate shot.

Lemonade

1 cup sugar   1 cup water

Boil five minutes. Add one cupful of lemon juice and the grated rind of one lemon. Add two quarts of ice water. Serve in tall glasses with crushed ice. Garnish with maraschino cherries and mint leaves.

Orangeade

1 cup sugar   1 cup water

Boil five minutes. Add one cupful of orange juice and the grated rind of one orange. Add two quarts of ice water. Serve in tall glasses with crushed ice. Garnish with whole mint leaf.

Punch

To one quart of tea add one bottle of ginger ale, juice of two lemons, juice of one orange. Add a few slices of lemon. Sweeten to taste. Serve with ice in tall glasses.

Summer Punch

1 cup lemon juice	2 cups loganberry juice
1 cup raspberry juice	3 mint leaves (crushed)

Mix thoroughly. Serve in tall glasses with crushed ice. Garnish with mint leaves.

Party Punch

4 bottles ginger ale	1 pint lemon ice

Put ginger ale in punch bowl with lemon ice. Serve some of the lemon ice with each glass of ginger ale. Whole fresh strawberries may be added.

Rhubarb Punch

Boil one cup of sugar and one-half cup of water for three minutes. Cool. Add to the syrup three cups of rhubarb juice, one cup of pineapple juice, juice of two lemons, and one cup of crushed strawberries. Mix thoroughly. Serve in tall glasses with crushed ice and mint leaves.

Reception Punch

Make a syrup of one cup of water and two cups of sugar. Boil ten minutes. Add the juice of five oranges, two cups of grated pineapple, juice of three lemons, one cup of cherries, two cups of strawberry juice. Let stand thirty minutes. Strain, and add enough ice water to make two gallons. Garnish with small green grapes.

Grapefruit Punch No. 1

Fill punch bowl two-thirds full of sweetened grapefruit juice. Add one pint of raspberry ice. Let stand several minutes. Serve in cups.

Grapefruit Punch No. 2

Fill tumbler with crushed ice. Fill one-half full of sweetened grapefruit juice. Add two maraschino cherries. Fill tumbler with ginger ale. Garnish with sprig of mint.

Tomato Punch

1 cup clear tomato juice	Juice of 1 lemon
⅛ teaspoon salt	2 tablespoons sugar

Mix ingredients and bring to a boil. Fill tumbler with crushed ice. Pour hot mixture over ice. Serve at once.

Breakfast Grape Juice

Fill tall glass with crushed ice. Add grape juice until glass is half full. Add grapefruit juice to fill glass. Serve at once.

Delicious Punch

2 cups strawberry juice	¼ cup lemon juice
1 cup pineapple juice	⅓ cup honey
4 cups cold water	

Mix all the ingredients thoroughly. Serve in tall glasses with crushed ice.

Ginger Ale Lemonade

1 cup loganberry juice	1 pint ginger ale
4 lemons (grated rind and juice)	1½ pints water
1 cup sugar	

Place small pieces of ice in pitcher. Mix loganberry juice, lemon juice, sugar, water, and ginger ale. Pour into pitcher and stir thoroughly. Allow to stand before serving. Garnish with sprig of mint and slices of lemon.

Porch Punch

½ cup apple jelly
1 cup grapefruit juice
1 pint ginger ale

¼ cup grenadine
Juice of 1 lemon
1 cup water

¼ teaspoon almond extract

Heat water and jelly. Add the rest of the ingredients. Stir. Pour into tall glasses filled with crushed ice.

Egg Nog, No. 1

1 glass milk (cold)
1 egg

⅛ teaspoon salt
1 teaspoon vanilla

Beat egg, add salt, vanilla, and milk. Beat well. Serve cold.

Egg Nog, No. 2

6 eggs
⅛ teaspoon salt

1 teaspoon vanilla
2 cups cream

4 tablespoons confectioners' sugar

Beat eggs separately. Whip cream. Combine cream with egg yolks. Lastly, fold in the beaten egg whites, add vanilla. Serve cold in tall glasses.

CHAPTER XII

Breads and Hot Breads

(SALAD ACCOMPANIMENTS)

White Bread

6 cups flour
2 cakes compressed yeast
2 teaspoons salt

2 teaspoons sugar
2 cups water or milk (lukewarm)
4 teaspoons shortening (melted)

Crumble yeast cake, dissolve in lukewarm water. Add salt and sugar. Mix well and add all of the flour. When partially mixed, add the shortening. Mix well with spatula. Turn out on slightly floured board and knead until the dough is smooth. Allow to stand in a greased bowl for two hours or until double in bulk. Knead down and let stand forty-five minutes. Knead again and let stand fifteen minutes. Divide dough for loaves, if more than one loaf is being made. Put in well-greased loaf pans. Allow to rise until light. Keep dough greased lightly while rising. Bake from fifty to sixty minutes in hot oven (425° F.). This will make two one-pound loaves.

Bread

2 cakes compressed yeast
2 tablespoons shortening
1 cup lukewarm water

1 tablespoon salt
4 tablespoons sugar
2 cups scalded milk

1 cup cold water

Break yeast into lukewarm water, add sugar, and stir until dissolved. Scald the milk, then add cold water to make the mixture lukewarm. Sift eight cups of flour and place in a bowl. Make a hollow in the center, put in shortening and salt. Add liquids. Mix to a soft dough. Put in a greased bowl and let rise until double in bulk. Knead thoroughly. Shape into loaves. Put into greased bread tins. Let rise until double in bulk. Bake from fifty to sixty minutes (425° F.).

Bran Bread

2 cups flour	1 cup molasses
2 cups bran	½ cup sugar
3 teaspoons salt	4 tablespoons melted shortening
1 egg	2 cups milk
2 teaspoons soda (dissolved in ½ cup warm water)	1 cup raisins
	½ cup walnut meats

Sift dry ingredients together. Add liquid ingredients. Mix well. Put into bread tins. Will make three small loaves. Bake an hour and a quarter in moderate oven (350° F.).

Shredded Wheat Bread

2 shredded wheat biscuits	1 tablespoon shortening
1 cup boiling water	½ yeast cake
¼ cup molasses	1 cup milk
¼ tablespoon salt	Flour

Put the crushed shredded wheat biscuits into a bowl with the boiling water, molasses, salt, and shortening. Let cool. Add the half yeast cake, the milk, and flour enough to make stiff sponge (five cups). Put into greased bowl in warm place and let rise until double in bulk. Toss on floured board. Knead thoroughly. Shape into loaves. Put into greased bread tins and set in warm place until light. Bake one hour in hot oven (400° F.).

Graham Nut Bread

2½ cups sour milk	1 cup nut meats
1 teaspoon salt	1 cup flour
3 cups graham flour	½ cup sugar
1 teaspoon soda	

Mix dry ingredients. Add sour milk to dry ingredients. Beat well. Add nut meats, cut small. Put into greased bread tins. Bake in moderate oven from fifty to sixty minutes (350° F.). Raisins may be used in place of nuts.

Nut Bread, No. 1

4 cups flour
¼ cup melted shortening
¼ cup sugar
2 eggs

1 teaspoon salt
1 cup chopped nuts
5 teaspoons baking powder
2 cups milk

Beat eggs. Add milk. Mix dry ingredients. Add nuts to dry ingredients. Combine liquid and dry ingredients. Put into well-greased bread tins. Allow to stand twenty minutes. Bake in moderate oven (350° F.).

Nut Bread, No. 2

4 cups flour
½ cup sugar
1 cup milk
1 teaspoon salt

1 egg
8 teaspoons baking powder
1 cup chopped nuts
½ cup chopped dates

Mix dry ingredients. Beat egg and milk. Add to dry ingredients. Add nuts and dates. Mix to smooth dough. Put in greased pans and let stand twenty minutes. Bake one hour in slow oven (325°–350° F.).

Whole Wheat Nut Bread

3 cups whole wheat flour
1 cup sugar
4 teaspoons baking powder
2 cups milk

1 egg
1 cup nut meats
1 cup flour
1 teaspoon salt

Beat egg, add milk. Add all ingredients to egg and milk mixture. Stir smooth. Put in pans and let stand twenty minutes. Bake forty-five minutes in moderate oven (350° F.). One cup dates, cut small, or raisins, may be added if desired.

Quick Graham Nut Bread

2 cups flour
4 teaspoons baking powder
1 teaspoon salt
1 egg

1 cup nuts
2 cups graham flour
1 cup sugar
2 cups milk

Mix dry ingredients. Gradually add the milk, then the well-beaten eggs, and mix thoroughly. Dredge the nuts in flour and add to the above mixture. Pour into well-greased loaf pan. Let stand twenty minutes and bake one hour in moderate oven (350° F.).

Quick Nut Bread

2 eggs	1 cup sugar
1 cup milk	½ teaspoon salt
1 cup chopped nuts	3½ cups flour

4 teaspoons baking powder

Beat eggs and sugar until light. Add milk, salt, and nuts and mix well. Add melted shortening. Sift flour and baking powder together. Stir into first mixture. Fill bread pans half full of mixture and let stand twenty minutes. Bake for sixty minutes in moderate oven (350° F.).

Graham Nut Bread with Molasses

1 teaspoon baking soda	1 teaspoon salt
½ cup molasses	1 cup flour
2 cups sour milk	2 cups graham flour
½ cup sugar	1 cup walnuts (cut fine)

Stir baking soda into molasses. Add other ingredients alternately. Mix well and bake in well-greased pan for sixty minutes in moderate oven (350° F.).

Orange Bread

2 eggs	½ cup sugar
1½ cups milk	4 cups flour
¼ cup shortening	4 teaspoons baking powder
1 teaspoon salt	1 cup candied orange peel

½ teaspoon almond extract

Mix and sift dry ingredients. Cut in the shortening. Add well-beaten eggs and milk. Beat well. Add the candied orange peel. Add almond extract. Put into greased bread pan and let stand ten minutes. Bake fifty minutes in moderate oven (350° F.).

Quick Bran Bread

2 cups bran	1 teaspoon salt
2 cups flour	3 teaspoons baking powder
2 cups sour milk	2 eggs
½ teaspoon soda	½ cup brown sugar

½ cup nuts

Mix dry ingredients. Add nuts. Beat eggs slightly and add to them the milk and brown sugar. Add to dry ingredients. Fill well-greased pan about one-half full and let stand ten minutes. Bake for forty-five minutes in moderate oven (350° F.). Raisins or dates may be substituted for the nuts.

Bran Date Loaf

2 cups flour	1 teaspoon soda
2 teaspoons baking powder	2 tablespoons molasses
2 cups bran	1 teaspoon salt
2 eggs	½ cup nuts
½ cup brown sugar	½ cup dates (cut fine)

2 cups sour milk

Sift flour, soda, baking powder, and salt together. Mix with bran. Add nuts and dates. Beat eggs slightly and add to them the milk, brown sugar, and molasses. Add to dry ingredients. Fill greased pan about half full. Let stand fifteen minutes. Bake forty-five minutes in moderate oven (350° F.).

Date Bread

2 cups flour	1 egg
½ teaspoon salt	¾ cup milk
4 teaspoons baking powder	1 tablespoon sugar
3 tablespoons shortening	½ cup dates (chopped)

Mix dry ingredients. Cut in shortening. Beat egg and milk. Combine mixtures. Mix well. Roll dough one-quarter inch thick, spread with melted butter, sprinkle with sugar and dates. Roll like a jelly roll, seal well, and cut into one-inch slices. Put onto greased baking sheet. Bake fifteen to eighteen minutes in moderate oven (350° F.). Serve hot.

Raisin Bread

2 cups flour	2 tablespoons shortening
½ cup sugar	¾ cup raisins, nuts, or dates
½ teaspoon salt	½ cup milk
3 teaspoons baking powder	1 egg

Mix dry ingredients. Cut in shortening. Add fruit to dry materials. Add beaten egg to milk. Combine mixtures. Shape into loaf. Put into greased bread tin. Let stand fifteen minutes. Bake thirty minutes in moderate oven (350° F.).

Boston Brown Bread, No. 1

1 cup flour	2 cups sour milk
½ teaspoon salt	3 teaspoons soda
1 cup graham flour	1 cup corn meal
1 cup molasses	½ cup raisins

Sift soda and salt with the flour. Mix with corn meal and graham flour. Add molasses to sour milk and stir into dry ingredients. Add raisins. Put into well-greased tins. Cover. Steam or bake three hours. Slow oven for baking (325° F.).

Boston Brown Bread, No. 2

1 cup corn meal	2 cups sour milk
1 teaspoon salt	1 cup rye flour
1 teaspoon soda	1 cup flour
1 cup molasses	

Mix dry ingredients, add molasses and milk. Stir until smooth. Put into well-greased tins. Cover. Steam for three hours.

Brown Bread

2 cups graham flour	1 cup flour
2 cups milk	½ cup molasses
½ cup brown sugar	1 teaspoon soda
½ teaspoon salt	1 cup walnuts (chopped)

Mix dry ingredients. Add chopped walnuts. Mix molasses and milk. Combine liquid and dry ingredients. Pour into greased bread pan. Let stand fifteen minutes. Bake one hour in moderate oven (350° F.).

Steamed Graham Bread

3 cups graham flour
3½ teaspoons soda
2½ cups sour milk

1 cup flour
1 teaspoon salt
2 tablespoons sugar

½ cup dates (cut fine)

Mix dry ingredients, add dates. Add sour milk to dry ingredients. Mix smooth. Put into greased tins. Cover. Steam two hours.

Steamed Raisin Bread

2 cups flour
3 teaspoons baking powder
1 egg
½ cup sugar

¾ cup raisins
2 tablespoons shortening
½ teaspoon salt
¾ cup milk

Mix and sift the dry ingredients. Cut in the shortening. Add raisins. Beat egg with milk. Add to dry ingredients. Place in greased bowl, cover with greased paper, and steam for one hour.

Corn Bread

1 cup flour
5 teaspoons baking powder
¾ teaspoon salt
1 cup milk

2 tablespoons shortening
¼ cup sugar
1 cup corn meal
1 egg

Mix and sift dry ingredients. Add corn meal. Add milk to well-beaten egg. Combine with dry ingredients. Add melted shortening. Mix thoroughly. Bake in a shallow pan thirty minutes in moderate oven (350° F.).

Spoonbread

1 pint milk
1 teaspoon salt

3 eggs
½ cup corn meal

1 teaspoon baking powder

Heat milk to boiling point. Add corn meal and cook five minutes. Cool slightly. Add baking powder, salt, and eggs.

Pour into shallow greased dish. Bake in hot oven (425° F.) for thirty minutes.

Spider Corn Bread

¾ cup corn meal
¼ cup flour
2 tablespoons sugar
1 teaspoon salt
½ teaspoon soda

1 teaspoon baking powder
1 egg
1 cup sweet milk
½ cup sour milk
2 tablespoons butter

Sift together the dry ingredients. Add beaten egg to one-half cup sweet milk, then add the sour milk. Combine dry and liquid ingredients. Melt butter in small frying pan, turn in mixture, and pour second half of sweet milk over this without stirring. Bake twenty-five minutes in moderate oven (350° F.). Serve hot.

Corn Meal Gems

1 cup milk
1 tablespoon shortening
¼ teaspoon salt
½ cup corn meal

2 eggs
¼ cup sugar
¼ cup flour
2 teaspoons baking powder

Scald milk, add butter and salt, and stir in corn meal. Stir and let thicken a few moments, then cool, add well-beaten eggs, and sugar, flour, and baking powder sifted together. Turn into hot buttered muffin pan and bake fifteen minutes in hot oven (400° F.).

Fancy Yeast Dough

4½ cups sifted flour
1½ cups scalded milk
   (cool to lukewarm)
1 tablespoon salt

½ cup sugar
2 cakes compressed yeast
½ cup butter
3 eggs

Crumble yeast into a bowl, add the milk, and stir until yeast is dissolved. Add sugar, beaten eggs, salt, and flour. Mix well, then add the melted butter and mix thoroughly. Turn out on floured board and knead to a smooth dough. Put into greased bowl. Let stand until double in bulk. Knead down and allow it to rise about forty-five minutes. Use for fancy breads.

Butterscotch Bread

Roll small piece of fancy yeast dough to one-half inch thickness. Put in square pan and let rise. Brush over with melted butter. At intervals of two inches, make parallel rows of inch depressions. Put a little butter and brown sugar in each. Cover top with brown sugar which has been mixed with cinnamon. Bake thirty to forty minutes in moderate oven (350° F.).

Filled Doughnuts

Turn fancy yeast dough on floured bread board and roll out to rectangular shape, one-quarter inch thick. Drop prune purée on half of the dough with a teaspoon, three or four inches apart. Fold the second half over the first. Cut out with a biscuit cutter and let rise until double in bulk. Fry in deep fat until brown (380° F.). Drain on unglazed paper and roll in granulated sugar. Be careful in cutting doughnuts to have prune filling in the center of each.

Fruit Loaf

After the fancy yeast dough has had the first rising, add one-half cup each of chopped nuts, seedless raisins, candied pineapple, citron, and candied cherries. Let rise forty-five minutes, mould into loaf. Put into greased bread pan, let rise until double in bulk. Bake in moderate hot oven for one hour (350° F.).

Apple Cake

Turn the fancy yeast dough on bread board. Divide dough in half. Roll to one-half inch thick. Place in two well-greased, shallow pans, shaping dough to the pans. Brush with butter; sprinkle with sugar. Cut apples in eighths and press into dough, sharp edge downward until dough is well covered. Sprinkle with cinnamon and sugar. Let rise one-half hour. Bake twenty minutes in moderate oven (350° F.).

Peaches, prunes or other fruit may be substituted for the apples.

Prune Cakes

Use fancy yeast dough. Drop dough with tablespoon on baking sheets, not too close together. Let rise until five inches in diameter. Prune mixture is made by putting cooked and drained prunes through a sieve. Spread on top of dough, leaving one-half inch at the edge. Sprinkle with grated cocoanut and then with powdered sugar. Let rise fifteen minutes. Bake twenty minutes in moderate oven (350° F.).

Swedish Tea Cake

Shape fancy yeast dough in oblong shape, and roll as thin as possible with pin. Brush with melted butter, sprinkle with sugar, and chopped almonds, cinnamon, raisins, or currants. Roll like jelly roll. Join ends to form a ring. Place on buttered sheet. Cut with scissors from outer part of roll toward center, but not entirely to center. Cut in half-inch slices. Then shape these slices by pulling out and flattening down, one over the other. Brush over with one egg slightly beaten. Sprinkle with finely chopped almonds, if desired. Bake in moderate oven (350° F.) for thirty minutes.

Parker House Rolls

Use bread dough or fancy yeast dough. Form dough into long roll; cut into slices, making each piece about one-half inch thick. Form each piece into ball and butter the top of each generously. Allow to stand ten minutes. Roll out or flatten out with hand. With round handle of wooden spoon make a deep crease in the center of dough and fold over. Place in greased pan and allow to rise until light. Bake twenty-five minutes in hot oven (400° F.).

Currant Rolls

2 tablespoons sugar   Flour to make soft dough
1 tablespoon butter   1 egg

Set sponge, using one cup milk, two cups flour, one teaspoon salt, one cake compressed yeast, and let rise overnight. In the morning add above ingredients and let rise. When light, roll out in rectangular shape one-fourth inch thick, spread with melted butter, sugar, cinnamon, and currants. Roll like jelly roll. Cut in pieces three-fourths inch thick. Place in buttered baking sheet cut side up and down. When light, bake one-half hour in moderate oven (350° F.). Brush over with beaten egg and return to oven to brown.

Coffee Cake

Use fancy yeast dough. After the first rising of the dough, knead in one-half cup raisins and let rise thirty minutes. Butter pan generously, line with chopped nuts. Put dough in pan over nuts. Let rise until double in bulk. Brush with melted butter and sprinkle with brown sugar. Bake one hour in moderate oven (350° F.).

Hot Cross Buns

1 cup scalded milk	1 yeast cake
3 tablespoons shortening	3 cups flour
¼ cup sugar	2 eggs (beaten)
½ teaspoon salt	¼ cup currants

Add shortening, sugar, and salt to milk. Heat until lukewarm, add yeast, flour, and eggs well beaten. When thoroughly mixed, add raisins, cover and let rise overnight. In the morning shape into large biscuits, place in greased muffin tins, let rise, brush over with beaten eggs, and bake in moderate oven (350° F.) thirty minutes. Cool and mark cross with frosting. May score cross with scissors before baking if desired.

Currant Buns

¼ cup melted butter	½ teaspoon salt
1½ cups scalded milk	½ cup currants (cleaned)
¼ cup sugar	4 cups flour
1 cake compressed yeast	

Scald milk. Cool to lukewarm temperature. Crumble yeast into milk. Stir. Add sugar, shortening, salt, currants, and flour. Mix well. Put into greased bowl. Let rise until double in bulk. Knead. Let rise forty-five minutes. Shape into biscuits. Put into greased muffin tins. Let rise until double in bulk. Bake in a moderate oven (350° F.) for thirty minutes. While hot, ice with a confectioners' sugar icing. If glazing is desired, brush biscuits with beaten egg before baking.

Cinnamon Rolls

Use fancy yeast dough. Roll to oblong shape one-fourth inch thick. Brush with butter. Spread with sugar and cinnamon. Roll like jelly roll and cut in pieces one-half inch thick. Grease muffin tins generously. Put layer of brown sugar three-quarters of an inch thick in muffin rings. Dot well with butter. Place cut surface of the roll over this filling. Let rise twenty minutes. Bake in moderate oven (350° F.) for twenty-five minutes. Invert pan, leaving pan over rolls for few minutes to allow the butterscotch to set.

Butterscotch Rolls

4¼ cups flour	¼ cup sugar
1 cup milk (scalded and cooled)	2 cakes compressed yeast
1½ teaspoons salt	⅓ cup butter
2 eggs	

Crumble yeast into bowl. Add the milk slowly and stir to soften the yeast. Add sugar, beaten eggs, salt, and flour. Mix thoroughly. Add melted butter and mix again. Turn onto a floured board and knead to a smooth dough. Place in a well-greased bowl, cover, and let rise until double in bulk. Knead and let rise fifty minutes. Turn on floured board. Roll to one-half inch thickness. Brush with butter. Sprinkle with one-half cup brown sugar. Roll as for jelly roll and cut into one-inch pieces. Butter a baking pan generously and cover the butter with a layer of brown sugar. Cover brown sugar with a layer of nut meats. Place rolls, cut side down, in nut meats. Let rise twenty-five minutes. Bake in oven (425° F.) twenty minutes. Invert pan.

Breakfast Crescents

Roll out fancy yeast dough to one-fourth inch thickness. Cut into triangular pieces, brush over with butter, sprinkle with mixture of cinnamon and sugar, and roll up into crescents so that the outer end is in the middle of the length on the outside of the roll. Seal well. Lay in crescent shape on well-greased baking sheets, allow to rise until double in bulk. Brush over with beaten egg and bake twenty minutes in moderate oven (350° F.). After baking, ice with confectioners' sugar icing, and sprinkle with chopped nuts.

Breakfast Tea Ring

Shape fancy yeast dough into a long roll. Roll to one-fourth inch thickness. Spread with melted shortening, sprinkle with sugar, chopped almonds, and raisins. Roll like a jelly roll and join ends to form ring. Place on buttered baking sheet and cut with scissors at one inch intervals. Pull out and overlay cut slices. Let rise. Brush top with egg slightly beaten. Bake for one-half hour in moderate oven (350° F.). While hot, ice with confectioners' sugar icing and sprinkle with chopped nut meats.

Dinner Crescents

2 cakes compressed yeast	2 teaspoons salt

3½ cups flour

Make sponge, using two cups milk. Let rise overnight. In the morning add two tablespoons sugar, one-half cup butter, and flour enough to knead. Make a very stiff dough. Put into greased bowl. Let rise until light. Turn onto moulding board. Roll dough thin as possible and cut in strips about seven inches wide. Cut these into squares, and then cut squares in two, making two triangles about ten inches at base. Brush with melted shortening. Then, commencing at base, roll up. Bring ends toward each other to form crescent, keeping the point in middle of roll. Place on greased pan some distance apart. When light, brush top with beaten egg. Bake fifteen to twenty minutes in hot oven (425° F.).

Ice Box Rolls

2 cakes compressed yeast
1 tablespoon salt
2 eggs

4 tablespoons shortening
¼ cup sugar
2 cups water (lukewarm)

6 cups flour

Crumble yeast into a bowl. Add sugar and salt. Add water. Add well-beaten egg. Add half of the flour and beat well. Add melted shortening. Mix in the rest of the flour. Let rise to double its bulk. Knead down, cover, and place in the ice box. Use dough from day to day as desired. Each time let rise to double in bulk and bake in hot oven (425° F.) for twenty minutes.

Cloverleaf Rolls

4 cups sifted flour
1 tablespoon salt
2 eggs

¼ cup butter
3 cakes compressed yeast
1 cup milk

¼ cup sugar

Crumble yeast into a bowl, add lukewarm milk, and stir to dissolve yeast. Add sugar, beaten eggs, salt, and flour. Mix well. Add melted butter and mix thoroughly. Turn out on floured board and knead to a smooth dough. Place in greased bowl. Cover and let rise until double in bulk; knead down and let rise twenty-five minutes. Form the dough into small balls. Grease muffin pans. Place three balls of the dough in each pan. Grease top of rolls and allow to rise until light. Bake twenty-five minutes in hot oven (400° F.).

Potato Biscuits

1 cup potato water
½ cup mashed potato
½ cup water (lukewarm)
½ cup sugar

1 yeast cake
1 teaspoon salt
4½ cups flour
¼ cup shortening

Crumble yeast; add salt, sugar, and water. Add potato and potato water. Stir in flour to make a stiff sponge. Add melted shortening. Add remainder of flour and knead until smooth.

Put into greased bowl. Let rise for two hours. Knead. Let rise for forty-five minutes. Shape into round balls. Put in muffin pans. Let rise again about thirty minutes and bake in a hot oven (425° F.) for twenty-five minutes.

Plain Muffins

1 egg	1 cup milk
½ teaspoon salt	1 tablespoon shortening
1½ cups flour	2 teaspoons baking powder

Beat egg with milk, add salt and shortening, and lastly the dry ingredients. Mix smooth. Bake twenty minutes in hot oven (375–400° F.) in greased muffin tins. Fill muffin pans two-thirds full.

Date Muffins

1 egg	1 cup milk
½ teaspoon salt	1 tablespoon shortening
1½ cups flour	2 teaspoons baking powder
½ cupful dates	

Beat egg with milk, add salt and shortening, and lastly the dry ingredients. Stir in the dates. Mix smooth. Bake twenty minutes in hot oven (375–400° F.) in greased muffin tins. Fill muffin pans two-thirds full. Raisins may be substituted for the dates.

Corn Meal Muffins

1 egg	1 cup milk
½ teaspoon salt	1 tablespoon shortening
2 tablespoons sugar	2 teaspoons baking powder
1 cup flour	½ cup yellow corn meal

Beat egg with milk, add salt and shortening, and lastly the dry ingredients. Mix smooth. Bake twenty minutes in hot oven (375–400° F.) in greased muffin tins. Fill muffin pans two-thirds full.

Bran Muffins

1 egg	½ cup bran or whole wheat
½ teaspoon salt	1 cup milk
1 cup flour	1 tablespoon shortening
2 teaspoon baking powder	

Beat egg with milk, add salt and shortening, and lastly the dry ingredients. Mix smooth. Bake twenty minutes in hot oven (375–400° F.) in greased muffin tins. Fill muffin pans two-thirds full. One-half cup raisins or dates will improve this recipe. Nuts may also be added.

Blueberry Muffins

1 egg	½ cup blueberries
½ teaspoon salt	1 cup milk
2 cups flour	1 tablespoon shortening
2 teaspoons baking powder	

Beat egg with milk, add salt and shortening, and lastly the dry ingredients. Stir in the blueberries. Mix smooth. Bake twenty minutes in hot oven (375–400° F.) in greased muffin tins. Fill muffin pans two-thirds full.

Oatmeal Muffins

1 cup cooked oatmeal	4 teaspoons baking powder
1½ cups flour	1 teaspoon salt
2 tablespoons sugar	1 cup milk
2 tablespoons shortening	1 egg

Mix and sift dry ingredients. Add one-half the milk and the well-beaten egg. Add the rest of the milk to the oatmeal. Combine mixtures. Beat thoroughly. Add shortening. Bake in greased muffin tins for twenty-five minutes in moderately hot oven (375° F.).

Potato Muffins

2 small potatoes boiled and put through ricer	2 eggs (well beaten)
1 cup scalded milk (cooled to lukewarm)	2 tablespoons shortening
	1 tablespoon sugar
1 yeast cake	2 teaspoons salt
	4 cups flour

Add yeast to lukewarm milk. Add salt, sugar, shortening, potatoes, eggs, and flour.

Mix as stiff as possible with a spoon. Let stand five hours in warm place. Turn onto floured board. Roll out, adding as little flour as possible. Roll one-half to three-fourths inch thick. Cut with biscuit cutter, place on buttered pans, grease top of muffins, and let stand two hours. Bake for ten minutes in hot oven (425° F.).

Indian Muffins

1 cup corn meal
1 cup flour
1 egg
2 tablespoons shortening

1 teaspoon salt
3 teaspoons baking powder
1½ cups milk
4 tablespoons bacon (fried and cut fine)

Beat egg and add shortening and milk. Mix the dry ingredients. Combine ham, liquid, and dry ingredients. Mix smooth. Bake in greased muffin tins for twenty-five minutes. Oven moderately hot (375° F.). Ham may be substituted for the bacon.

Mincemeat Muffins

3 cups whole wheat flour
3 teaspoons baking powder
1 teaspoon soda
4 teaspoons sugar
1 teaspoon salt

1¾ cups milk
1 cup mincemeat
2 teaspoons grape juice
2 teaspoons melted butter
1 egg

Beat egg with milk, add shortening. Mix dry ingredients. Add to liquid. Add mincemeat. Mix thoroughly. Fill greased muffin tins two-thirds full. Bake twenty-five minutes in moderately hot oven (375° F.).

Raspberry Muffins

¾ cup sugar
3 tablespoons shortening
1 egg
1 cup sour milk

½ teaspoon salt
1½ cups flour
1 teaspoon soda
1 cup raspberries

Cream shortening and sugar. Add egg. Beat well. Mix dry ingredients. Add alternately with liquid. Add raspberries.

Fill greased muffin tins two-thirds full. Bake thirty minutes in moderate oven (350° F.).

Bran Muffins with Molasses

1 cup flour	1 egg
1 teaspoon salt	1 teaspoon soda
1¼ cups milk	2 cups bran

½ cup molasses

Mix dry ingredients. Beat egg, add milk and molasses. Add to dry ingredients. Put in well-greased muffin tin. Bake twenty-five minutes in moderate oven (350° F.).

Berry Muffins

2 cups flour	1 egg
¼ teaspoon salt	1 cup milk
3 teaspoons baking powder	2 teaspoons melted shortening
¼ cup sugar	1 cup berries

Beat the egg, add the milk and melted shortening. Mix the dry ingredients. Combine liquid and dry ingredients. Mix smooth. Add the berries. Fill greased muffin tins two-thirds full of muffin mixture. Bake twenty-five minutes in moderately hot oven (375° F.).

Sour-Milk Muffins

2 cups flour	2 teaspoons baking powder
¼ teaspoon soda	½ teaspoon salt
2 tablespoons sugar	1 egg
1 cup sour milk	2 tablespoons shortening

Sift flour once before measuring. Mix flour, baking powder, soda, salt, and sugar together. Beat the egg, add milk, and stir into the dry ingredients. Add the melted shortening last. Bake in greased muffin pans twenty to twenty-five minutes in moderately hot oven (375° F.).

Popovers

1 cup flour	½ teaspoon salt
2 eggs	1¼ cups milk

Add milk to well-beaten eggs. Add this mixture to flour and salt. Beat well. Put in hot, well-greased popover or muffin tins and bake forty minutes. Have oven hot for first ten minutes, then decrease heat to finish baking. Start 500° F., decrease to 375° F.

Whole-Wheat Biscuits

1 cup flour	1 teaspoon salt
1 cup whole wheat flour	3 tablespoons shortening
4 teaspoons baking powder	1 cup milk

Mix dry ingredients. Cut in shortening. Add milk to make soft dough. Roll on slightly floured board to one-inch thickness. Cut with biscuit cutter. Bake fifteen minutes in hot oven (400° F.).

Sour-Milk Baking-Powder Biscuits

2 cups flour	1 teaspoon salt
1 teaspoon soda	3 teaspoons baking powder
4 tablespoons shortening	¾ cup sour milk

Sift flour once before measuring. Mix dry ingredients. Cut in shortening. Add the milk gradually to form soft dough. Roll out and cut with biscuit cutter. Bake fifteen minutes in hot oven (400° F.).

Sour-Cream Biscuits

2 cups flour	½ teaspoon soda
4 teaspoons baking powder	1 teaspoon salt
¾ cup sour cream	2 tablespoons shortening

Mix dry ingredients. Cut in shortening and stir into the dough the sour cream. Turn dough onto moulding board. Pat the dough to one-half inch thickness. Cut with biscuit cutter. Bake in hot oven until light brown (400° F.).

Orange Tea Biscuit

2 cups flour	¾ cup milk
½ teaspoon salt	4 teaspoons baking powder
2 tablespoons sugar	Grated rind of orange
3 tablespoons shortening	

Mix the dry ingredients. Cut in the shortening, add the grated orange rind. Add liquid to dry ingredients. Mix thoroughly. Turn dough onto floured moulding board. Pat to one-half inch thickness. Cut with small cutter, put into greased baking pan. Before putting into the oven take one-half pieces loaf sugar and dip into orange juice and press down into the top of each biscuit. Bake in quick oven (425° F.) and serve at once.

Best Baking-Powder Biscuits

2 cups flour	¾ cup liquid
4 teaspoons baking powder	1 teaspoon salt
3 tablespoons shortening	

Mix the dry ingredients. Cut in shortening. Add the liquid. Turn onto a floured moulding board. Pat to one-half inch thickness. Cut with biscuit cutter. Place on a greased baking sheet. Bake in a hot oven (400° F.) fifteen to twenty minutes.

Pigs in Clover

2 cups flour	4 tablespoons shortening
1 teaspoon salt	¾ cup milk
4 teaspoons baking powder	

Sift flour, salt, and baking powder together. Cut in the shortening. Add milk to make a soft dough. Turn on floured moulding board. Roll out to one-fourth inch thickness. Cut in squares. Wrap each square around frankfurter or pork sausage which has been previously cooked. Place in rows on baking sheet and bake in hot oven (400° F.) fifteen to twenty minutes. Serve with mustard.

Ham Roll

2 cups flour	1 teaspoon salt
4 teaspoons baking powder	3 tablespoons shortening
¾ cup milk	

Mix the dry ingredients. Cut in the shortening. Add liquid. Mix well. Turn dough onto floured moulding board. Pat into oblong shape one-half inch thick. Spread with shortening and then with deviled ham. Roll like jelly roll. Seal well. Cut into one-inch slices and put on greased baking sheet cut side up. Brush top with melted shortening. Bake in hot oven (400° F.) fifteen minutes or until nicely browned.

Butterscotch Biscuits

2 cups flour	1 teaspoon salt
⅔ cup milk	4 teaspoons baking powder
4 tablespoons shortening	½ cup broken nut meats

Mix and sift dry ingredients. Cut in shortening. Add the milk gradually to form soft dough. Roll thin, spread with one-third cup creamed butter and three-fourths cup brown sugar. Cover with nut meats. Roll like a jelly roll. Cut into pieces one inch thick and put in greased muffin pans cut side up and bake fifteen minutes in hot oven (400° F.).

Cheese Biscuits

2 cups flour	4 teaspoons baking powder
1 teaspoon salt	3 tablespoons shortening
¾ cup milk	¼ pound American Cheese (grated)

Sift flour, salt, and baking powder together. Add cheese. Cut in shortening, add milk to make a soft dough. Turn onto floured moulding board, roll out to one inch thickness. Cut with biscuit cutter. Bake on greased baking sheet in hot oven (400° F.) fifteen to twenty minutes.

Cinnamon Pin Wheels

2 cups flour	3 tablespoons shortening
1 teaspoon salt	4 teaspoons baking powder
2 tablespoons sugar	¾ cup milk

Mix the dry ingredients. Cut in the shortening. Add milk and mix thoroughly. Turn out onto floured moulding board. Roll dough to one-eighth inch thickness. Brush with melted butter. Sprinkle with sugar which has been mixed with cinnamon. Roll like a jelly roll. Cut into one-inch pieces. Place cut side on greased baking sheet. Bake in hot oven (400° F.) for fifteen to twenty minutes.

Baking-Powder Coffee Cake

2 cups flour	½ teaspoon salt
2 tablespoons sugar	4 teaspoons baking powder
4 tablespoons shortening	¾ cup milk
1 egg (well beaten)	1 teaspoon vanilla

Mix and sift the dry ingredients. Cut in shortening and add the vanilla, egg, and the milk to make a soft dough. Place in a well-greased pan. Sprinkle with mixed sugar and cinnamon and dot with butter. Bake twenty-five minutes in moderate oven (375° F.).

Tea Biscuit Filled with Lobster

2 cups flour	1 teaspoon salt
4 teaspoons baking powder	3 tablespoons shortening
¾ cup milk	

Mix and sift flour, baking powder, and salt. Cut in shortening. Add liquid. Mix thoroughly and turn onto floured moulding board. Pat to one-half inch thickness. Bake on greased baking sheet fifteen minutes in hot oven (400° F.). When done, while hot, cut center from top of biscuit. Fill center with lobster salad. Return crust to biscuit and serve at once.

Something New for Breakfast
Eggs in Bacon Nests

Tea Dainties, No. 1

2 cups flour
2 tablespoons sugar
1 teaspoon salt
4 teaspoons baking powder
¼ cup stoned dates

¼ cup walnuts (chopped)
4 tablespoons shortening
¾ cup milk
20 marshmallows

Sift the flour, sugar, salt, and baking powder together. Cut in the shortening. Add the milk gradually, forming soft dough. Place a teaspoon of dough in small greased muffin tins, then a marshmallow; then a stoned date, and lastly a few walnut meats. Cover with another spoonful of dough and bake in a hot oven (400° F.) for fifteen minutes. While hot, ice with confectioners' sugar icing.

Tea Dainties, No. 2

2 cups flour
2 tablespoons sugar
1 teaspoon salt
4 teaspoons baking powder

¼ cup walnuts (chopped)
4 tablespoons shortening
¾ cup milk
10 apricots

Sift the flour, sugar, salt, and baking powder together. Cut in the shortening. Add the milk gradually, forming soft dough. Place a teaspoon of dough in small greased muffin tins. Cut the apricots in half and remove stones; place one-half in each tin, then a few walnut meats. Cover with another spoonful of dough and bake in a hot oven (400° F.) for fifteen minutes. Ice with confectioners' sugar icing while hot. Pitted stewed prunes may be used instead of apricots.

Breakfast Bread

½ cup sugar
¼ teaspoon salt
⅔ cup milk
1½ cups flour
½ cup raisins

2 tablespoons shortening
1 egg
1 teaspoon vanilla
4 teaspoons baking powder
½ cup citron (cut fine)

Mix the dry ingredients. Beat the egg with the milk. Add the melted shortening. Combine liquid and dry ingredients.

Add the fruit. Pour into a shallow cake pan that has been well greased. Spread with unbeaten white of egg, sprinkle with sugar and cinnamon. Dot with butter. Bake in moderately hot oven (375° F.) for twenty-five minutes.

Cheese Puffs

3 tablespoons grated cheese	1 egg
½ teaspoon salt	1 tablespoon butter
½ cup hot water	½ cup flour

Put cheese, salt, water, and butter into saucepan and boil. Add flour and beat till it leaves the pan. Add egg and beat. Drop by spoonfuls on greased baking sheet. Bake fifteen minutes in hot oven (425° F.).

Cheese Straws

½ pound grated American cheese	2 cups flour
1 teaspoon baking powder	½ pound butter

Put flour, baking powder, cheese, and butter together in the bowl. Mix thoroughly to a smooth paste. Chill. Roll as for pie crust. Cut into fancy shapes or squares and bake in hot oven (400° F.). Bake on ungreased baking sheets.

Cheese Sticks

1 cup flour	½ teaspoon baking powder
⅓ cup shortening	¼ teaspoon salt

Mix baking powder, flour, and salt. Cut in shortening. Add ice water to form ball. Turn onto a floured baking board. Roll to one-quarter inch thickness. Cover with one tablespoon grated American cheese. Fold edges of dough together. Roll out. Add 1 tablespoon grated cheese. Fold edges together. Repeat until 4 tablespoons grated cheese have been added. Chill. Roll to one-eighth inch thickness. Cut in strips one by two and one-half inches. Bake in hot oven (450° F.) until brown. Bake on ungreased baking sheets.

Salad Tarts

¼ pound cream cheese   ¼ pound sweet butter
1 cup flour   1 teaspoon baking powder

Mix the above ingredients. Mould into ball. Let stand in
ice box overnight. Toss on floured board. Roll thin and cut
in three-inch squares. Put a piece of cooked lobster on one
half, turn other half over, making a little turnover. Seal
thoroughly. Bake on a baking sheet in a hot oven (400° F.).
Chicken may be substituted instead of lobster.

Rye Gems

1 cup rye flour   1 teaspoon salt
¼ cup sugar   1 cup flour
1 egg   2 teaspoons baking powder
                   1½ cups milk

Mix dry ingredients. Beat egg and milk. Add to dry ingredients. Bake in well-greased gem pans for twenty-five
minutes in hot oven (400° F.).

CHAPTER XIII

Cakes

Burnt Sugar Cake

½ cup shortening
1 cup sugar
⅛ cup milk
1½ cups flour

½ teaspoon salt
3 eggs
2 teaspoons baking powder
2 tablespoons caramelized sugar

Cream shortening. Add sugar and mix until well blended. Add the eggs and salt and beat thoroughly. Mix baking powder with the flour. Add caramelized sugar to milk. Add dry and liquid ingredients alternately to first mixture. Stir until smooth. Pour into a greased and flour-dusted cake tin. Bake thirty-five minutes in a moderate oven (350° F.). Turn out of pan. Cool. Ice.

To caramelize sugar put one cup of sugar into a skillet. Stir until sugar melts and turns brown. Add one-half cup boiling water. Cook until sugar dissolves. Will keep.

Cocoa Cake

⅛ cup butter
1¼ cups sugar
3 eggs
⅔ cup milk

⅛ cup cocoa
¼ teaspoon salt
2 teaspoons baking powder
½ teaspoon vanilla

1½ cups flour

Cream shortening. Add sugar and salt gradually. Mix until well blended. Add the eggs. Beat thoroughly. Mix cocoa and baking powder with the flour. Add vanilla to milk. Add dry and liquid ingredients alternately to first mixture. Mix until smooth. Pour into a greased and flour-dusted cake tin. Bake thirty-five minutes in a moderate oven (350° F.). Turn out of pan. Cool. Ice.

Chocolate Cake, No. 1

½ cup shortening   1 square chocolate (melted)
1 cup sugar   ½ teaspoon salt
2 eggs   1 teaspoon vanilla
3 teaspoons baking powder   ¾ cup milk
                  2 cups flour

Cream shortening. Add sugar gradually. Add well-beaten eggs and vanilla. Sift flour and baking powder together. Add this mixture alternately with the milk to first mixture. Bake in well-greased layer cake pans. Bake twenty-five minutes in moderate oven (350° F.).

This cake may be baked as a sheet or loaf cake if desired.

Chocolate Cake, No. 2

1 cup shortening   ½ cup yeast dissolved in
1 cup sweet milk   ¼ cup warm water
2 cups sugar   1 cup nuts (chopped)
3 eggs   3 cups flour
2 squares chocolate (melted)   1 teaspoon soda dissolved in
½ teaspoon salt   3 tablespoons boiling water

Cream shortening. Add sugar and salt gradually. Mix until well blended. Add the eggs and beat thoroughly. Mix flour and nut meats. Add yeast mixture to first mixture. Add flour and nuts alternately with the milk. Add the melted chocolate. Mix well. Let stand in ice box overnight. In the morning add the soda dissolved in boiling water. Mix well. Pour into a greased and flour-dusted cake pan. Bake forty-five minutes in a moderate oven (350° F.). Cool. Ice with coffee icing.

Delicious Chocolate Cake

½ cup milk   ½ cup sugar
                3 squares chocolate

Cook these ingredients until chocolate is melted. Bring to a boil. Cool.

1 cup sugar

½ cup butter

3 eggs

½ cup milk

2 cups flour

¾ teaspoon soda

1 teaspoon cream of tartar

Cream butter. Add sugar gradually. Add egg yolks and beat thoroughly. Add soda and cream of tartar to flour. Add dry ingredients to first mixture alternately with the milk. Add boiled mixture which has been cooled to this. Fold in stiffly beaten egg whites. Pour into greased and flour-dusted layer cake pans. Bake twenty-five minutes in a moderately hot oven (375° F.). This will make three layers.

Put layers together with a chocolate cream filling.

4 squares chocolate

3 tablespoons milk

¾ cup sugar

2 teaspoons butter

2 egg yolks

¼ teaspoon salt

1 teaspoon vanilla

Mix ingredients and cook until thick. Stir constantly. Cool. Spread between layers. Ice cake with boiled icing.

Boston Fudge Cake

3 squares chocolate

3 tablespoons butter

½ cup boiling water

1 cup sugar

1 egg

¼ cup sour milk

¾ teaspoon soda

½ teaspoon vanilla

1 cup flour

¼ teaspoon salt

Melt chocolate and butter together over hot water. Add boiling water and mix thoroughly. Add sugar. Mix well. Add eggs well beaten. Stir until well mixed. Mix soda and salt with the flour. Add alternately with the sour milk to other ingredients. Mix thoroughly. Pour into a greased and flour-dusted cake pan. Bake thirty minutes in a moderate oven (350° F.). Ice with fudge frosting. Top with nuts.

Jelly Roll

3 eggs

1 cup sugar

1 teaspoon baking powder

3 tablespoons milk

Jelly (preferably currant)

1 cup flour

Beat egg yolks until light. Add sugar. Mix well. Beat egg whites until stiff. Mix baking powder with flour. Add milk to first mixture. Fold in egg whites. Stir in flour. Mix well. Pour into shallow pan which has been lined with waxed paper. Bake twenty minutes in a moderate oven (350° F.). Turn out onto a towel covered with confectioners' sugar. Remove waxed paper. Spread with jelly. Roll. Dust with confectioners' sugar. Serve hot or cold.

Chocolate Roll

3 eggs	¼ teaspoon salt
⅔ cup water	1 cup sugar
½ cup cocoa	1¾ cups flour
3 teaspoons baking powder	

Beat egg yolk until thick and lemon colored. Add sugar and salt. Mix well. Mix cocoa, baking powder, and flour. Add alternately with water to first mixture. Fold in stiffly beaten egg whites. Pour into shallow pan which has been lined with waxed paper. Bake twenty minutes in a moderate oven (350° F.). Turn out onto a towel covered with confectioners' sugar. Remove waxed paper. Spread with sweetened whipped cream. Roll. Dust with confectioners' sugar. To serve, cut in slices and top each slice with vanilla ice cream. Marshmallow fluff may be used instead of whipped cream.

Plain Cake

½ cup shortening	⅔ cup milk
1 cup sugar	1 teaspoon vanilla
2 eggs	2 cups flour
3 teaspoons baking powder	½ teaspoon salt

Cream shortening and sugar. Add eggs and beat thoroughly. Add salt and baking powder to flour. Add vanilla to milk. Add liquid and dry ingredients alternately to first mixture. Spread batter into greased cake pan to one-quarter inch thickness. Cover dough with one-quarter cup broken nut meats, one-half cup sugar, and cinnamon mixed together. Bake in moderate oven (350° F.) twenty-five minutes. Serve hot. Cut cake into pieces with a fork.

French Pastry, No. 1

1½ cups shortening
1 cup sugar
2 eggs

⅔ cup milk
1 teaspoon vanilla
2 cups flour

3 teaspoons baking powder

Cream shortening and sugar. Add eggs and beat thoroughly. Add salt and baking powder to flour. Add vanilla to milk. Add liquid and dry ingredients alternately to first mixture. Spread batter into greased cake pan to one-quarter inch thickness. Bake in a moderate oven (350° F.) twenty-five minutes. Turn out onto cake rack. When cool, cut with fancy cookie cutters. Ice all the way around. Decorate with candies, cocoanut, nut meats, or colored shot. Candies representing flowers or fruits may be used for decoration. Icing may be tinted with vegetable coloring and thereby be made more effective.

Devil's Food Cake, No. 1

½ cup shortening
2 eggs
½ teaspoon salt
1 cup milk

2 teaspoons vanilla
1¼ cups sugar
1¾ cups flour
2 teaspoons baking powder

4 squares chocolate

Cream shortening. Add sugar and mix until well blended. Add eggs and beat thoroughly. Mix salt, baking powder, and flour. Add vanilla to the milk. Add liquid and dry ingredients alternately to the first mixture. Add vanilla and melted chocolate. Mix until smooth. Pour into a greased and flour-dusted cake tin eight by twelve inches, and bake forty minutes in a moderate oven (350° F.).

Devil's Food Cake, No. 2

½ cup shortening
2 eggs
½ teaspoon salt
1 cup sour milk

1 teaspoon vanilla
1¼ cups sugar
1¾ cups flour
1 teaspoon soda

3 squares chocolate

Cream shortening and sugar together. Add the well-beaten eggs. Mix flour, salt, and baking powder together. Add to the creamed mixture, alternately with the milk. Add melted chocolate and vanilla. Mix well and pour into greased flour-dusted oblong pan or layer-cake tins. Bake forty minutes in moderate oven (350° F.). Bake thirty minutes for layer cake.

Fruit Cake

½ pound shortening
½ pound brown sugar
6 egg yolks
½ pound citron
1 pound raisins
1 pound currants
½ pound almonds (cut fine)
½ pound candied cherries

1 teaspoon cinnamon
½ teaspoon nutmeg
1 teaspoon mace
½ teaspoon allspice
1 teaspoon cloves
6 egg whites
½ pound flour
¼ cup orange juice

1 slice candied pineapple (cut fine)

Cream shortening, add sugar, and egg yolks. Beat thoroughly. Then add floured fruit, liquid and flour. Fold in the stiffly beaten egg whites. Line pan with three or four thicknesses of well-greased paper. Bake four or five hours in a very slow oven (300° F.) or steam four hours and bake one.

White Fruit Cake

1 pound sugar
½ pound butter
1 cup fruit juice
1 pound flour
2 teaspoons baking powder
½ teaspoon salt
1 pound white raisins
½ pound Brazil nuts

½ pound citron
½ pound red cherries (candied)
1 large cocoanut (grated)
½ pound pineapple (candied)
½ pound orange peel (candied)
½ pound lemon peel (candied)
8 egg whites
1 pound blanched almonds

Cream the butter, add sugar gradually. Mix baking powder and salt with half the flour and add alternately with liquid to first mixture. Add remaining flour to fruit and nuts cut fine. Add floured fruit to cake mixture. Fold in the beaten egg whites. Bake in loaf pan or round cake pan lined with heavy oiled paper. Bake for three and one-half hours in a slow oven (300°

F.).   This makes four one-pound cakes or two two-pound cakes.

Christmas Fruit Cake

½ pound shortening	6 eggs
½ pound brown sugar	1 teaspoon cinnamon
½ pound flour	1 teaspoon mace
½ pound citron	½ teaspoon nutmeg
½ pound almonds	½ teaspoon allspice
½ pound walnuts (chopped)	¼ teaspoon cloves
1 pound raisins (seedless)	¼ cup fruit juice
1 pound currants	2 teaspoons baking powder
½ pound cherries (candied)	1 teaspoon salt

Shave and chop the heated citron.   Wash the raisins and currants.   Blanch and cut almonds.   Halve the cherries.   Mix all these together and dredge with flour.   Mix the remainder of the flour with salt, spices, and baking powder.   Cream shortening and add sugar gradually.   Add egg yolks well beaten. Add the flour mixture and fruit juice alternately.   Stir in fruit and nuts.   Fold in stiffly beaten egg whites.   Line pans well with three layers of oiled paper.

Put the cake mixture in the pans.   Bake three hours in slow oven (325° F.).

Date Cake

¾ cup flour	3 eggs
½ teaspoon baking powder	1 cup brown sugar
1 cup dates (cut fine)	1 teaspoon vanilla
1 cup broken walnut meats	2 tablespoons melted shortening
½ teaspoon salt	

Beat eggs until light.   Add sugar and shortening.   Mix thoroughly.   Add dates and nut meats, stir in flour which has been mixed with salt and baking powder.   Bake in a shallow cake pan, eight by twelve inches, that has been greased and dusted with flour.   Bake thirty minutes in a moderate oven (350° F.).   While hot, ice with confectioners' sugar and milk icing.   Cool before serving.   May be baked in layers.   Serve with whipped cream between layers and on top.   Decorate with cherries or nuts.

Almond Cake

12 eggs	1 pound granulated sugar
1 teaspoon vanilla	1 pound almonds
2 teaspoons baking powder	

Beat egg yolks until thick and lemon colored. Add sugar gradually, beating continually. Beat sugar and egg yolks together fifteen minutes. Add vanilla, baking powder, and ground almonds. Fold in beaten egg whites. Pour into a greased spring mould and bake in slow oven (325° F.) one hour. Remove side of pan. Cool. Ice with boiled frosting or dust with confectioners' sugar.

Delicious Tea Cake

½ pound butter	1 teaspoon vanilla
½ pound sugar	½ pound flour
6 eggs	2 teaspoons baking powder
⅛ teaspoon salt	½ cup almonds
½ cup sugar and cinnamon	

Cream butter until soft and creamy. Add sugar and mix until thoroughly blended. Add egg yolks and beat hard until well mixed and light. Add salt and baking powder to flour. Combine mixtures. Add vanilla. Fold in stiffly beaten egg whites. Mix until smooth. Pour into a greased and flour-dusted cake pan eight by twelve inches. Sprinkle with chopped almonds, and a mixture of sugar and cinnamon. Bake forty minutes in a slow oven (325° F.). Do not remove from pan before serving. Cool and dust with confectioners' sugar before serving.

Spice Cake

¼ cup butter	½ teaspoon soda
1 cup sugar	1½ teaspoons cinnamon
1 egg	½ teaspoon nutmeg
1 cup sour milk	¾ cup raisins
2 cups flour	

Mix raisins with two tablespoons flour which is to be used in the cake. Mix the remainder of the flour, soda, and spices.

Add egg and mix. Cream butter and sugar. Add the milk and flour mixtures alternately and mix well. Fold in the floured raisins. Pour into a greased and flour-dusted cake pan eight by ten inches. Bake thirty-five minutes in a moderate oven (350°F.).

Nut Cake

½ cup shortening
1½ cups sugar
3 teaspoons baking powder
½ teaspoon salt

2 cups flour
¾ cup water
1 cup nuts (chopped)
Whites 4 eggs

1 teaspoon almond extract

Cream shortening. Add sugar and mix until well blended. Mix salt and baking powder with the flour. Add flavoring to water. Add dry and liquid ingredients alternately to first mixture. Add nuts. Fold in stiffly beaten egg whites. Mix smooth. Pour into greased and flour-dusted cake pan eight by twelve inches. Bake thirty-five minutes in a moderate oven (350° F.). When done turn out of pan. Cool. Ice.

Orange Cake

2¼ cups flour
½ cup shortening
1 cup sugar
½ teaspoon salt

3 teaspoons baking powder
2 eggs
½ cup milk
½ cup orange juice

2 tablespoons grated orange rind

Cream the shortening, add sugar gradually. Mix until blended. Mix flour, salt, and baking powder. Add the well-beaten eggs to the first mixture. Add the flour to dough alternating with the milk and orange juice. Add the grated orange rind. Bake in layer cake pans. Bake forty-five minutes in a moderate oven (350° F.). This amount will make two layers.

Filled Cup Cakes

½ cup butter
2 eggs
1¾ cups flour
3 teaspoons baking powder

1 teaspoon vanilla
1 cup sugar
½ cup milk
½ teaspoon salt

Cream the butter and sugar. Add the eggs. Add the milk alternately with the dry ingredients which have been mixed together. Add the flavoring. Mix well. Bake in well-greased muffin tins, being careful not to fill more than two-thirds full. Bake for twenty minutes in a hot oven (400° F.). As soon as cakes are cool, cut off the top. Scoop out inside, and fill with cocoa cream icing. Replace the top and ice.

Lemon, chocolate, butterscotch, or orange filling may be used for these cakes instead of cocoa cream.

Plain Cup Cakes

1 cup butter	½ teaspoon salt
2 cups sugar	1 cup milk
4 eggs	3 teaspoons baking powder
1 teaspoon vanilla	3½ cups flour

Cream butter, add sugar and continue creaming. Add yolks of eggs. Mix flour, salt, and baking powder. Add alternately with the milk. Beat the egg whites and fold into mixture.

Bake in greased muffin pans twenty minutes in a hot oven (400° F.). Cool. Ice. One teaspoon vanilla may be added if desired. May be baked as a sheet if desired.

Rich Tea Cakes

3 tablespoons butter	1 cup flour
½ cup sugar	1 teaspoon baking powder
5 egg yolks	¼ teaspoon salt
¼ cup milk	Grated rind of 1 orange

Cream butter. Add sugar and mix until well blended. Add eggs. Beat until mixture is light. Add salt and baking powder to flour. Add alternately with milk to first mixture. Add orange rind. Mix until smooth. Bake in greased muffin pans twenty minutes in a hot oven (400° F.). Remove from pans. Cool. Ice.

Silver Cake

⅓ cup butter
1¼ cups sugar
4 egg whites
½ teaspoon salt

¼ cup milk
1½ cups flour
2 teaspoons baking powder
½ teaspoon almond extract

Cream butter. Add sugar and mix until well blended. Add almond extract to milk. Mix salt and baking powder with the flour. Add liquid and dry ingredients alternately to first mixture. Fold in stiffly beaten egg whites. Mix smooth. Pour into greased and flour-dusted cake pan six by ten inches. Bake thirty-five minutes in a moderate oven (350° F.). Turn out of pan. Cool. Ice.

Gold Cake

¼ cup shortening
½ cup sugar
Yolks of 5 eggs
Grated rind 1 lemon

¼ cup milk
⅞ cup flour
1½ teaspoons baking powder
1 teaspoon lemon juice

Cream butter, add sugar gradually. Add the yolks of the eggs beaten until thick and lemon colored. Add lemon juice and rind. Mix flour and baking powder. Add alternately with the milk to the first mixture. Pour dough into greased and flour-dusted cake pan six by ten inches. Bake forty-five minutes in moderate oven (350° F.).

Sandwich Cake

½ cup butter
2 eggs
1 teaspoon vanilla
1 cup nuts

1 teaspoon baking powder
1 cup sugar
½ teaspoon salt
1 cup dates

1½ cups flour

Cream butter. Add sugar and blend thoroughly. Add eggs and stir until well mixed. Mix baking powder and salt with the flour. Combine mixtures. Add flavoring. Mix smooth. Spread to one-half inch thickness in greased and flour-dusted cake pan. Cover with dates cut fine. Put nuts over dates. Beat one egg white until stiff. Add one cup brown sugar to beaten egg white. Spread over layer of nuts. Bake twenty-five minutes in a moderate oven (350° F.). Cut into squares after cake has cooled.

Ice-Box Cake

2 dozen lady fingers	1 teaspoon vanilla
1 quart cream	1 package gelatine
Whites of 5 eggs	½ cup cold water
¾ cup sugar	½ cup boiling water

Split lady fingers and arrange around sides and bottom of pudding dish. Crumb part of the lady fingers to sprinkle on top and bottom. Mix whipped cream, whites of eggs well beaten, sugar, and vanilla. Add cold water and then boiling water to gelatine. Let this stand while whipping the cream. Combine mixtures. Drain one can crushed pineapple. Add to other ingredients. Mix well. Pour into pudding dish. Be careful not to disarrange lady fingers. Sprinkle crumbed lady fingers over top. Set in refrigerator overnight. Serve very cold. Other fruits may be used instead of the pineapple.

Ribbon Cake

3 eggs	1 teaspoon vanilla
2 cups sugar	⅔ cup butter
3 cups flour	1 cup milk
2 teaspoons cream of tartar	1 teaspoon soda
½ teaspoon salt	

Cream the butter. Add sugar and stir until well blended. Add eggs and beat thoroughly. Mix salt, soda, and cream of tartar with the flour. Add vanilla to milk. Add dry and liquid ingredients alternately to first mixture. Mix smooth. Grease and flour-dust three layer-cake pans. Pour cake mixture into two of them. To remaining cake mixture add one tablespoon molasses, one-half cup raisins, one-half cup sliced citron, one teaspoon cinnamon, one-half teaspoon each of cloves, allspice, and nutmeg. Add one tablespoon flour and mix well. Pour into third cake pan. Bake twenty-five minutes in a moderate oven (350° F.). Turn out of pans. Cool. Put layers together with jelly. Dust top layer with confectioners' sugar.

Lady Baltimore Cake

½ cup shortening
1¼ cups sugar
2⅔ cups flour
½ teaspoon salt

3 teaspoons baking powder
1 cup milk
1 teaspoon almond extract
Whites of 5 eggs

Cream shortening thoroughly. Add sugar gradually. Stir until blended. Mix and sift flour, salt, and baking powder. Add to the creamed mixture alternately with the milk. Add the flavoring and mix well. Fold in the well-beaten egg whites. Bake in layer-cake pans, well greased and floured, forty-five minutes in a moderate oven (350° F.). Turn cake out of pans. Cool. Put layers together with Lady Baltimore filling. Ice sides and top of cake with boiled frosting.

Minnesota Layer Cake

1 cup sugar
½ cup butter
1 cup water
½ teaspoon salt

1 teaspoon vanilla
3 teaspoons baking powder
3¼ cups flour
Whites of 4 eggs

Cream butter. Add sugar and mix until well blended. Mix salt, baking powder, and flour. Add vanilla to water. Add dry and liquid ingredients alternately to first mixture. Fold in stiffly beaten egg whites. Mix smooth. Pour into greased and flour-dusted layer-cake pans. Bake twenty-five minutes in a moderate oven (350° F.). Turn cakes out of pans. Cool. Ice with butterscotch icing and decorate with walnut meats.

New England Sponge Cake

6 eggs
1 cup sugar
1 cup flour

½ teaspoon salt
2 tablespoons lemon juice
1 tablespoon water

Separate the eggs. Beat yolks until thick and lemon colored. Add sugar gradually. Beat thoroughly. Add lemon juice and water. Add salt to flour. Combine mixtures. Mix smooth. Fold in stiffly beaten egg whites. Pour into an ungreased tube tin. Bake in a slow oven (275° F. to 350° F.) for one hour. Increase heat gradually after the first fifteen minutes. Invert tin.

Let cake cool. Remove carefully with a spatula. Dust with confectioners' sugar.

English Sponge Cake

6 eggs
1 cup flour
1 cup sugar

¼ teaspoon salt
1 tablespoon lemon juice
Grated rind 1 lemon

Beat the egg whites until stiff. Add half the sugar. Beat the egg yolks until thick and lemon colored. Gradually add the remainder of the sugar, lemon juice, and grated rind. Fold the egg yolk mixture into the egg whites. Then fold in the flour and salt. Put into ungreased tube tin and bake in slow oven (275° to 350° F.), for one hour. Increase the heat gradually after the first fifteen minutes. Invert cake and let cool. Remove with spatula. Dust with powdered sugar.

Inexpensive Sponge Cake

2 eggs
½ teaspoon salt
1½ cups sugar

1 cup flour
½ cup water
2 teaspoons baking powder

Beat eggs. Add the sugar and salt. Beat thoroughly. Add the flour mixed with the baking powder. Add the water. Add one teaspoon lemon juice. Mix well. Bake in tube pan in moderate oven (350° F.) for forty-five minutes.

Chocolate Sponge Cake

2 cups sugar
4 eggs
1 cup milk
½ teaspoon salt

2 teaspoons baking powder
1 cup flour
1 teaspoon vanilla
½ pound chocolate

Separate eggs. Beat yolks and add sugar. Mix thoroughly. Heat milk and chocolate until chocolate melts. Cool. Mix the dry ingredients. Add alternately with milk and chocolate to the first mixture. Fold in stiffly beaten egg whites. Add vanilla. Bake in a greased and flour-dusted cake pan one hour in a slow oven (325° F.). Remove cake from pan and dust with confectioners' sugar before serving.

Sunshine Cake

Whites of 10 eggs	1 teaspoon lemon juice
Yolks of 6 eggs	1 cup flour
1½ cups confectioners' sugar	1 teaspoon cream of tartar

Beat whites of eggs stiff and dry. Add sugar and continue beating. Beat yolks of eggs until thick and lemon colored. Combine mixtures. Add lemon. Fold in flour which has been mixed with cream of tartar. Mix until smooth. Pour into an ungreased tube tin. Bake one hour in a slow oven (275° to 350° F.). Increase heat gradually after first fifteen minutes. Invert cake until cool. Remove carefully with a spatula. Dust with confectioners' sugar.

Glorified Sunshine Cake

⅞ cup sifted flour	⅓ cup of water
½ teaspoon cream of tartar	5 egg whites (stiffly beaten)
¼ teaspoon salt	5 egg yolks (beat until creamy)
1¼ cups sugar	1 teaspoon vanilla

Sift flour twice. Measure. Add cream of tartar and salt. Sift together three times. Boil sugar and water to 238° F. Pour syrup slowly over egg whites, beating constantly. Continue beating as mixture cools. Fold in egg yolks and flavoring. Add flour gradually. Pour into ungreased tube pan. Bake in slow oven (350° F.) for forty minutes. Then reduce heat to 325° F. and bake twenty minutes more. Remove from oven. Invert pan until cold. Carefully remove cake with a spatula. Dust with confectioners' sugar.

Angel Food

1 cup egg whites	1 teaspoon cream of tartar
1 cup flour	1 teaspoon salt
1½ cups granulated sugar	1 teaspoon almond extract

Beat egg whites until stiff. Add cream of tartar while beating. Continue beating until the egg white is stiff enough to hold its shape. Gradually fold in the sugar which has been sifted. Add the flavoring. Fold in the flour which has been sifted with the salt three times. Pour into ungreased tube cake pan. Bake in slow oven one hour gradually increasing heat from 250° to 350° F. Invert pan until cake is cool. Remove cake carefully with a spatula. Dust with confectioners' sugar.

Chocolate Angel Food

1¼ cups egg whites
1½ cups sugar
⅔ cup flour

1 teaspoon vanilla
1 teaspoon cream of tartar
¼ teaspoon salt

½ cup cocoa

Sift cocoa with the flour. Sift the sugar. Beat egg whites. Add cream of tartar and salt and beat until stiff but not dry. Add the sugar gradually, beating all the time. Add the vanilla. Fold in the flour and cocoa mixture. Put in a cool oven and bake at 250° F. for the first fifteen minutes, 275° F. for the next fifteen, 300° F. for the third fifteen, and finish baking at 350° F. Bake one hour. Invert pan to cool cake.

Angel Cake

8 egg whites
1 teaspoon cream of tartar
1 cup sugar

¼ teaspoon salt
¾ teaspoon vanilla
¾ cup flour

Add salt to egg whites and beat. Add cream of tartar and beat until stiff. Add flavoring. Mix sugar and flour, and sift several times. Sift over egg whites, and fold in as quickly as possible. Pour into ungreased tube tin and bake fifty minutes in slow oven (325° F.). When done, invert pan until cake cools.

Angel Food Delight

Cut the top from a large angel food cake about two inches down from top. Then cut out the inside. Fill the cavity with the following mixture:

2 cups whipped cream
½ cup pineapple (diced)
¼ pound quartered marshmallows

½ cup candied cherries
½ cup pecans (chopped)
1 teaspoon vanilla

Place top back on the cake. Ice the sides and top of cake. Decorate cake if desired. Chill in refrigerator two hours. Serve. Each slice will have a chilled cream center.

White Layer Cake

½ cup shortening
1½ cups sugar
1 cup liquid
3 egg whites

3 teaspoons baking powder
1 teaspoon vanilla or almond
   flavoring
⅛ teaspoon salt

2¼ cups flour

Cream sugar and shortening together. Add liquid alternately with the flour that has been mixed with the baking powder and salt. Add flavoring. Mix well. Fold in well-beaten whites of eggs. Pour into greased and flour-dusted layer-cake tins. Bake thirty-five minutes in moderate oven (350° F.).

Cocoanut Cake

¼ cup shortening
¾ cup sugar
½ cup milk
½ teaspoon salt
1½ cups flour

2 teaspoons baking powder
½ teaspoon vanilla
4 egg whites
4 tablespoons grated fresh
   cocoanut

Cream shortening. Add sugar and mix well. Add salt and baking powder to flour. Add vanilla to milk. Add liquid and dry ingredients alternately to first mixture. Add cocoanut. Fold in stiffly beaten egg whites. Pour into greased and flour-dusted layer cake pans. Bake thirty minutes in a moderate oven (350° F.). Ice cake before serving.

Little White Cakes

2 cups sugar
2 cups flour
½ teaspoon salt

8 teaspoons baking powder
Whites of 2 eggs
1 teaspoon vanilla

1 cup milk

Sift sugar, flour, baking powder, and salt together four times. Heat milk. Add to dry ingredients. Mix thoroughly. Add whites of eggs beaten stiff. Bake in greased muffin tins. Bake in a hot oven (400° F.) ten minutes. Remove from tin. Ice.

Yellow Cake

½ cup shortening
1 cup sugar
2 eggs
⅛ teaspoon salt

1 teaspoon vanilla
¾ cup milk
2 cups flour
3 teaspoons baking powder

1 tablespoon water

Cream shortening and sugar together. Add the egg yolks, which have been beaten until light, with the water and flavoring. Mix thoroughly. Mix the dry ingredients together and add to the first mixture alternately with the milk. Fold in the beaten egg whites. Bake either as a loaf cake or in layers in greased and flour-dusted pans. Bake forty minutes at 325° F., for loaf cake, and twenty minutes at 375° F., for layer cake. Cool before icing.

Black Walnut Cake

1½ cups sugar
½ cup shortening
1 cup milk
½ teaspoon salt

3 cups flour
3 teaspoons baking powder
1 teaspoon vanilla
½ cup black walnuts (chopped)

Whites of 5 eggs

Cream sugar and shortening together. Mix dry ingredients. Add milk alternately with dry ingredients. Add vanilla and nuts. Mix well. Fold in beaten whites of eggs. Put into greased and flour-dusted layer tins. Bake thirty minutes in moderate oven (350° F). Turn out of pans. Cool. Put layers together with a cream filling. Ice top and sides of cake.

Pound Cake, No. 1

¾ pound butter
1 pound sugar
1 cup milk
3 teaspoons vanilla

1 pound flour
4 teaspoons baking powder
Whites of 8 eggs
1 teaspoon salt

Cream butter. Add sugar gradually. Mix until well blended. Add vanilla to milk. Add salt and baking powder to flour.

Add dry and liquid ingredients alternately to first mixture. Add beaten egg whites last. For a close-grained cake, beat after adding eggs. For a light cake, fold in whites carefully. Bake in greased and flour-dusted bread pans one hour in a moderate oven (350° F.).

For assorted small cakes use pound cake. Cut in fancy shapes, ice with colored fondant. Decorate also with candies, cherries, nuts, and candied peel.

Pound Cake, No. 2

1½ cups sugar	1½ cups flour
1 cup butter	1 teaspoon vanilla
1 teaspoon salt	2 teaspoons baking powder

2 eggs

Mix baking powder with flour. Cream butter and sugar. Add the well-beaten egg. Mix thoroughly. Add flour and milk alternately to first mixture. Bake in tube pan which has been greased and dusted with flour from fifty to sixty minutes in moderate oven (350° F.). Cool. Ice.

Loaf Cake

⅓ cup shortening	1⅔ cups flour
¾ cup sugar	¼ teaspoon salt
2 eggs	2 teaspoons baking powder
½ cup milk	1 teaspoon vanilla

Cream the shortening, add sugar gradually. Add the eggs and beat thoroughly. Mix the baking powder with the flour. Add the vanilla to the milk. Add the liquid and dry ingredients alternately to the egg mixture, adding the dry ingredients first and last. Mix well.

Place in greased flour-dusted loaf pan. Bake forty-five minutes in moderate oven (350° F.).

One-half cup citron or candied pineapple cut fine and one-half cup candied cherries, halved, may be added to this recipe if desired.

Apple-Sauce Cake

½ cup butter
1 cup sugar
½ teaspoon cloves
1 teaspoon cinnamon
½ teaspoon nutmeg
½ cup raisins (chopped)

½ cup currants
1 teaspoon soda
1 cup hot apple sauce
2 cups flour
½ teaspoon salt

Cream butter. Add sugar and mix until well blended. Mix spices, soda, and salt with the flour. Add raisins to flour mixture. Add dry ingredients and apple sauce alternately to creamed mixture. Stir until smooth. Pour into greased and flour-dusted oblong cake pan six inches by ten inches. Bake forty-five minutes in a moderate oven (350° F.). Turn out of pan. Cool. Serve either plain or iced.

Pineapple and Cherry Butterscotch Cake

½ cup shortening
1 cup sugar
3 eggs
2 cups flour

3 teaspoons baking powder
½ teaspoon salt
⅔ cup milk
1 teaspoon vanilla

Mix the dry ingredients. Cream sugar and shortening. Add well-beaten eggs. Add milk alternately with the dry ingredients to creamed mixture. Add the vanilla and mix well. Grease generously a round pudding pan. Line with brown sugar about one-half inch deep. Dot with three tablespoons butter. Place in the pan slices of pineapple with maraschino cherry in center of each. Pour the cake batter over the mixture in the pan. Bake fifty minutes in moderate oven (350° F.). Turn out onto chop plate. Serve hot with whipped cream topped with cherries.

Filled Cake

1 cup sugar
⅔ cup milk
1½ cups flour
¼ teaspoon salt

½ cup butter
3 eggs
3 teaspoons baking powder
1 teaspoon vanilla

Cream the butter, add sugar gradually. Add the eggs and beat thoroughly. Mix the baking powder with the flour. Add the vanilla to the milk. Add the liquid and the dry ingredients alternately to the egg mixture, adding the dry ingredients first and last. Mix until smooth. Pour into greased and flour-dusted layer cake pans. Bake thirty-five minutes in a moderate oven (350° F.). Turn out of pans. Cool. Put layers together with lemon filling. Ice top and sides of cake or serve with whipped cream.

Cheese Cake

4 cups crumbs	3 tablespoons butter
3 tablespoons sugar	4 eggs (yolks and whites
½ pint cream	beaten separately)
1 cup sugar	1 pound cream cheese
¼ teaspoon salt	3 tablespoons flour
1 teaspoon vanilla	

Roll the crumbs very fine. Add to butter and sugar which have been creamed together. Blend thoroughly. Put mixture in the bottom of a baking pan and press down even all around. A spring form is best, but any other pan may be used. Beat yolks, add remaining ingredients. Beat egg whites stiff and add to mixture. Mix thoroughly. Pour into baking pan on top of the crumbs. Bake one hour in a slow oven (325° F.).

Rich Cream Cake

1 cup sour cream	½ teaspoon soda
1 cup sugar	1½ teaspoons baking powder
3 eggs	1 tablespoon lemon juice
1½ cups flour	Grated rind one lemon
½ teaspoon salt	

Beat the eggs, add sugar, and beat thoroughly. Add sour cream, lemon juice, and grated rind. Mix the dry ingredients and add to the egg mixture. Stir until well mixed. Pour into a greased and flour-dusted cake pan six by ten inches. Bake thirty minutes in a moderate oven (350° F.). Turn out of pan. Cool. Cover top with quartered marshmallows. Put boiled frosting over marshmallows. Ice sides of cake. Cool before serving.

Shortbread

½ pound butter	1 egg
¼ pound shortening	1¼ pounds flour
1 cup sugar	¼ teaspoon soda
1 teaspoon nutmeg	½ teaspoon cream of tartar

Mix until soft the butter and shortening. Mix with sugar and egg. Beat well. Mix the flour, soda, cream of tartar, and nutmeg. Combine mixtures. Sprinkle sugar on moulding board and rolling pin. Toss dough onto board. Roll thin and cut in shapes. Bake on greased baking sheets. Bake in moderate oven (350° F.) ten minutes.

Scotch Shortbread

2 cups flour	1 cup butter
½ cup brown sugar	

Mix sugar and flour. Add butter. Mix thoroughly. Mould into ball. Toss onto floured moulding board. Roll to one-eighth inch thickness. Cut into diamond shapes. Prick top with a fork. Bake on greased baking sheets in a moderate oven (350° F.) fifteen minutes.

Bishop Bread

1 cup sugar	1½ teaspoons baking powder
3 eggs	1 cup almonds
1½ cups flour	1 cup raisins
1 teaspoon vanilla	½ teaspoon salt

Beat the eggs until light. Add the sugar and continue beating until well mixed. Add vanilla, salt, and baking powder to flour. Cut almonds and mix with raisins. Combine mixtures. Stir until well mixed. Pour into a greased and flour-dusted cake pan six by ten inches. Bake thirty-five minutes in a moderate oven (350° F.). While hot ice with a confectioners' sugar and milk icing. Cool. Cut into squares before serving.

Coffee Cake

½ cup butter
1½ cups brown sugar
2 squares melted chocolate
2 egg yolks
¾ teaspoon vanilla

1¾ cups flour
1 teaspoon baking powder
¾ teaspoon soda
1 cup sour cream mixed with
½ cup cold coffee (strong)

Cream butter and sugar. Add chocolate and egg yolks well beaten. Mix thoroughly. Mix flour, baking powder, and soda. Add to the chocolate mixture, alternating with sour cream and coffee. Add vanilla. Fold in one stiffly beaten egg white. Mix well. Bake in square greased and flour-dusted pan. Bake forty minutes in a moderate oven (350° F.). Turn out of pan. Cool. Ice before serving.

Hot Milk Cake

2 well-beaten eggs
1 cup sugar
1 cup flour

1 teaspoon baking powder
½ cup hot milk
1 teaspoon vanilla

¼ teaspoon salt

Beat eggs and add sugar. Beat thoroughly. Add the flour mixed with the salt and baking powder. Add the hot milk and vanilla. Stir until smooth. Bake in a greased and flour-dusted cake pan eight inches by eight inches. Bake thirty-five minutes in a moderate oven (350° F.). Turn out of pan. Cool. Ice.

Quick Cup Cakes

3 eggs
1 cup sugar
2 tablespoons butter

½ cup milk
2 teaspoons baking powder
1½ cups flour

1 teaspoon vanilla

Beat eggs until light. Add sugar gradually. Stir in melted butter. Mix baking powder and flour. Add flour and milk alternately to first mixture. Pour into greased muffin tins. Bake twenty-five minutes in a moderate oven (350° F.). Remove from pans and roll each cake in sifted confectioners' sugar. Serve as a fresh fruit or berry accompaniment.

Molasses Cake

1 cup brown sugar
1 cup sour milk
⅓ cup molasses
1 teaspoon cinnamon
½ teaspoon salt

½ cup shortening
½ cup raisins
1 egg
½ teaspoon nutmeg
1½ teaspoons soda

2 cups flour

Cream shortening. Add sugar. Mix until well blended. Mix salt, soda, and spices with the flour. Beat egg with molasses and sour milk. Add dry and liquid ingredients alternately to creamed mixture. Add raisins. Mix smooth. Pour into greased and flour-dusted cake pan eight inches by twelve inches. Bake forty minutes in a moderate oven (350° F.). Turn out of pan. Cool. Ice.

Graham Cake

1 cup granulated sugar
½ cup butter
3 eggs
¾ cup milk

1½ teaspoons baking powder
½ cup flour
1½ cups graham crackers
(rolled fine)

Cream butter. Add sugar and mix until well blended. Add the eggs and beat thoroughly. Mix flour and baking powder with the graham cracker crumbs. Add dry and liquid ingredients alternately to the creamed mixture. Stir until smooth. Pour into greased and flour-dusted layer cake pans. Bake twenty-five minutes in a moderate oven (350° F.). Remove from pans. Cool. Put butter filling or whipped cream between the layers. Cover top layer with whipped cream. Sprinkle with chopped nuts.

Gingerbread

⅓ cup shortening
1 cup molasses
1 egg
½ cup sour milk

1¾ teaspoons soda
2 teaspoons cinnamon
1 teaspoon ginger
½ teaspoon salt

1¾ cups flour

Heat shortening and molasses. Beat egg and sour milk. Mix dry ingredients. Combine mixtures. Beat until smooth. Pour into shallow cake pan which has been greased and dusted with flour. Bake twenty minutes in a hot oven (400° F.). Serve hot with whipped cream, ice cream, or hard sauce. One-quarter cup chopped candied ginger added to the batter before baking is a delicious addition.

Gingerbread Cakes

½ cup sugar
¼ cup shortening
2 eggs
1 teaspoon soda
1 teaspoon ginger

2 teaspoons cinnamon
½ cup sour milk
1¾ cups flour
¼ teaspoon salt
½ cup molasses

Cream the shortening and add the sugar gradually. Add the well-beaten egg. Mix well. Mix flour, soda, salt, cinnamon, and ginger. Add alternately with the liquid ingredients to the creamed mixture. Mix smooth. Pour into greased muffin pans. Bake twenty minutes in a moderate oven (350° F.). Top each cake with a marshmallow. Return to oven until marshmallow is toasted. Serve at once.

Fairy Gingerbread

½ cup butter
1 cup sugar
½ cup milk

1 egg
1½ cups flour
¼ teaspoon soda

2 teaspoons ginger

Cream butter. Add sugar and mix until well blended. Mix soda and ginger with the flour. Add egg to milk and beat well. Add dry and liquid ingredients alternately to creamed mixture. Mix well. With a spatula spread onto inverted side of baking pan that has been greased. Spread to one-quarter inch thickness. Bake fifteen minutes in a moderate oven (350° F.). While hot cut into squares and serve at once with butter.

ICINGS AND FILLINGS

White Frosting

2½ cups sugar
1½ teaspoons vanilla
1 cup syrup
½ cup water
2 egg whites

Boil the sugar, syrup, and water together until syrup spins a thread (234° F.). Pour the hot syrup slowly into the beaten egg whites, beating continually. Add the vanilla and continue to beat until the mixture will hold its shape. For chocolate boiled frosting add four squares melted chocolate during final beating.

Seven-Minute Icing

1 egg white (unbeaten)
⅞ cup granulated sugar
½ teaspoon baking powder
3 tablespoons cold water

Put all ingredients in top of double boiler. Place over boiling water and beat with rotary beater for seven minutes. Remove from fire. Beat until thick.

Boiled Frosting, No. 1

2 cups sugar
½ cup cold water
2 egg whites

Boil sugar and water to (238° F.). Pour into the stiffly beaten egg whites very slowly. Beat until thick enough to spread. Flavor with one teaspoon of vanilla.

Boiled Frosting, No. 2

⅓ cup water
1 cup sugar
½ teaspoon cream of tartar
1 egg white

Boil the water, sugar, and cream of tartar until it forms a soft ball in cold water. Pour in a fine stream on egg white beaten very stiff. Beat as you pour. Continue beating until stiff and smooth.

Pineapple Icing

2 cups sugar   ⅔ cup cream

Boil sugar and cream together for ten minutes. Remove from fire and beat until smooth and thick.

To one-half of icing add two-thirds cup grated pineapple and spread between layers of cake. To the remainder of icing add enough pineapple juice to make it spread smoothly.

Confectioners' Sugar Icing

1 cup confectioners' sugar   1 teaspoon vanilla
                    ⅛ teaspoon salt

Add enough milk to mix smooth. Stir vigorously.

Use for cake, fancy yeast bread, or cookies. May be colored with cocoa, chocolate, or vegetable colorings.

Cocoa Cream Icing

⅓ cup butter   3 tablespoons dry cocoa
1 cup confectioners' sugar   1 teaspoon vanilla
                    ⅛ teaspoon salt

Cream butter. Add salt and sugar and mix until well blended. Add cocoa and vanilla. Mix smooth. Use for filling or for icing.

Coffee Frosting

½ cup butter   1 tablespoon strong black coffee
2 cups confectioners' sugar   1 teaspoon vanilla

Cream butter. Add sugar and mix until well blended. Add coffee and vanilla. Mix smooth. Use for filling or icing.

Uncooked Chocolate Frosting

1 egg white   ¼ teaspoon salt
1 teaspoon vanilla   Confectioners' sugar
              7 tablespoons grated sweet chocolate

Beat egg white until stiff. Add salt and enough confectioners' sugar to spread easily. Add chocolate and vanilla. Mix thoroughly. Dipping the knife into milk will aid in spreading this icing and giving it gloss.

Cooked Chocolate Frosting

1½ cups sugar   1 teaspoon vanilla
½ cup water   ¼ teaspoon cream of tartar
1 tablespoon butter   2 squares chocolate

Combine above ingredients. Stir to mix thoroughly. Cook without stirring to 238° F., or to soft ball stage. Let stand until cold. Beat. Thin with cream until of right consistency for spreading.

Banana Icing

Pulp of one banana   1 teaspoon lemon juice
               2 cups confectioners' sugar

Mix banana, lemon, and sugar. Stir well for two minutes. Spread on cake. To make chocolate banana icing, add one square melted bitter chocolate. Any tint may be added to this icing. The icing keeps moist and retains its gloss.

Twice-Cooked Icing

1 cup sugar   ½ teaspoon cream of tartar
½ cup water (boiling)   1 egg white

Dissolve sugar in water. Boil to hard-ball stage (246° F.), or until syrup spins a long thread. Remove from fire. Beat egg white in top of double boiler with rotary beater. Pour syrup slowly over egg, beating with beater as long as possible. Then beat with spoon until mixture is light and stiff. Set dish over hot water and allow to cook, beating constantly until bubbles rise from bottom and mixture gives slight scraping sound on bottom of dish. Remove at once from hot water. Beat until ready to spread.

Chocolate Icing

2 cups sugar
¾ cup milk
1 teaspoon vanilla

4 ounces bitter chocolate
¼ teaspoon salt
1 tablespoon butter

Put all ingredients in saucepan. Mix well and cook until a small amount dropped in cold water will form a very soft ball. Allow to cool and then beat until thick enough to spread on cake.

Chocolate Marshmallow

¼ pound chocolate
½ cup sugar

1 cup milk
6 marshmallows

Heat chocolate, milk, and sugar in saucepan until chocolate melts. Bring to boiling point and cook for ten minutes. Add marshmallows, remove from fire, and beat until the mixture is smooth and thick. Cool slightly before spreading on cake. To build up a thick frosting spread the chocolate mixture on in layers, letting each one "set" before adding the next.

Chocolate Fluff

1 cup cream
1 teaspoon vanilla

4 tablespoons cocoa
¼ teaspoon salt
¾ cup sugar

Mix well and beat until thick. Chill. Serve on sheet or loaf cake, layer cake, or cup cakes.

Fudge Frosting

1 cup sugar
1 tablespoon butter

½ teaspoon baking powder
½ cup cocoa
¼ cup milk

Mix ingredients thoroughly and let come to boil. Cook ten minutes. Add one teaspoon vanilla and beat until thick enough to spread.

Cake and Punch for Light Refreshments

Fudge Frosting for Cookies

2 cups sugar
⅔ cup milk

2 squares chocolate
2 tablespoons butter

Boil sugar, milk, and chocolate together to soft-ball stage. Add butter. Cool. Beat. Put in vessel of hot water to keep soft enough to spread on cookies.

Chocolate Cream

¾ cup granulated sugar
2 squares chocolate

⅛ teaspoon salt
½ teaspoon vanilla

¼ cup cream

Mix chocolate, sugar, and cream. Cook until chocolate melts. Simmer three minutes. Add salt and vanilla. Beat until thick enough to spread.

Almond Butter Icing

½ cup butter
2 cups confectioners' sugar

1 teaspoon almond extract
⅛ teaspoon salt

Cream butter until soft and smooth. Add salt and sugar. Add flavoring. Mix thoroughly. Use for cake icing.

Mocha Icing

1½ cups confectioners' sugar
3 tablespoons butter

2 tablespoons coffee
1 teaspoon vanilla

Cream butter and sugar. Add coffee and vanilla. Mix smooth. Spread on cake. Chill cake.

Butter Icing, No. 1

1½ cups confectioners' sugar
⅓ cup butter

Cream butter, add sugar. When thoroughly blended, place over hot water for five minutes. Spread on cake. Let stand until icing sets before serving.

Butter Icing, No. 2

1½ cups confectioners' sugar   2 tablespoons cream
3 tablespoons butter   1 teaspoon vanilla

Cream together the butter and sugar. Add cream. Add the vanilla. Mix smooth. Spread on cake. Chill cake to set icing.

Caramel Icing

1 cup sugar   2 tablespoons butter
¼ cup milk   1 teaspoon vanilla
½ cup sugar for caramelizing

Caramelize one-half cup of sugar. Add milk. Dissolve sugar. Cook until it forms a soft ball in water. Remove and add butter and vanilla. Beat until thick enough to spread.

Butterscotch Filling

This may also be used as a frosting.

2 cups sugar   ¾ cup cream
¾ cup brown sugar

Cook together slowly the white sugar and cream without stirring. Bring to boiling point gradually and cook until the soft-ball stage (238° F.). In the meantime melt the brown sugar slowly in an iron skillet, stirring to prevent burning. Add the melted sugar to the bubbling, hot cream mixture, stirring rapidly. When cooked, remove from fire and beat until smooth, creamy, and stiff enough to spread. If milk has been used instead of cream, add butter on removing from fire. One-half cup chopped nuts is a good addition.

Butterscotch Icing

1 pound brown sugar   2 tablespoons butter
¾ cup cream   1 pound walnuts
⅛ teaspoon salt

Mix salt, sugar, and cream. Boil until a little dropped into water forms a soft ball. Remove from fire. Add butter. Beat until creamy. Spread on cake. Cover with halves of walnuts.

Caramel Marshmallow

2 cups brown sugar
½ cup milk

¼ cup butter
½ cup nuts (chopped)

16 marshmallows

Boil sugar and milk to the soft-ball stage (238° F.). Add butter and marshmallows cut into small pieces. After the marshmallows have melted, cool the mixture. Beat until creamy and add nuts. Spread on cake.

Marshmallow Icing

2½ cups sugar
½ cup water

4 tablespoons marshmallow
cream

3 egg whites

Boil sugar and water to soft-ball stage (238° F.). Add to the syrup the marshmallow cream. Pour the syrup in a fine stream over the stiffly beaten egg whites. Beat until stiff enough to spread.

Mocha Frosting

1½ tablespoons butter
½ tablespoon cocoa
1½ cups confectioners' sugar

2½ tablespoons strong coffee
1 tablespoon cream
1 teaspoon vanilla

Cream the butter. Add the cocoa and sugar. When thick, add alternately the coffee, cream, and one cup more of sugar. Enough to make it spread easily. Add vanilla.

Strawberry Frosting

1 cup strawberries (fresh or canned)   ½ cup butter
3 cups confectioners' sugar

Cream the butter. Add part of the sifted sugar. Add the strawberries which have been mashed. Add remainder of the sugar. Stir until well blended. Spread on the cake.

A little orange or lemon juice may be added to the frosting.

Orange Icing

2 cups confectioners' sugar	2 tablespoons melted butter
¼ cup hot orange juice	1 tablespoon grated orange rind

Add the hot orange juice and melted butter gradually to the sugar. Mix well. Add the freshly grated rind of orange. Mix well. Ice the cake.

Almond Filling

1 cup milk	¼ cup sugar
2 tablespoons flour	4 egg yolks
⅛ teaspoon salt	1 teaspoon vanilla
1 tablespoon butter	½ cup finely chopped almonds

Mix sugar, salt, and flour. Add milk. Cook for ten minutes, stirring constantly. Add beaten egg yolks. Cook to consistency of thick cream. Cool, add vanilla and finely chopped nuts. Spread between layers of cake.

Raisin and Nut Filling

⅔ cup milk	¼ cup water
2 tablespoons flour	1 egg white
1 tablespoon sugar	1¼ cups raisins and nuts (chopped)
	1 cup sugar

Cook flour, sugar, and milk until thick. Boil the sugar and water to soft-ball stage. Pour over beaten egg white. Beat well. When well beaten, add the cooked mixture and beat until thoroughly smooth. Add raisins or nuts. Use for filling.

Fig Filling

½ pound figs (chopped)	⅓ cup boiling water
⅓ cup sugar	1 tablespoon lemon juice

Mix ingredients and cook in double boiler until thick enough to spread. Spread while hot. Dates may be used instead of figs.

Cream Filling

½ cup sugar   4 tablespoons flour
⅛ teaspoon salt   1 egg
1 teaspoon vanilla   1 cup milk

Mix sugar, flour, and salt together. Add eggs, mix well.
Add to scalded milk. Cook in double boiler, stirring constantly
until it thickens. Flavor and spread between layers. Sprinkle
confectioners' sugar on top of cake.

Flavor may be varied by using almond extract, cocoanut, or
fruit juice instead of vanilla.

Lady Baltimore Icing, No. 1

2 cups sugar   2 egg whites
¾ cup water   ⅓ cup nuts
¼ teaspoon cream of tartar   ⅓ cup raisins
⅓ cup dates or figs   ½ cup candied cherries (halved)

Boil together sugar and water with the cream of tartar until
it spins a fine thread (238° F.). Pour over the well-beaten egg
whites. Beat thoroughly. When just past the soft-stage add
three-fourths cup of frosting to the chopped nuts, raisins,
cherries, and figs. Spread this between layers of cake. Continue beating the remainder of the frosting until fluffy and
glossy. Spread on top and sides of cake.

Lady Baltimore Icing, No. 2

1½ cups sugar   ½ cup raisins (chopped)
¾ cup water   ½ cup dates (chopped)
2 eggs   ½ cup figs (chopped)
              ½ cup nuts (chopped)

Boil sugar and water until it spins a thread (238° F.). Pour
over two whole eggs beaten together. Beat until mixture begins
to stiffen. Add chopped fruit. Beat until icing reaches spread
consistency. Put between layers, on top of cake, and on the
sides.

Rich Cake Filling

1 cup butter icing 　　　　　　½ cup whipped cream
2 squares melted chocolate 　　½ cup nuts (chopped)

Mix ingredients thoroughly. Use for cake filling. One teaspoon vanilla may be added if desired.

Lemon Filling

1 cup boiling water 　　　　　　½ cup sugar
1 lemon juice and rind 　　　　　4 tablespoons flour

1 egg

Mix sugar, flour, and water. Cook until thick. Add egg. Beat well. Add lemon juice and rind. Mix well. Cool. Use for cake filling. Orange or pineapple juice may be used instead of the lemon.

CHAPTER XIV
Candies and Confections

Chocolate Taffy

1 cup water	1 cup molasses
2 ounces grated chocolate	3 tablespoons butter
1 cup sugar	1½ teaspoons vanilla

Cook water, chocolate, sugar, molasses, and butter together until the syrup forms a hard ball (260-270° F.) when dropped into cold water. Add vanilla and pour into a buttered pan to cool and harden. When partially hard, mark off in squares with a knife; and when cold and brittle, break off on marked lines.

Taffy

4 cups sugar	⅔ cup boiling water
⅓ cup vinegar	2 tablespoons butter

Melt the butter. Add sugar, hot water, and vinegar. Stir until sugar is dissolved. Boil until the mixture turns brittle in cold water. Turn into a buttered pan to cool. Pull until white. Cut into cubes.

Fondant

2½ pounds sugar   ½ teaspoon cream of tartar
1½ cups hot water

Put ingredients into stewpan. Stir, and heat gradually to boiling point. Boil without stirring until, when tried in cold water, a soft ball will be formed that will just keep shape. After boiling for a few minutes, sugar will adhere to sides of kettle, and should be washed off with a cloth dipped in cold water. Pour slowly on a slightly oiled marble slab or large platter. Let stand a few minutes, but not long enough to become hard around the edge. Scrape fondant to one end of the marble or dish and work with a wooden spatula until white and creamy. It will quickly change from this consistency and begin to lump, then it should be kneaded with the hands until perfectly smooth. Put into bowl, cover with oiled paper, and let stand twenty-four hours.

Chocolate Creams

Mould fondant into balls, squares, and oblong pieces. Allow it to set. Dip carefully into melted dipping chocolate. When entirely covered with chocolate remove to parafin paper and let it dry. Candied cherries, cocoanut, and nut meats may be moulded into the fondant, or they may be used to decorate the top of the dipped candies.

Peppermint Patties

Melt one-half cup of fondant in top of double boiler. Add one-half teaspoon mint extract. Drop with a teaspoon onto parafin paper. Cool.

Wintergreen Patties

Melt one-half cup of fondant in top of double boiler. Add one-fourth teaspoon oil of wintergreen and a bit of red vegetable coloring. Drop with a teaspoon onto parafin paper. Cool.

Quick Fondant

3½ cups confectioners' sugar	½ teaspoon almond extract
2 egg whites	

Beat the egg whites slightly. Add the sugar gradually, beating until stiff, then knead. As the sizes of eggs differ, a little more or less sugar may be necessary. Add flavoring. Mould into balls. Roll in chopped nuts. Chill.

Walnut Creams

1½ cups granulated sugar	⅛ teaspoon salt
1½ cups light brown sugar	1 cup walnuts (chopped)
1 cup milk	½ teaspoon almond extract

Put the sugar and milk in a large saucepan and stir until the sugar is dissolved. Boil until a soft ball is formed when the mixture is tested in cold water. Let stand until lukewarm, then beat vigorously; when it begins to get creamy, add the nuts and extract. Pour into a buttered pan, and when hard cut into squares with a knife which has been dipped in boiling water.

Apricot Candies

¾ cup dried apricots   ¼ teaspoon salt
½ cup nut meats   1 teaspoon vanilla
¾ cup fresh cocoanut (grated)   1 teaspoon lemon rind (grated)
1 tablespoon lemon juice   1 teaspoon orange rind (grated)

Wash the apricots and put them through a food chopper with the nut meats. Add the cocoanut, lemon juice, and grated orange and lemon rinds. Mix and knead well; roll out on a sugared board to about one-fourth inch thickness. Cut in squares and roll in confectioners' sugar.

Pop-corn Balls

Mix three tablespoons of butter with two cups of molasses and two-thirds cup of corn syrup. Boil until a little syrup dropped into cold water forms a brittle mass. Quickly stir in four cups of pop corn. Form into balls. Allow balls to set and cool.

Puffed Rice Confection

2 tablespoons butter   2 cups molasses
⅔ cup corn syrup

Mix the ingredients thoroughly. Boil until a little syrup dropped into cold water forms a brittle mass. Quickly add four cups of puffed rice. Pour into greased baking pan. When cool, break into pieces. Puffed wheat may be used instead of puffed rice.

Stuffed Dates, No. 1

Remove stone from dates. Insert small roll of fondant. Roll in confectioners' sugar. Allow to set before serving.

Stuffed Dates, No. 2

Remove stone from dates. Insert whole nut meat. Roll in granulated sugar.

Chocolate-covered Raisins

Melt one-quarter pound sweet dipping chocolate in top of double boiler. Add two cups of seedless raisins. Drop with a teaspoon onto parafin paper. Cool and allow to set.

Chocolate-covered Peanuts

Melt one-quarter pound sweet dipping chocolate in top of double boiler. Add two cups of shelled peanuts. Stir until peanuts are covered with chocolate. Drop with a teaspoon onto parafin paper. Cool and allow to set.

Delicious Fruit Paste

1 pound dates	3 tablespoons lemon juice
1 pound figs	3 tablespoons confectioners' sugar
1 teaspoon vanilla	1 pound nut meats

Put dates, figs, and nuts through a food chopper. Add sugar, vanilla, and lemon juice. Shape into small balls and roll in confectioners' sugar. Allow to set and cool.

Peanut Brittle

2 cups sugar	¼ teaspoon salt
	1 cup shelled peanuts

Put sugar in a frying pan. Place over a slow fire and stir until melted. Scrape sugar from the sides of the pan and off the spoon. Have a warm buttered pan ready. As soon as sugar is melted, add chopped peanuts which have been sprinkled with salt. Pour at once into warm pan.

Candied Orange Peel

Cut peel into strips one-fourth inch wide. Boil three times in salted water (one teaspoon salt to one quart water). Pour off water each time and put on fresh. The last time, boil peel until tender. Plunge into ice water to crisp. Drain. Boil in sugar syrup until, when lifted, the peel dries. Roll in granulated sugar. Make syrup of one-fourth cup water and one cup sugar for each cup orange peel. Grapefruit peel may be used instead of orange.

Candied Cranberries

3 cups large cranberries   3 cups sugar
2 cups water

Select large, firm cranberries. Make three small slits in each berry. Boil the sugar and water together until clear. Allow this syrup to cool, then add the berries and bring very slowly to the boiling point. If the berries are heated too quickly, the skin will burst before the syrup soaks into the pulp. As soon as the syrup boils, take the dish off the stove and let it stand overnight.

Next day drain the syrup from the berries and reduce it to about half its original volume by boiling. Cool the syrup, then place the berries in it and heat again slowly. Boil very gently for three or four minutes and allow to stand for two hours.

Boil gently a third time for five minutes. Allow the berries to stand in the thick syrup overnight. Warm once more so that the syrup will be thin enough to pour easily and drain the berries. Spread them on oiled paper to dry. When dry, the berries should be bright, firm, plump, and semitransparent.

Fudge

1 cup granulated sugar   2 squares chocolate (unsweetened)
1 cup brown sugar   ⅔ cup milk
2 tablespoons butter   1 teaspoon vanilla
⅛ teaspoon salt

Put all the ingredients except the vanilla into a saucepan. Stir until the chocolate is melted and the sugar dissolved. Boil without stirring until the mixture forms a soft ball when dropped into cold water. Cool. Beat until creamy. Add vanilla and pour into greased pan. Cut into squares while fudge cools.

Fudge with Nuts

2 cups granulated sugar   2 squares bitter chocolate
⅛ teaspoon salt   ⅔ cup milk
3 tablespoons butter   1 teaspoon vanilla
1 cup walnut meats (cut fine)

Put all of the ingredients, except the vanilla and nuts, into a saucepan. Stir until chocolate is melted and sugar dissolved. Boil without stirring until the mixture forms a soft ball when dropped into cold water. Cool. Beat until creamy. Add vanilla and nuts. Pour into a greased pan. Cool. Cut into squares.

Chocolate Fudge

2 cups sugar
⅔ cup cream
2 tablespoons butter

2 squares chocolate
¼ teaspoon salt
1 teaspoon vanilla

Add the sugar to the liquid. Add butter, grated chocolate, and salt. Put over the fire and stir until sugar is dissolved. Boil without stirring until candy forms soft ball when dropped into cold water. Add vanilla and cool to room temperature. Do not stir until cool, then beat vigorously until the mixture sets. Drop with a teaspoon onto a greased pan or waxed paper.

Penuche

2 cups brown sugar
⅔ cup milk
⅛ teaspoon salt

1 teaspoon vanilla
4 tablespoons butter
½ cup walnut meats
(cut fine)

Mix the ingredients in a saucepan. Boil slowly until a little dropped into cold water forms a soft ball. Cool. Beat until creamy. Add vanilla and nut meats. Pour into a greased pan. Cool. Cut into squares.

Salted Almonds

1 cup almonds (blanched)　　　　2 tablespoons butter

Place melted butter in shallow pan. Add almonds and stir until coated with fat. Place in a moderate oven (350° F.). Bake twenty-five minutes, stirring constantly. Drain on brown paper. Sprinkle with salt.

CHAPTER XV

Canning and Preserves, Pickles and Relishes,
Jams and Jelly Making

Apple Jelly

Quarter apples. Wash and add one-third as much water as apples. Bring to the boiling point. Strain through a jelly bag. Measure juice and boil twenty minutes. Add equal amount of heated sugar. Boil five minutes. Skim. Pour into sterilized jelly glasses. Cool. Cover with paraffin. Crab-apple jelly is made according to this rule.

Apple and Almond Jelly

To one quart of apple jelly (measured after sugar has been added) add one teaspoon of almond extract. Pour into sterilized jars and cover with paraffin.

Apple and Plum Jelly

Mix one quart of plum juice with one quart of apple juice. Boil twenty minutes. Add an equal amount of heated sugar. Boil five minutes. Skim. Pour into sterilized jars. Seal with paraffin.

Spiced Apple Jelly

1 quart apples	1 teaspoon whole cloves
1½ cups vinegar	1½ cups cranberries
1 teaspoon stick cinnamon	

Tie spices in cheesecloth. Cook all together, drain through a jelly bag. Measure juice. Boil twenty minutes. Add equal amount of heated sugar. Cook five minutes. Skim. Pour into sterilized jars. Seal with paraffin.

Currant Jelly

Wash currants, but do not remove from stems. Put into preserving kettle, mash slightly. Heat until currants lose their color. Put through jelly bag. Measure juice, bring to the boiling point and boil twenty minutes. Add an equal amount of heated sugar. Boil five minutes. Skim. Pour into sterilized glasses and when cold cover with paraffin.

Currant and Raspberry Jelly

Mix one quart of currant juice with one quart of raspberry juice. Boil twenty minutes. Add equal amount of heated sugar. Boil five minutes. Skim. Pour into sterilized jars. Seal with paraffin.

Mint Jelly

To one quart of apple jelly (measured after sugar has been added) add one teaspoon of mint extract and a little green coloring. Pour into sterilized jars and cover with paraffin.

Cranberry Jelly

4 cups cranberries 2 cups sugar
2 cups water

Pick over and wash cranberries. Place in saucepan with the water and boil twenty minutes. Strain through a sieve, rubbing through as much pulp as possible. Cook three minutes. Add two cups sugar and boil two minutes. Turn into bowl or jars. Chill and allow to set before using.

Quince and Cranberry Jelly

1 dozen quinces 3 quarts cranberries

Cook the fruits separately, drain, combine juices. Boil twenty minutes. Add equal amount of heated sugar. Boil five minutes. Skim. Pour into sterilized jars. Seal with paraffin.

Grape Jelly

Mix one quart of grape juice with one quart of apple juice. Boil twenty minutes. Add equal amount of heated sugar. Boil five minutes. Skim. Pour into sterilized jars. Seal with paraffin. To make blackberry jelly, substitute blackberry juice for the grape juice.

Rhubarb Jelly

Mix one quart of rhubarb juice with one quart of apple juice and one cup of orange juice. Boil twenty minutes. Add an equal amount of heated sugar. Boil five minutes. Skim. Pour into sterilized jars. Seal with paraffin.

Rhubarb and Strawberry Jelly

Mix one quart of rhubarb juice with one quart of strawberry juice and two quarts of apple juice. Boil twenty minutes. Add an equal amount of heated sugar. Boil five minutes. Skim. Pour into sterilized jars. Seal with paraffin.

Grape Juice

3 quarts grapes	1 pint water
	Sugar

Wash ripe grapes and free from stems. Measure, and to every three quarts grapes use one pint water. Put into kettle and let come slowly to boiling point, stirring constantly. Remove from fire and strain through thick cloth. Measure and put juice back in kettle. Add one cup sugar to every three quarts of juice. Let come quickly to boiling point and turn at once into sterilized bottles. Seal.

Grape Fudge

7 pounds of grapes	1 pound raisins
7 pounds of sugar	1 pound walnuts

Wash and pulp the grapes. Cook the pulp until seeds can be removed. Put through a coarse strainer. Chop the skins, cut raisins and nuts in small pieces. Then mix ingredients and cook until thick. The time depends on the juice. Pour into sterilized jars. Seal with paraffin.

Grape Marmalade

1 pint grape pulp
½ cup sugar
¼ teaspoon ground cloves

½ teaspoon cinnamon
¼ teaspoon allspice
Rind of ¼ lemon

Boil slowly for about thirty minutes. Stir constantly. Before putting in jars remove the lemon rind. Pour into sterilized jars. Seal with paraffin.

Orange Marmalade

9 oranges
4 quarts water

6 lemons
Sugar

Peel the fruit. With a sharp knife or scissors cut the peel in thin strips. Slice the fruit as thin as possible. Remove the seeds. Place the fruit and peel in a kettle. Pour the hot water over the fruit and let stand thirty-six hours. Boil two hours. Measure the cooked fruit and add an equal amount of hot sugar. Cook until the mixture jells. Pour into sterilized glasses. When cold cover with hot paraffin.

Crab Apple Marmalade

Use pulp left over from crab-apple jelly. Rub it through strainer and for each cup of fruit add three-quarters cup sugar. Add lemon cut fine, allowing one-half lemon to every six cups pulp. Cook very slowly. Stir constantly until thick. Pour into sterilized jars. Seal with paraffin.

Any fruit pulp left from jelly making, or any combination of fruit pulp may be used instead of the crab apple. One-half teaspoon of ground cinnamon may be used to flavor the marmalade instead of the lemon.

Plum Conserve

5 pounds blue plums
5 pounds sugar
1½ pounds seeded raisins

Juice of 3 oranges
Rind of 1 orange
Juice of 2 lemons

½ pound blanched almonds

Pit plums, but do not peel. Dissolve sugar in fruit juice and add fruits. Cook until a glaze forms over the surface. Add nuts to mixture. Pour into sterilized jars and seal with paraffin.

Rhubarb Conserve

3 pounes rhubarb   1 cup blanched almonds
3 quarts strawberries   6 pounds sugar

Cut rhubarb into cubes. Hull the strawberries. Wash.
Cook fruit and sugar until thick. Stir constantly. Add nuts.
Pour into sterilized jars. Seal with paraffin.

Rhubarb and Orange Conserve

2 pounds rhubarb   3 pounds sugar
4 oranges   1 cup blanched almonds

Peel oranges. Cut pulp into cubes. Cube rhubarb. Add
sugar to fruit. Cook until thick. Add nuts. Pour into sterilized
jars. Seal with paraffin.

Apricot Conserve

20 apricots, (cut in halves)   4 cups sugar
1 pint canned pineapple   Juice of 2 oranges
    or 1 fresh pineapple   ¼ pound blanched almonds

Peel and halve apricots. Cut pineapple in small pieces. Add
sugar and orange juice. Cook from thirty to forty minutes. Add
blanched almonds and pour into sterilized jars and when cool
cover with paraffin.

Prune Conserve

2 pounds prunes   5 oranges
Grated rind of 1 orange   ¼ pound pecans (cut fine)
Juice of ½ lemon   1 teaspoon cinnamon

Wash prunes thoroughly. Cover with water and let soak
three hours. Cook in the same water until tender. Remove
pits and return the pulp to any juice that is left. Add oranges
cut in small pieces. Add the rind. Cook twenty minutes.
Measure and add an equal amount of sugar. Cook twenty
minutes. Add lemon juice and cinnamon just before the mixture is done. Pour into sterilized jars and when cold seal with
hot paraffin.

Gooseberry Jam

1 pound gooseberries   1 pound sugar

Remove stem and blossom end from gooseberries. Wash.
Mix with sugar. Cook slowly over low flame one hour. Put
into sterilized jars. When cold seal with hot paraffin.

Rhubarb and Strawberry Jam

1 pound rhubarb   1 pound strawberries
2 pounds sugar

Hull strawberries. Cut rhubarb in small pieces. Cook rhubarb and strawberries and sugar over low flame for one hour.
Pour into sterilized jars and when cold seal with paraffin.

Strawberry Jam, No. 1

2 pint boxes of strawberries   ½ cup lemon juice
5 cups sugar

Let stand one-half hour. Cook ten minutes. Pour into
sterilized jars. Seal with paraffin.

Strawberry Jam, No. 2

4 cups strawberries   4 cups sugar

Mix strawberries with sugar. Cook seventeen minutes. Let
stand overnight. In the morning heat, pour into sterilized jars.
Seal with paraffin. This rule is used to make raspberry, blackberry, black raspberry, peach or plum jam.

Peach Jam

12 pounds peaches   1 cup vinegar
8 pounds sugar

Peel peaches. Cut into small pieces. Add sugar and vinegar.
Cook slowly until thick. Pour into sterilized jars. Seal with
paraffin.

Spiced Cranberry

4 cups cranberries	1 cup raisins
½ cup currants	½ cup candied orange peel
2 cups sugar	½ cup water
1 teaspoon cinnamon	¼ teaspoon ginger

Mix cranberries with sugar and other ingredients. Cook slowly for forty minutes. Pour into sterilized jars. Seal with paraffin.

Cranberry Sauce

3 cups cranberries	1 cup boiling water
	3 cups sugar

Pick over and wash the cranberries. Boil the sugar and water together five minutes. Add cranberries and cook until transparent.

Spiced Pears

Cut four pounds of pears into quarters. Cover with two pounds sugar and two tablespoons ground ginger, two tablespoons cinnamon. Mix thoroughly. Let stand overnight.

In the morning bring to the boiling point slowly. Boil fifteen minutes. Add one pint diced pineapple, one diced lemon with peel, one-half pound blanched almonds. Heat thoroughly. Put into jars and seal.

Ginger Pears

Cut eight pounds of pears into small pieces of uniform size and discard the stems and cores. Add one-quarter pound canton ginger cut in small pieces and four pounds granulated sugar. Cover and let stand overnight. In the morning add juice of two lemons. Cook slowly two and one-half hours. Pour into sterilized jars. Seal with paraffin.

Watermelon Pickle

Watermelon rind should be cut in small pieces and soaked overnight in brine; one tablespoon salt to one quart water. In the morning drain and cook in boiling water until tender.

To two quarts of cooked watermelon rind add:

1½ cups vinegar
½ cup water
2 cups brown sugar

1 stick cinnamon
1 teaspoon ground ginger
½ teaspoon ground cloves

Cook twenty minutes. Drain. Put watermelon rind into sterilized jars. Boil syrup ten minutes. Pour over watermelon rind. Seal.

Sweet Pickled Crab Apples

1 peck crab apples
1 quart vinegar

3 pounds brown sugar
1 teaspoon whole cloves

1 stick cinnamon

Wash the crab apples and remove blossom ends. Steam until tender. Make syrup of vinegar, sugar, and spices. Cook in this syrup ten minutes, put into jars, boil down syrup and pour over fruit. Seal.

Sweet Pickled Peaches

3 cups vinegar
4 cups sugar

¼ cup (scant) mixed whole spices
½ peck peaches

Scald peaches. Remove skins. Make a syrup of sugar, vinegar, and spices; skim, and boil twenty minutes. Remove spices. Cook peaches a few at a time in syrup until tender, put in jar, let stand twenty-four hours. Reheat three times. At the end of the third time, cover with the syrup cooked down until thick. Seal.

Pickled Peaches

4 pounds brown sugar
1 stick cinnamon

1 pint vinegar
Whole cloves

1 teaspoon ground ginger

Boil sugar, ginger, vinegar, and stick cinnamon. Peel small peaches. Stick four cloves (whole) into each peach. Cook peaches in syrup until tender. Pack peaches into wide-mouthed jars. Pour syrup over them to cover. Seal.

Canned Peaches

8 quarts of peaches   1 quart sugar
                    3 quarts water

Select firm peaches. Put into boiling water just long enough
to loosen skins. Remove skins, cut in halves, and remove
stones.

Cook fruit at once. A few of the stones may be cooked with
it for the almond flavor. Put sugar and water in preserving
kettle and cook to syrup. Add fruit, cook slowly until it is soft
enough to be easily pierced. Put fruit into sterilized jars,
arranging outer surface of peach to the glass, fill to overflowing
with boiling syrup and seal. This same rule is used to can
pears.

Canned Tomatoes

Wipe tomatoes, cover with boiling water, and let stand until
skins may be easily removed. Put them in kettle and cook
thirty minutes. Skim frequently. Pour into sterilized jars and
seal. Salt may be added if desired.

Canned Rhubarb, No. 1

String rhubarb, and cut into one-inch pieces, pack in a jar,
place jar under cold water faucet, and let water run twenty
minutes. Fill jar full of cold water. Seal.

Canned Rhubarb, No. 2

6 quarts rhubarb   1½ quarts sugar
                    1 pint water

String rhubarb and cut into cubes. Add water and sugar.
Cook fifteen minutes. Pour into sterilized jars and seal.

Bar le Duc

Wash one quart of currants picked from the stem. Cook
one-half cup water, one and one-half cups sugar. Boil until
thick. Add currants one cup at a time. Cook three minutes.
Skim. Put into sterilized jars. After all the currants have

been cooked pour the syrup over the currants in the jars.
When cold seal with paraffin.

Corn Relish

2 dozen ears sweet corn	3 green peppers
½ pound cabbage	½ cup salt
4 onions	3 tablespoons mustard
1 quart vinegar	3 pimentos
2 cups sugar	½ teaspoon pepper

Cut corn from ear. Chop cabbage, onions, peppers, and
pimentos. Mix all ingredients together and boil one hour.
Pour into sterilized jars and seal.

Uncooked Tomato Relish

1 peck ripe tomatoes (cut in small pieces)	3 cups celery (cut fine)
	½ cup salt

2 cups onions (chopped fine)

Mix onions and celery. Cover with salt. Add tomatoes.
Let stand one hour. Then add:

2 large red peppers (chopped)	2 teaspoons cinnamon
3 cups light brown sugar	1 teaspoon cloves
¾ cup mustard seed	2 pints vinegar

Mix thoroughly. Chill. Pour into sterilized jars and seal.

Pepper Relish

Two dozen red and two dozen green peppers, twelve onions.
Chop onions. Remove seeds from peppers, and chop fine.
Pour boiling water over peppers and onions and let stand five
minutes, drain, and again cover with boiling water, let stand
ten minutes. Drain. Add two quarts of vinegar, five cups
sugar, one tablespoon salt. Boil fifteen minutes. Pour into
sterilized jars. Seal.

Beet Relish

2 cups cooked beets (chopped fine)	½ cup horseradish sauce
2 cups raw cabbage (chopped)	½ cup sugar
½ tablespoon salt	½ teaspoon pepper

Enough vinegar to mix smooth. Put into jars. Keep cool.

Olive Oil Pickles

4 quarts small cucumbers   1 pint small white onions
  (sliced)   (sliced)

Let stand in weak brine overnight. Drain, rinse in cold water, and add:

2 tablespoons white mustard seed   2 tablespoons celery seed
                   1 cup olive oil

Mix well, put in sterilized jars, and add vinegar to cover. Seal.

Chopped Pickle

1 gallon green tomatoes (chopped)   1 quart white onions (chopped)
1 gallon cabbage (chopped)   ½ cup salt

Pack in layers in stone crock and leave for six hours. Drain in cheesecloth bag overnight. Add one and one-half quarts of water and one pint vinegar and bring to boiling point. Add two large green peppers, chopped, one tablespoon white pepper. Mix thoroughly. Bring to boiling point. Put into sterilized jars. Seal.

Piccalilli

½ peck green tomatoes   1 teaspoon celery seed
8 large onions   ½ cup mustard seed
3 red peppers   1 pound brown sugar
2 pounds cabbage   3 pints vinegar
1 bunch celery   ½ cup salt

Chop vegetables fine. Mix all of the ingredients. Let stand overnight. Drain. Cook ten minutes. Put into sterilized jars. Seal.

Sweet Pickles

7 pounds small cucumbers   1 cup water
5 pounds sugar   ¾ cup mixed spices
1 pint vinegar   ¼ whole clove
         ½ whole cinnamon

Boil sugar, water, vinegar, and spices to syrup. Pack washed cucumbers into sterilized jars. Fill jars with hot syrup. Seal.

Dill Pickles

Select uniform cucumbers. Brush clean. Pack cucumbers into sterilized quart jars. Add one cup dill pickles cut fine to each jar. Heat to boiling point, one quart vinegar, three quarts water and one cup of salt. Pour over cucumbers to overflowing. Seal.

Small Pickles

Fill ten sterilized quart jars with very small cucumbers that have been carefully washed. Heat five cups of water and one cup vinegar to boiling point. Add one cup salt. Pour over pickles in jar to overflowing. Seal.

Sliced Pickles

1 peck cucumbers	3 pounds sugar
1 cup salt	1 pint vinegar

Brush cucumbers and slice fine. Cover with salt. Let stand three hours. Drain. Make syrup of sugar and vinegar. Pour over sliced cucumbers. Cook until cucumber becomes transparent. Put into sterilized jars. Seal.

Catsup

½ bushel ripe tomatoes	½ cup sugar
1 pint vinegar	¼ cup salt
2 tablespoons whole allspice	2 tablespoons paprika
3 tablespoons cinnamon	2 tablespoons cloves
2 tablespoons ground mustard	6 onions

Cut tomatoes and onions fine. Add other ingredients. Simmer one hour. Drain. Strain through fine sieve. Bring to boiling point. Put into sterilized bottles. Seal.

Chili Sauce

12 ripe tomatoes (peeled)	2 tablespoons brown sugar
2 large onions (chopped)	1 tablespoon cinnamon
4 large green peppers (chopped)	1 tablespoon mustard
2 tablespoons salt	4 cups vinegar

Mix and boil together until reduced about one-half. Put into sterilized jars. Seal.

CHAPTER XVI
Cookies

Sour Cream Cookies

1 cup sugar
½ cup butter
½ cup sour cream
2 eggs
2 teaspoons soda

2 teaspoons cream of tartar
1 teaspoon lemon juice
2½ cups flour
¼ teaspoon salt

Cream shortening. Add salt and sugar and blend thoroughly. Add beaten egg. Beat well. Mix lemon juice with sour milk. Mix soda and cream of tartar with flour. Add liquid and dry ingredients alternately to egg mixture. Mix thoroughly. Chill. Toss onto floured moulding board. Roll thin as possible. Cut into fancy shapes. Bake on a greased baking sheet ten minutes in a moderately hot oven (375° F.).

Crisp Cookies

¾ cup butter
¾ cup other shortening
2 cups brown sugar
3 eggs
¼ teaspoon salt

1 teaspoon cinnamon
½ cup chopped almonds
5 cups flour
2 teaspoons baking powder
1 teaspoon vanilla

Cream shortening thoroughly. Add sugar gradually and continue creaming. Add the well-beaten eggs. Sift the flour once before measuring. Mix and sift flour, cinnamon, soda, and salt. Add gradually to the creamed mixture. Add the vanilla and the chopped almonds. Mix thoroughly and shape into two rolls. Let stand in the ice box or cold place overnight. In the morning slice thin and bake fifteen minutes in moderately hot oven (375° F.).

German Crisps

1 cup butter	2 cups brown sugar
2 eggs	3½ cups flour
¼ teaspoon salt	1 teaspoon soda

1 cup chopped walnuts

Cream butter and sugar, add egg and beat thoroughly. Mix flour and soda. Add flour mixture, vanilla, and nuts to creamed sugar and shortening. Mix thoroughly. Form into roll. Flatten top. Let stand in the ice box or a cold place overnight. In the morning, slice thin. Bake on greased cookie sheets ten minutes in a moderately hot oven (375° F.).

Chocolate Cookies, No. 1

1 pound sugar	1 pound grated sweet chocolate
1 pound butter	1 lemon (juice and rind)
1 pound ground almonds	1½ pounds flour
6 eggs	2 teaspoons baking powder

Cream shortening. Add sugar. Blend thoroughly. Add the eggs and beat well. Add the almonds, lemon juice, and rind. Mix baking powder with the flour. Add to first mixture. Mix thoroughly. Chill. Roll to one-eighth inch thickness on a floured moulding board. Bake on a greased baking sheet in a moderately hot oven for ten minutes.

Chocolate Cookies, No. 2

1 cup sugar	½ cup butter
1 egg	2 teaspoons baking powder
½ cup milk	2 squares chocolate (melted)
1½ cups flour	1 teaspoon vanilla
⅛ teaspoon salt	1 cup nuts (halved)

Cream shortening. Add sugar gradually. Add the egg and beat thoroughly. Mix vanilla with milk. Add baking powder and salt to flour. Add liquid and dry ingredients alternately to the first mixture. Add chocolate. Mix well. Drop from a teaspoon onto a greased baking sheet. Top each cookie with one-half nut meat. Bake ten minutes in a moderately hot oven (375° F.).

Brownies

½ cup shortening
2 eggs
2 squares bitter chocolate
½ teaspoon baking powder

1 cup sugar
½ teaspoon salt
1 cup nut meats (broken)
¾ cup flour

1 teaspoon vanilla

Melt chocolate and butter together over hot water. Add sugar and eggs and beat thoroughly. Add vanilla and nut meats. Mix baking powder with the flour. Add to first mixture. Mix thoroughly. Pour into a greased baking pan eight inches by twelve inches and bake twenty-five minutes in a moderate oven (350° F.).

Chocolate Fudge Cookies

1¼ cups brown sugar
½ cup butter
1 egg
½ cup milk

2 teaspoons baking powder
2 cups flour
1 teaspoon vanilla
¼ teaspoon salt

2½ squares chocolate (melted)

Cream the shortening, add sugar gradually. Add the egg and beat. Mix the baking powder with the salt and flour. Add the vanilla to the milk. Add the liquid and the dry ingredients alternately to the egg mixture, adding the dry ingredients first and last. Add melted chocolate. Drop from a teaspoon onto greased baking sheets. Bake ten minutes in a moderately hot oven (375° F.). Serve cookies plain or iced with chocolate frosting.

Date Bars

1 pound dates
1 cup walnut meats
½ cup flour
¼ teaspoon baking powder

¼ teaspoon salt
1 cup sugar
2 eggs
¼ cup melted shortening

Pit dates and cut into quarters. Mix together flour, baking powder, salt, and sugar. Add dates and nuts to flour mixture. Beat eggs. Add melted butter. Combine mixtures and bake in eight inch by twelve inch pan thirty minutes in moderate oven

(350° F.). When slightly cool, cut in bars. Roll each bar in powdered sugar.

Date and Nut Cookies

2 egg whites
1 cup confectioners' sugar
1 tablespoon cocoa

⅛ teaspoon salt
1 cup chopped nut meats
1 cup dates (cut in small pieces)

Beat egg whites until stiff. Mix sugar, cocoa, and salt. Fold into the beaten egg whites. Fold in nuts and dates. Drop from a teaspoon onto a greased baking sheet. Bake twenty minutes in a moderate oven (350° F.).

Peanut Cookies

1 cup flour
¼ cup butter
½ cup sugar
2 eggs

1 teaspoon vanilla
2 teaspoons baking powder
½ teaspoon salt
1 tablespoon milk

1 cup chopped peanuts

Cream the butter and sugar. Add well-beaten eggs. Sift and mix dry ingredients. Add milk, peanuts, and dry ingredients to egg mixture. Add vanilla. Mix thoroughly. Drop from teaspoon onto greased baking sheet. Bake in moderately hot oven (375° F.) until brown. Ten minutes.

Peanut Wafers

¾ cup shortening
1½ cups brown sugar
1 egg
½ teaspoon salt

2 teaspoons baking powder
3 tablespoons milk
2 cups peanuts
3 cups flour

Cream shortening. Add sugar gradually. Add the well-beaten eggs. Sift the flour once before measuring. Mix together flour, salt, and baking powder. Add to the creamed mixture alternating with the liquid. Add the peanuts chopped fine. Roll out on a floured board to one-eighth inch thickness. Cut and place on a greased baking sheet. Bake ten minutes in a hot oven (400° F.).

Peanut Butter Drop Cookies

½ cup sugar
2 tablespoons butter
1 egg
2 tablespoons milk

2 teaspoons baking powder
⅛ teaspoon salt
¾ cup peanut butter
1 cup flour

Cream sugar and butter. Add egg and beat. Add milk and flour sifted with salt and baking powder. Add peanut butter. Drop on greased baking sheet and bake fifteen minutes in hot oven (400° F.). One-half cup nuts may be added.

Walnut Patties

1 egg
1 cup brown sugar
1 cup walnuts (chopped)

6 tablespoons flour
1 teaspoon vanilla
⅛ teaspoon salt

Beat the egg, salt, and sugar together until light. Stir in the nuts, then the flour, and the vanilla. Drop on a greased baking sheet. Bake in a hot oven (400° F.) fifteen minutes.

Dainty Nut Wafers

4 tablespoons shortening
¾ cup sugar
1 egg
1⅓ cups flour
1 teaspoon baking powder

½ teaspoon salt
2 tablespoons milk
1 teaspoon vanilla
½ cup chopped nut meats

Cream shortening. Add sugar gradually and continue creaming. Add the egg. Beat well. Mix flour, baking powder, and salt. Add to the creamed mixture, alternately with the liquid. Add vanilla. Mix thoroughly.

Spread very thin on bottom of greased baking pan and sprinkle with finely chopped nuts. Bake fifteen minutes in moderate oven (350° F.). When done remove from oven and cut in strips two inches by four inches. While hot place each strip over the handle of a wooden spoon. If strips become crisp or wrinkled before shaping, soften by warming in oven.

Almond Bars

½ pound almonds   2 egg whites
                ½ pound confectioners' sugar

Beat egg whites stiff. Mix ground almonds and sugar. Fold in beaten whites. Toss onto sugared moulding board. Mould into roll. Flatten, spread with meringue. Cut into strips one inch by three inches and bake in moderate oven (350° F.) twenty minutes.

Meringue:

1 beaten egg white   ¼ cup sugar
                ½ teaspoon vanilla

Nantucket Cookies

1 cup butter   2 cups brown sugar
2 eggs   3½ cups flour
1 teaspoon soda   ½ teaspoon salt
                1 cup walnuts (chopped fine)

Cream shortening. Add sugar and blend thoroughly. Add the eggs. Beat well. Mix salt and soda with the flour. Add nuts and flour mixture to first mixture. Mix thoroughly. Put into parafin-paper-lined bread tin in ice chest overnight. In the morning slice very thin and bake on greased baking sheets ten minutes in a moderately hot oven (375° F.).

Oatmeal Cookies

2 cups brown sugar   ½ teaspoon salt
1 cup shortening   1½ teaspoons cinnamon
2 eggs   2½ cups flour
¾ cup milk   ½ cup nut meats
1 teaspoon soda   ½ cup raisins
                3 cups rolled oats

Cream shortening. Add sugar and mix until well blended. Add the eggs and beat thoroughly. Mix soda, salt, and cinnamon with the flour. Add to first mixture alternately with the milk. Add nuts and raisins. Add rolled oats. Mix well. Drop from spoon onto greased baking sheets. Bake ten minutes in a hot oven (400° F.).

Rocks

1 cup sugar
1 cup shortening
2 eggs
1½ cups flour
2 cups rolled oats

1 teaspoon cinnamon
1½ cups currants
1 teaspoon soda
2 tablespoons grape juice
½ cup buttermilk

½ teaspoon salt

Cream shortening. Add sugar and salt and mix until thoroughly blended. Add eggs and beat thoroughly. Mix soda and cinnamon with the flour. Add to first mixture alternately with the butter milk. Add the currants. Add the rolled oats. Mix thoroughly. Drop from a spoon onto greased baking sheets. Bake ten minutes in a hot oven (400° F.). One-half cup currants may be omitted and one-half cup nuts added instead if desired.

Hermits

¾ cup shortening
1½ cups brown sugar
3 eggs
1 teaspoon soda
2 cups flour

1 teaspoon cinnamon
1 cup walnuts
¼ teaspoon salt
½ cup raisins
½ cup currants

Cream shortening. Add salt and sugar. Mix until well blended. Add the eggs. Beat thoroughly. Add nuts, currants, and raisins. Mix flour with soda and cinnamon. Add to first mixture. Mix well. Drop from a spoon onto greased baking sheets. Bake in a moderately hot oven (375° F.) ten minutes. One-quarter cup chopped citron may be added to this rule if desired.

Graham and Fig Wafers

1 cup cream
3 tablespoons sugar
¼ teaspoon salt

2 teaspoons baking powder
2½ cups graham flour
½ pound figs or dates

Sift together sugar, salt, and baking powder. Add to cream. Add graham flour. Chill. Roll half the dough on floured moulding board. Spread with chopped figs or dates. Roll other half of dough and place on layer of fruit. Roll top lightly. Cut into strips with sharp knife.

Bake on greased baking sheets in a moderate oven (350° F.) for fifteen minutes.

Tea Cookies

¼ cup shortening
1 cup flour
⅛ teaspoon salt

¼ teaspoon baking powder
½ cup confectioners' sugar
¼ cup milk

½ teaspoon vanilla

Cream shortening and sugar. Add milk gradually to prevent curdling. Add baking powder to flour. Add flour, salt, and flavoring. Spread very thin on a buttered inverted pan. Crease in three-inch squares and bake in slow oven (325° F.) until a delicate brown. Remove from oven. Roll quickly while still hot. Roll on handle of wooden spoon. Work quickly, as wafers become brittle when cool.

Finely chopped almonds may be added to top of cookie before baking, if desired.

Drop Cookies

1 cup butter
2 cups sugar
2 teaspoons salt
4 eggs

1 cup sour cream
1 teaspoon soda
4 cups flour
4 teaspoons baking powder

1 teaspoon vanilla

Cream shortening. Add sugar and mix until well blended. Mix salt, soda, and baking powder with the flour. Add vanilla to sour cream. Add eggs to shortening and sugar. Beat thoroughly. Add liquid and dry ingredients alternately. Mix well. Drop from a spoon onto greased baking sheets. Top each cookie with one-half nut meat. Bake ten minutes in a moderately hot oven (375° F.).

Molasses Cookies, No. 1

½ cup sugar
½ cup molasses
½ cup sour milk
½ cup shortening

1 egg
1 teaspoon cinnamon
1 teaspoon soda
2 cups flour

Cream shortening. Add sugar and mix until well blended. Add the egg and beat thoroughly. Mix soda and cinnamon with the flour. Add molasses to sour milk. Combine mixtures. Mix well. Chill. Toss onto floured moulding board. Roll to one-quarter inch thickness. Cut with round cutter. Bake on greased baking sheets fifteen minutes in a moderate oven. Ice with confectioners' sugar and milk icing.

Molasses Cookies, No. 2

1½ cups molasses
½ cup sugar
1 cup shortening
2 teaspoons soda
½ teaspoon cinnamon

1 tablespoon boiling water
1 teaspoon salt
½ teaspoon ginger
½ teaspoon allspice
¼ teaspoon cloves

3 cups flour

Boil molasses and sugar for five minutes. Add the shortening. Cool. Then add soda dissolved in the boiling water. Mix flour, spices, and salt. Add to molasses mixture. Mix thoroughly. Chill. Toss onto a floured moulding board. Roll as thin as possible. Cut with a round cutter. Bake on greased baking sheets ten minutes in a moderately hot oven (375° F.).

Wisconsin Molasses Cookies

2 cups molasses
1 cup shortening
½ cup sugar
2 tablespoons butter
¼ pound almonds (chopped fine)

1½ teaspoon soda
½ teaspoon salt
½ teaspoon cinnamon
½ teaspoon cloves
½ teaspoon nutmeg

4 cups flour

Mix shortening, sugar, and molasses. Heat to boiling point. Mix soda, salt, spices, and flour. Combine mixtures. Add nuts.

Mix thoroughly. Toss onto floured moulding board. Knead into roll. Grease dough and chill over night in refrigerator. In the morning slice and bake on greased baking sheets ten minutes in a moderately hot oven (375° F.).

Mincemeat Cookies

2 cups shortening
5 eggs
1 teaspoon salt
6½ cups flour

3 cups mincemeat
3 cups brown sugar
2 teaspoons soda
3 tablespoons hot water

1 cup nuts

Cream shortening. Add sugar and mix until well blended. Add eggs and beat thoroughly. Mix salt and soda with the flour. Add water to first mixture. Add mincemeat and flour mixture alternately to first mixture. Add nuts. Mix thoroughly. Drop with a spoon onto greased baking sheets. Bake ten minutes in a moderately hot oven (375° F.).

Butterscotch Whistles

1 egg
⅛ teaspoon salt
2 tablespoons flour

½ cup brown sugar
¼ teaspoon vanilla
1 tablespoon chopped nuts

Beat egg. Add sugar and salt. Beat thoroughly. Add nut meats and flour. Drop mixture from teaspoon onto greased baking sheets. Bake in hot oven (400° F.) until brown (one to two minutes). Remove quickly with spatula. Roll over handle of spoon. Cool.

Sponge Drops

Whites 3 eggs
⅓ cup sugar
Yolks 3 eggs

½ cup flour
½ teaspoon salt
1 teaspoon vanilla

Beat whites of eggs until stiff. Add sugar gradually and continue beating. Add beaten yolks and vanilla. Fold in the flour sifted with salt. Drop from teaspoon onto greased baking sheets. Bake ten minutes in moderate oven (350° F.).

Christmas Cookies

1 cup butter	1 cup milk
2 cups sugar	½ teaspoon salt
4 eggs	3 teaspoons baking powder
	6 cups flour

Cream the shortening. Add sugar gradually. Add the eggs and beat thoroughly. Mix salt and baking powder with the flour. Add the liquid and the dry ingredients alternately to the egg mixture, adding the dry ingredients first and last. Mix thoroughly. Chill dough overnight. In the morning roll thin on a floured moulding board. Cut into various shapes with cookie cutters. Bake on greased baking sheets ten minutes in a moderately hot oven. Cool. Ice with confectioners' sugar and milk icing. Decorate with colored sugars and candies.

Orange Cookies

½ cup butter	1 egg
1 cup sugar	½ cup orange juice
Grated rind 1 orange	3 cups flour
3 teaspoons baking powder	⅛ teaspoon salt

Cream shortening. Add sugar and mix until well blended. Add the egg and beat thoroughly. Add grated orange rind. Mix baking powder and salt with flour. Add to first mixture alternately with orange juice. Mix thoroughly. Chill dough overnight. Roll thin on a floured moulding board. Cut with round cutter. Brush with unbeaten white of egg. Sprinkle with granulated sugar. Bake on greased baking sheets ten minutes in a moderately hot oven (375° .). Lemon may be used instead of orange.

Brandy Snaps

8 tablespoons flour	8 tablespoons butter
8 tablespoons sugar	4 tablespoons light syrup
1 teaspoon ginger	4 tablespoons molasses

Mix flour, sugar, and ginger. Mix the molasses and syrup. Heat to boiling point, add butter, stir until melted. Add the remaining ingredients and heat for a second or two. Drop from a spoon onto greased baking sheets. Bake three minutes in a moderate oven (350° F.). Remove quickly with a spatula and roll around handle of wooden spoon. Cool. May be filled with sweetened whipped cream before serving if desired. Delicious either with cream or plain.

Sand Tarts, No. 1

½ cup shortening	2 teaspoons baking powder
1 cup brown sugar	White of 1 egg (unbeaten)
1 egg	Blanched almonds
1¾ cups flour	1 tablespoon sugar
¼ teaspoon cinnamon	

Cream shortening and brown sugar. Add well-beaten egg, then flour, mixed and sifted with baking powder. Mix thoroughly. Chill. Roll out thin as possible. Cut with small cutter and brush over with white of egg. Sprinkle with sugar mixed with cinnamon. Place split almond in center. Put onto greased baking sheets. Bake eight minutes in moderate oven (350° F.).

Sand Tarts, No. 2

½ cup shortening	1 egg
1 cup sugar	2 cups flour
1 tablespoon water	2 teaspoons baking powder
¼ cup almonds	

Cream shortening and sugar. Add egg and water. Beat thoroughly. Add flour and baking powder. Mix well and chill. Roll very thin, cut into squares and sprinkle with sugar and cinnamon. Place two or three blanched almonds on top and bake on greased baking sheets ten minutes in a moderate oven. (350° F.).

Gold Cookies

1 cup sugar	½ cup shortening
4 egg yolks	1½ cups flour
2 teaspoons baking powder	1 teaspoon vanilla
½ teaspoon salt	

Cream shortening. Add salt and sugar and mix until well blended. Add egg yolks and beat well. Mix baking powder with flour. Combine mixtures. Add vanilla. Mix thoroughly and chill. Roll into balls the size of a walnut. Then roll in a mixture of sugar and cinnamon, or ground nuts. Bake on greased baking sheets three inches apart in moderate oven (350° F.) fifteen minutes.

Cocoanut Kisses

1 pound shredded cocoanut	½ pound confectioners' sugar
¼ cup flour	1 teaspoon vanilla
4 egg whites (unbeaten)	

Mix the cocoanut, flour, and sugar. Add vanilla and whites of eggs. Mix thoroughly. Roll into balls size of a walnut. Bake on greased baking sheet in a moderate oven (350° F.) fifteen minutes.

Kisses

3 egg whites	1 teaspoon vanilla
2½ cups granulated sugar	

Beat egg whites until stiff. Fold in the sugar. Add vanilla. Drop from a teaspoon onto waxed paper. Bake on wooden board until firm and dry. This will take thirty minutes in a slow oven (300° F.–325° F.).

One-quarter cup cocoanut or one square of melted chocolate may be added if desired.

Bachelor Buttons

½ cup butter	2 eggs
2¼ cups flour	2 teaspoons baking powder
1½ cups sugar	1 teaspoon vanilla

Mix baking powder and flour. Cream butter until soft and smooth. Add flour mixture. Stir well. Beat eggs until light. Add vanilla and sugar. Add to first mixture. Mix thoroughly. Chill. Drop from a spoon onto greased baking sheets. Bake ten minutes in a moderately hot oven (375° F.). Each cookie may be topped with a raisin or nut meat before baking if desired.

CHAPTER XVII

Desserts

Apple Dessert

2 cups flour	¼ cup shortening
3 teaspoons baking powder	1 cup milk
½ teaspoon salt	1 egg
1 tablespoon sugar	1 teaspoon vanilla

6 apples

Sift flour and baking powder. Cut in shortening. Add salt and sugar. Add milk, vanilla, and beaten egg. Mix well. Drop tablespoon of batter into well-greased muffin tins. Peel and cut apples in half. Remove core. Press apples down into batter. Cover with sugar and cinnamon. Bake in hot oven (400° F.) twenty-five minutes. Serve hot with ice cream or whipped cream.

Apple Sponge

Grease an eight by ten-inch cake tin generously. Fill the bottom one inch deep with apples — sliced as for pie. Put one-half pound brown sugar over the apples. Cover apples with a batter made from:

3 eggs (well beaten)	Grated rind of 1 lemon
2 tablespoons water	¾ cup flour
½ cup sugar	1 teaspoon baking powder

Bake forty minutes in a moderate oven (350° F.). Serve with whipped cream. Garnish with cherries.

Apple Dumpling

Roll pie crust not too thin. Cut in squares to fit apples. Pare and core medium apples and place an apple in each square. Fill core with sugar and cinnamon. Dot with butter. Fold points of pastry over apples. Seal edges well. Place in pan. Pour water to which sugar, butter, and cinnamon have been added around dumplings. Bake in hot oven (450 F°.) until apples are soft. Reduce heat to (350° F.) after first fifteen minutes. Serve with whipped cream or hard sauce.

Banana Dessert

3 bananas (peeled)   3 teaspoons cocoa
                 3 teaspoons granulated sugar

Mix cocoa with sugar. Roll bananas in this mixture. Chill thoroughly in refrigerator. Serve with whipped cream.

Custard

1 pint scalded milk   ⅛ teaspoon salt
2 eggs   ½ teaspoon vanilla
                 4 tablespoons sugar

Beat egg and sugar slightly. Add milk gradually. Mix well. Put into a double boiler and cook until it coats the spoon. Cool before serving.

Baked Custard

1 cup milk   1 egg
1 tablespoon sugar   ⅛ teaspoon salt

Beat egg. Add salt, sugar, and milk. Mix thoroughly. Pour into greased custard cups. Put cups in pan of hot water. Bake in slow oven (325° F.), until knife inserted in custard comes out clean, thirty to forty minutes. One teaspoon vanilla may be added if desired. Custard may be dusted with nutmeg before baking if desired.

Caramel Custard

3 cups scalded milk   ½ teaspoon salt
1 teaspoon vanilla   ½ cup sugar
                 5 eggs

Caramelize the sugar, add milk. Cook over low flame until sugar dissolves. Add mixture to beaten egg. Add salt and flavoring. Pour into custard moulds. Bake from thirty to forty minutes in oven of (300°–325° F.). Put moulds in pan of water while baking.

Butterscotch Custard

½ cup brown sugar	4 tablespoons flour
2 cups milk	1 tablespoon butter
⅛ teaspoon salt	2 eggs

Mix sugar with flour, salt, and milk. Cook fifteen minutes in top of a double boiler. Pour slowly over beaten egg yolks and return to boiler for two minutes' cooking. Longer time of heating is liable to curdle the mixture. Remove from fire, add butter, and cool. Add stiffly beaten egg whites. Put into dish for serving. This is good served plain. It may be garnished with chopped nuts, maraschino cherries, or whipped cream. One teaspoon vanilla may be added, if desired.

Floating Island

2 cups hot milk	⅛ teaspoon salt
3 eggs	½ teaspoon vanilla
2 tablespoons sugar	

Beat egg yolks slightly. Mix with sugar and salt. Add slowly the scalded milk, stirring constantly. Cook over water just below boiling point until thick. Flavor and cool. If custard should curdle from over cooking, place in a pan of cold water and beat with a rotary egg beater.

Beat the egg whites until stiff. Add vanilla and one tablespoon confectioners' sugar. Mix thoroughly. Drop by spoonfuls into pan of hot water. Cook slowly until white sets. Serve on top of custard.

Custard Soufflé

3 tablespoons butter	⅛ teaspoon salt
4 tablespoons flour	1 cup scalded milk
¼ cup sugar	4 eggs

Melt butter, add flour, and hot milk gradually. When thick, pour over yolks of eggs beaten until thick and lemon colored. Add salt, sugar. Cool. Fold in whites of eggs beaten stiff and dry. Turn into buttered pudding dish, and bake from thirty to thirty-five minutes in slow oven (325° F.). Serve at once. Dust with confectioners' sugar before serving. Serve with whipped cream.

Almond Soufflé

Crumble eight macaroons and six lady fingers into a bowl and pour over them one cup of hot milk. Let stand for one-half hour. Then add one teaspoon vanilla, the beaten yolks of two eggs, one-eighth teaspoon salt, one-third cup sugar, and one-half cup chopped blanched almonds. Lastly fold in the stiffly beaten egg whites. Turn into a buttered baking dish. Set in pan of hot water and bake forty minutes in slow oven (300°–325° F.). Serve at once with whipped cream.

Chocolate Soufflé

2 tablespoons butter	⅛ teaspoon salt
2 tablespoons flour	1½ squares bitter chocolate
¾ cup milk	½ cup sugar
3 eggs	2 tablespoons hot water
1 teaspoon vanilla	

Melt the shortening in double boiler, add the flour, then add the milk. Cook until thick. Add the sugar, hot water, and melted chocolate. Cool. Add vanilla and beaten egg yolks. Fold in the stiffly beaten egg whites. Bake thirty-five minutes. Slow oven (325° F.). Dust with confectioners' sugar before serving.

Vanilla Soufflé

3 tablespoons butter	⅛ teaspoon salt
4 tablespoons flour	1 cup scalded milk
¼ cup sugar	4 eggs
1 tablespoon vanilla	

Melt butter, add flour, salt, and hot milk. Cook until thick. When thick pour over egg yolks beaten until thick and lemon colored. Add sugar. Add vanilla. Fold in stiffly beaten egg whites. Put into a buttered pudding dish and bake thirty to thirty-five minutes in a slow oven (325° F.). Serve at once. Dust with confectioners' sugar before serving. Serve with whipped cream.

Prune Whip, No. 1

½ cup prune pulp   ¼ cup sugar
3 egg whites (beaten stiff)

Mix prune pulp with sugar thoroughly. Fold in beaten egg whites. Chill. Serve with whipped cream. May be baked before serving if desired. Time thirty minutes. Slow oven (325° F.).

Prune Whip, No. 2

1½ cups prune purée   ¼ cup sugar
Whites of 4 eggs   ½ tablespoon lemon juice

Add sugar to prune purée and cook five minutes. Beat whites of eggs until stiff, and add prune mixture gradually. Add lemon juice. Put into buttered pudding dish, and bake thirty minutes in slow oven (325° F.). Serve cold with custard sauce. Apricots may be used instead of prunes.

Custard Sauce

1 cup hot milk   1 tablespoon sugar
2 eggs (yolks)   ⅛ teaspoon salt
½ teaspoon vanilla

Beat egg yolks slightly. Mix with sugar and salt. Slowly add scalded milk. Stir constantly. Put into double boiler. Cook until it thickens over water just below the boiling point. Flavor and cool. If custard should curdle, place in a pan of cold water and beat with rotary egg beater.

Jellied Prunes

½ pound prunes   1 cup sugar
2 cups cold water   ¼ cup lemon juice
(to soak prunes)   2½ tablespoons granulated
Boiling water   gelatine
½ cup cold water (to soak gelatine)

Soak prunes for several hours in two cups cold water. Cook in same water until soft. Pit prunes and cut in quarters. To prune water add enough boiling water to make two cups. Soak gelatine in half cup cold water. Dissolve in hot liquid. Add sugar and lemon juice. Strain, add prunes. Pour into moulds. Chill. Unmould and serve with whipped cream.

Blanc Mange

¾ cup flour   ¼ teaspoon salt
6 tablespoons sugar   3 cups milk
            1½ teaspoons vanilla

Scald two cups milk. Mix dry ingredients with one cup milk. Add slowly to scalded milk. Cook in double boiler until thick, stirring constantly. Then cover and cook thirty minutes longer. Remove from fire, add vanilla, and pour into cold, wet moulds. Chill thoroughly. Unmould. Serve with cream and sugar or with sliced or crushed fruits. Two squares of chocolate melted may be added if chocolate blanc mange is desired.

Rice Suprême

2 cups cold cooked rice   2 cups whipped cream
            1 cup pineapple (cut fine)

Mix pineapple and rice with whipped cream. Chill. Serve in sherbet glasses, garnished with cherries or strawberries. Apricots may be substituted for the pineapple.

Baked Apple

Core but do not pare apples. Fill center with brown sugar and raisins. Put into shallow baking pan. Add enough water to cover bottom of pan. Bake in moderate oven (350° F.). Dates may be used instead of raisins.

Top with marshmallow five minutes before removing from oven. Serve hot with cream.

Pineapple Delight

1 cup cream   8 slices pineapple (cut fine)
12 marshmallows (quartered)   10 maraschino cherries
1 teaspoon vanilla   (cut in quarters)

Whip the cream. Fold in pineapple, maraschino cherries, and marshmallows. Add vanilla. Chill thoroughly. Serve in sherbet glasses. Two cups of halved strawberries may be substituted for the cherries and pineapple.

Spanish Cream

1¼ tablespoons gelatine
¼ cup cold water
1 teaspoon vanilla
⅛ teaspoon salt

¾ cup boiling water
3 egg yolks and whites
3 tablespoons sugar
1 pint milk

Soak the gelatine in cold water. Dissolve in boiling water. Beat yolks of eggs with sugar and add salt. Add hot milk slowly. Cook in double boiler until it thickens. Add gelatine, vanilla, and whites of eggs, stiffly beaten. Turn into moulds. Chill and let set. Unmould. May be served plain or with custard sauce.

Bavarian Cream

2½ tablespoons granulated gelatine
½ cup cold water
½ cup orange juice

½ cup lemon juice
½ cup sugar
1 pint heavy cream

1 teaspoon vanilla

Soak the gelatine in water for a few minutes. Heat the fruit juice and add sugar. Combine with gelatine. Cool the mixture. When it begins to harden fold in stiffly beaten cream. Add vanilla. Pour into wet moulds. Chill and let set. Unmould before serving.

Pineapple Bavarian Cream

1 cup pineapple (diced)
2 cups boiling water

¼ cup sugar
2 tablespoons gelatine

1 cup whipped cream

Soak gelatine in cold water. Add boiling water. Stir until gelatine dissolves. Cool. When film forms on top, beat with egg beater until white. Add whipped cream, then pineapple. Pour into moulds and allow to set.

Chocolate Charlotte

¼ cup cold water	2 tablespoons granulated gelatine
4 tablespoons hot water	⅓ cup scalded cream
2 cups cream	⅔ cup confectioners' sugar
1½ squares chocolate	1 teaspoon vanilla
6 lady fingers	

Melt chocolate. Add half the sugar. Add hot water. Soak gelatine in cold water. Dissolve in scalded cream. Add chocolate mixture. Add vanilla and rest of sugar. Mix well. Fold in whipped cream. Pour into individual mould. Chill until firm. Unmould before serving. Serve plain or with whipped cream. Moulds may be lined with lady fingers before adding chocolate mixture if desired.

Charlotte Russe

Whip one quart heavy cream. Set aside in cold place. Beat eight yolks of eggs well with one-half pound confectioners' sugar. Dissolve four tablespoons gelatine in cold water. Dissolve gelatine over hot water. Then stir slowly into eggs and sugar. Add one tablespoon vanilla and stir slowly into whipped cream. If fruits are desired, add one cup of any fruit such as peaches, apricots, or strawberries. Sugar the fruit very little as there must not be much juice. Pile mixture into sherbet glasses and chill thoroughly before serving.

Strawberry Shortcake

2 cups flour	2 tablespoons sugar
4 teaspoons baking powder	1 egg
1 teaspoon salt	1 teaspoon vanilla
4 tablespoons shortening	¾ cup milk

Mix dry ingredients. Cut in shortening. Beat egg. Add milk and vanilla to egg. Add to dry ingredients. Mix smooth and turn onto floured board. Pat to one-half inch thickness. Cut with biscuit cutter. Bake on greased cookie sheet fifteen to twenty minutes. Hot oven (400° F.). Split biscuit, butter, and fill with fruit. Top with whipped cream or ice cream. Five cups of strawberries halved and sweetened are needed for this recipe.

For shortcake you may use fresh crushed strawberries, with sugar, raspberries, peaches, or any fresh fruit or berries in season. Stewed rhubarb is also delicious.

Quick Prune Dessert

1 cup flour	2 teaspoons baking powder
2 tablespoons sugar	2 tablespoons shortening
1 egg	½ teaspoon vanilla
	⅓ cup milk

Mix and sift flour, baking powder, salt, and sugar. Cut in shortening. Beat egg with milk and vanilla. Add to flour mixture. Stir until smooth. Put into greased pie tin, and cover with a generous layer of pitted stewed prunes. Bake twenty-five minutes in a moderately hot oven (375° F.). Serve hot with meringue or whipped cream. Apples, peaches, or apricots, either fresh or stewed, may be used instead of prunes.

Apricot Slices

⅓ cup milk	1 egg
2 tablespoons shortening	2 tablespoons sugar
½ teaspoon vanilla	1 cup flour
2 teaspoons baking powder	⅛ teaspoon salt

Mix and sift flour, baking powder, salt, and sugar. Cut in shortening. Beat egg with milk and vanilla, and add to flour mixture. Stir until smooth. Put into greased pie tin. Cover dough with a generous layer of halved apricots. Bake in a moderately hot oven (375° F.). When done, while hot, cover with confectioners' sugar icing. Sprinkle with nut meats and cut in slices.

Lemon Soufflé

1½ cups shortening	1 cup sugar
2 eggs	⅔ cup milk
1 teaspoon vanilla	2 cups flour
	3 teaspoons baking powder

Cream shortening and sugar. Add egg. Beat thoroughly. Mix flour and baking powder. Add vanilla to milk. Add wet and dry ingredients alternately to shortening and sugar. Mix thoroughly. Spread batter into greased cake tin to one-quarter inch thickness. Bake in moderate oven (350° F.) twenty to twenty-five minutes. Leave cake in tin. Make filling as follows:

⅓ cup flour	1⅓ cups water
⅔ cup sugar	⅛ teaspoon salt
2 egg yolks	Juice and rind 1 lemon

Mix sugar, salt, and flour. Cook until thick. Add egg yolks and beat thoroughly. Add juice and rind of lemon. Cool. Spread filling over cake after cake has cooled. Top with meringue, made from two egg whites, one-half teaspoon baking powder, and one-half cup granulated sugar. Put in low oven (325° F.) to brown meringue. Cool and serve.

Blackberry Roll

2 cups flour	¼ cup sugar
4 teaspoons baking powder	2½ cups blackberries (sweetened
½ teaspoon salt	with ¾ cup sugar)
¾ cup milk	4 tablespoons shortening

Sift flour, baking powder, and salt together. Cut in shortening. Add milk. Mix well. Toss on floured moulding board. Roll out to one-quarter inch thickness. Spread with sweetened berries. Roll. Place in well-greased pan. Bake twenty-five minutes in a moderate oven (350° F.). Serve with whipped cream. Apples may be used instead of berries.

Schaum Torte

Whites 6 eggs	2 cups sugar
1 teaspoon vinegar	1 teaspoon vanilla

Beat egg whites until stiff. Fold in sugar, vinegar, and vanilla. Mix carefully. Pour into greased spring form. Bake one hour in a slow oven (300°–325° F.). When done cool. Remove side of pan. Fill torte with ice cream.

Cover ice cream with fresh fruit or berries. Strawberries, raspberries, or sliced peaches are best. Garnish or decorate top with whipped cream and sherbet.

Russian Loaf

Whip one quart heavy cream. Set aside in cold place. Beat eight egg yolks well and add one-half pound confectioners' sugar. Dissolve two tablespoons gelatine in cold water. Dissolve gelatine over hot water. Stir slowly into the eggs and sugar. Add one tablespoon vanilla and stir slowly into whipped cream.

If fruits are desired, add one cup fruit such as peaches or strawberries. Sugar the fruit very little, as there must not be much juice.

Cut loaf angel or sponge cake into three slices of equal thickness. Put generous layers of filling between each slice. Cover outside of loaf with rest of filling. Put aside to chill and set. Serve cold.

Work quickly when putting filling on cake to prevent mixture setting while working.

Meringues or Kisses

6 egg whites   2 cups sugar
                          1 teaspoon vanilla

Beat egg whites until stiff. Fold in sugar and vanilla. Drop by spoonfuls onto wax paper. Put paper on board or baking sheet. Bake fifty minutes in a slow oven (275°–300° F.).

Fruit Meringues

Beat six egg whites until stiff. Gradually fold in two cups granulated sugar. Bake meringues on wax paper. Put paper on board or baking sheet. Bake in slow oven (275° F.) from fifty to sixty minutes.

Cut and remove top very carefully. Fill inside with ice cream and seasonable fresh fruits. Put back top and serve.

Brown Betty

2 cups bread crumbs   2 tablespoons butter
2 cups sliced apples   ⅔ cup brown sugar
2 teaspoons cinnamon   ½ cup water

Mix bread crumbs with melted butter. Arrange ingredients in alternate layers in buttered baking dish. Add water last.

A Sunday Night Buffet Supper

Bake forty-five minutes in a moderate oven (350° F.). Serve hot with whipped cream. Rhubarb, peaches, raspberries, or blackberries may be used instead of apples.

Danish Apple Cake

4 cups crumbs	3 tablespoons butter
1 quart mushy apple sauce	Whipped cream

Jelly

Butter baking dish. Line with crumbs one-fourth to one-half inch thick. Add layer of apple sauce, dot with butter, then add a second layer of crumbs three-fourths inch thick, then a layer of apple sauce one inch thick. Dot with butter. Continue with alternate layers until dish is full and all ingredients used. Have crumbs as top layer. Pat mixture until firm. Bake forty-five minutes in a slow oven (325° F.). Cool. Turn out of dish and ice with whipped cream. Dot top with jelly.

Date Torte

4 eggs	1 teaspoon baking powder
1 cup sugar	1 package dates (pitted and halved)
1 cup bread crumbs	1 cup walnut meats
	1 teaspoon vanilla

Beat the eggs; add sugar gradually. Add vanilla. Add bread crumbs, which have been mixed with the baking powder. Add dates and walnuts which have been cut fine. Mix well. Bake in a greased cake tin. Moderate oven (350° F.) for thirty-five minutes. Serve with whipped cream or ice cream.

Individual servings of date torte may be covered with fresh raspberries before topping with whipped cream. Berries are a delicious addition.

Cream Puffs

1 cup flour	½ cup butter
1 cup boiling water	4 eggs

Heat water and shortening together in a small saucepan to the boiling point. Add the flour all at once and beat thoroughly.

The dough will form a stiff ball in pan. Remove from fire. Add eggs one at a time, unbeaten. Beat thoroughly after each egg is added. Bake forty-five minutes, 500° F. for first fifteen minutes. Reduce heat to 350° F. last thirty minutes.

A greased baking sheet is best for cooking cream puffs. Drop dough with a spoon, allowing enough space for puff to spread.

Cream Puff Delight

Cut cream puffs in half, crosswise. Fill with vanilla ice cream. Pour hot chocolate sauce over cream puff. Sprinkle with chopped nuts.

Butterscotch sauce may be used instead of chocolate if desired.

Cream Filling for Cream Puffs

½ cup flour	2 tablespoons butter
2 cups scalded milk	⅛ cup sugar
2 eggs	½ teaspoon salt
1 teaspoon vanilla	

Mix the flour with some of the cold milk. Add to hot milk. Cook fifteen minutes in double boiler. Beat eggs, sugar, and salt together. Add to the hot liquid. Add butter. Return to double boiler and cook until thick. Cool. Cut slice from top of cream puff. Fill with cream filling. Cover with top. Dust with confectioners' sugar or ice with chocolate frosting.

Gingerbread Gems with Apples

3 tablespoons brown sugar	2 cups flour
1 egg	¾ cup molasses
1 teaspoon soda	½ teaspoon ginger
¼ cup shortening	1 teaspoon cinnamon
2 apples	½ teaspoon salt
1 tablespoon milk	¼ cup raisins or currants

Mix and sift dry ingredients. Add molasses and melted shortening. Then add egg beaten with milk. Add raisins or currants. Into greased muffin tins put apples cut in eighths.

Pour the mixture over the apples and bake in moderate oven (350° F.) twenty-five minutes.

Serve with whipped cream or hard sauce.

Blitz Torte

½ cup shortening
¾ cup sugar
4 eggs
¼ teaspoon salt

1 cup flour
1½ teaspoons baking powder
3 tablespoons milk
¼ pound blanched almonds

1 teaspoon vanilla

Cream the shortening and add sugar. Add the beaten egg yolks and vanilla. Beat well. Add the flour mixed with the salt and baking powder alternately with the milk. Spread in two shallow greased layer cake pans. Cover with a meringue made by beating the whites of the eggs very stiff and adding gradually one cup of sugar and one teaspoon baking powder. Sprinkle this with the almonds, cut fine. Bake in a moderate oven (350° F.) thirty-five minutes.

When cool put the layers together with a lemon, custard, or cream filling.

Washington Pie

1 egg
4 teaspoons baking powder
⅔ cup sugar
½ teaspoon salt

1 cup milk
¼ cup melted shortening
2 cups flour
1 teaspoon vanilla

Beat egg well with sugar and salt. Mix baking powder with the flour. Add vanilla to milk. Add liquid and dry ingredients alternately to egg and sugar mixture. Add melted shortening. Mix thoroughly. Pour into greased layer cake tins. Bake thirty-five minutes in a moderate oven (350° F.). Turn out of tin and cool.

Put layers together, and cover top with custard filling, whipped cream, or Chocolate Fluff.

CHAPTER XVIII
Fish and Fish Sauces

Salmon Loaf

2 cups flaked salmon	2 eggs
1 cup bread crumbs	1 tablespoon chopped parsley
1 tablespoon chopped onion	1 teaspoon salt

¼ teaspoon pepper

Put all the ingredients into a bowl and mix thoroughly. Shape into loaf. Add one-half cup water. Bake in moderate oven (350° F.) for thirty-five minutes. Tuna, haddock, swordfish, or halibut may be substituted for salmon.

Broiled Salmon Steak

Put salmon steak on rack of broiler. Cook under medium flame until entirely brown. Turn and brown both sides. Serve with drawn butter, parsley, and lemon.

Salmon Steak

6 slices fresh salmon steak,	4 tablespoons flour
1 inch thick	4 tablespoons butter
¾ cup milk	Salt and pepper

Remove skin from salmon. Roll in the flour which has been seasoned with salt and pepper. Place in buttered baking dish, add milk. Dot with butter. Bake one hour in moderate oven (350° F.). Baste frequently during baking.

Boiled Salmon

Soak salmon in cold water; then let it come to a boil. Change water twice. Let it boil fifteen minutes slowly. Pour off all the water. Put two tablespoons of butter and two tablespoons of flour into a pan, brown, and add one quart of milk. Cook until thick. Take off stove and stir in two well-beaten eggs. Pour over salmon. Do not let it curdle.

Salmon Casserole

4 potatoes	1 onion
4 slices bacon	2 cups salmon
1 egg	¾ cup milk
¼ cup crumbs	Salt and pepper

Put layer of peeled, sliced potatoes into buttered pan, then layer of salmon, onion, and bacon. Mix egg and milk and pour over salmon. Sprinkle with crumbs and bake fifty to sixty minutes in moderate oven (350° F.).

Fried Oysters

Drain off liquor. Roll each oyster in bread crumbs then dip in egg, again roll in crumbs, and fry.

Oysters may be fried in deep fat or in fat at least an inch deep in the frying pan. As soon as they are golden brown remove from fat and place on a brown paper to drain. Serve hot.

Serve with catsup or chilli sauce.

Pigs in Blankets

Roll each oyster in a thin slice of bacon and hold together with toothpick. Add salt and pepper and bake in oven (350° F.) until nicely browned.

Creamed Oysters

Make two cups medium white sauce of butter, flour, and milk. Season with salt and pepper, add three cups oysters. Cook fifteen minutes. Serve hot.

Sauté Oysters

Roll the oysters in beaten egg and season with salt and pepper. Then cover with bread crumbs and fry in butter until nicely browned. Bacon fat or lard may be used in place of butter.

Oyster Cocktail

50 small oysters
2 teaspoons grated horse
  radish
¼ teaspoon tabasco sauce
2 tablespoons vinegar

5 tablespoons lemon juice
1½ tablespoons Worces-
  tershire sauce
3 tablespoons tomato
  catsup

½ teaspoon salt

Chill and wash oysters. Mix with other ingredients. Serve in cocktail glasses.

Oyster Stew

1 pint oysters
1 quart milk

½ teaspoon salt
2 tablespoons butter

Heat oysters in own liquid. Add salt, butter, and scalded milk. Serve in bowl with heated crackers.

Scalloped Oysters

1 pint oysters
1 teaspoon salt
¼ cup butter

1 cup crumbs
1 teaspoon pepper
4 tablespoons cream

4 tablespoons oyster liquid

Place a layer of the crumbs in a buttered baking dish. Add a layer of oysters. Season with salt and pepper and dot with butter. Add another layer of crumbs, then more oysters, and season as before. Pour over the cream and liquor. Cover with another layer of crumbs. Bake in moderate oven thirty minutes (350° F.).

Fried Smelts

To clean smelts, spread open outer gills, and with the fore-finger take hold of the inner gills and pull gently; the parts unfit for food are all attached to these inner gills, and come away to-gether, leaving the smelt in perfect shape. Rinse thoroughly and wipe dry. If smelts are small, dip in milk and roll in flour, or in egg and bread crumbs. Fry in deep fat.

Broiled Salt Mackerel

Let soak in cold water twelve hours, skin side up. Drain, and wipe dry. Brush over with melted shortening. Broil on a well-greased broiler, skin side down, basting with butter once or twice. Remove carefully to serving dish and serve with hot white sauce. Sprinkle with finely chopped parsley.

Lobster à la Newburg

3 pounds lobster (boiled)	½ teaspoon salt
¼ cup butter	Dash cayenne
2 tablespoons sherry flavoring	½ cup cream
Yolks 3 eggs	

Cut lobster in slices. Melt butter, add lobster, and cook five minutes. Add seasonings and sherry flavoring. Cook one minute, then add cream and beaten egg yolks. Cook until thick. Serve on toast or in timbales.

Lobster Cutlet

3 pounds lobster (boiled)	¼ teaspoon grated nutmeg
2 tablespoons butter	1 teaspoon lemon juice
2 tablespoons flour	1 egg
½ cup milk	Salt and pepper
Bread crumbs	

Cut lobster meat as fine as possible. Cream butter and flour in a saucepan, and when mixed, add the milk and cook until thick. Add the salt, pepper, lemon, and nutmeg. Mix well. While still hot, add the lobster and spread on a plate to cool. When cool, shape into cutlet form, dip in egg and bread crumbs. Fry golden brown in hot fat. Drain well before serving. Garnish with lemon, parsley, watercress, caper, aspic, or olives.

Boiled Lobster

Put lobster into boiling, salted water. Be sure that lobster is completely submerged. Boil twenty to thirty minutes. Serve with drawn butter and lemon.

Broiled Live Lobster

Split live lobster through the middle. Wash thoroughly. Fill with a bread dressing. Put on to broiler rack and broil twenty minutes. Serve with drawn butter and lemon.

Lobster Stew

2 cups lobster meat cut into cubes	4 tablespoons butter
1 quart milk	1 cup cream

Melt butter. Add lobster. Cook ten minutes. Add scalded milk and cream. Season with salt and pepper. Serve at once.

Fillet of Sole, No. 1

Dredge slices of fillet of sole in flour. Pat into shallow greased baking dish. Season with salt and pepper. Dot with butter. Bake in a moderately hot oven (350° F.) thirty minutes. Put under broiler to brown before serving. Garnish with parsley and lemon.

Fillet of Sole, No. 2

Roll slices of fillet of sole in beaten egg, then in cracker crumbs. Sauté in butter. Turn once while cooking. Serve with salt and pepper. Garnish with parsley and lemon.

Deviled Crabs

2 tablespoons butter	2 egg yolks
2 tablespoons flour	1 cup chopped crab meat
1 cup soup stock	¼ cup chopped mushrooms
Salt and pepper	1 teaspoon parsley

Make a sauce of butter, flour, and stock, and add other ingredients, except parsley, and cook several minutes. Add parsley. Wash and trim crab shells, fill rounding with mixture, and sprinkle with buttered crumbs. Crease on top with case knife, making three parallel lines, and three short lines branching from outside parallel lines. Bake till crumbs are brown. Moderate oven (350° F.).

Baked Halibut, No. 1

6 thin slices salt pork
2 pounds sliced halibut
3 tablespoons flour

1 small onion
Salt and pepper
3 tablespoons butter

¾ cup bread crumbs

Place four slices pork in baking pan. Slice onion in thin slices over pork. Wipe halibut steak. Lay on top of the pork and onion. Season with salt and pepper. Mix butter and flour to a paste and spread over the halibut. Cover with crumbs. Cut remaining pork in narrow strips and lay over the crumbs. Bake fifty minutes in moderate oven (350° F.).

Baked Halibut, No. 2

1 pound halibut
½ cup water
Sprig of parsley
1 tablespoon flour

1 cup tomatoes
1 onion
3 cloves
1 tablespoon butter

Salt and pepper

Clean fish, dry thoroughly, and put in baking pan. Mix tomatoes, water, onion, parsley, and cloves. Cook ten minutes. Melt butter, add the flour, and gradually add the hot mixture. Add salt and pepper to taste. Cook four minutes and strain. Pour one-half the sauce on the fish and bake in a moderate oven (350° F.) until fish separates from the bone, basting often. Serve on hot platter and pour around it the remainder of the sauce. Garnish with parsley.

Broiled Halibut

Wipe slices of halibut clean. Put onto a greased broiler rack. Broil under medium flame until brown. Turn once while broiling. Serve with drawn butter and slices of lemon.

Broiled Swordfish

Cut slices two inches thick. Wipe fish clean. Put onto a greased broiler rack. Broil under medium flame until brown. Turn once while broiling. Serve with drawn butter and slices of lemon.

Broiled Mackerel

Split the mackerel and wash it. Spread it onto a greased broiler rack. Broil under medium flame until brown. Serve with drawn butter and lemon.

Baked Mackerel

Split the mackerel and wash it. Spread wide and put into a greased baking pan. Season with salt and pepper. Dot with butter. Cover with milk. Bake forty minutes in a moderate oven (350° F.). Serve with lemon.

Creamed Codfish

Soak codfish in cold water. Let it come to a boil. Change water three times, then let it boil fifteen to twenty minutes slowly. Pour off all water. Put two tablespoons butter and two tablespoons flour in a pan. Brown and add one quart milk. Cook until thick, and stir in two well-beaten eggs. Pour over codfish; do not let it curdle. Serve at once.

Boiled Cod

Wipe fish clean. Boil thirty minutes, slowly in salted water. Drain. Serve with medium thick white sauce and garnish with hard cooked eggs.

Fried Cod

Wipe fish clean. Cut into individual servings. Roll cod in corn meal. Fry in deep fat. Drain. Serve at once.

Cod may be fried in a frying pan in either butter or bacon drippings.

Fish Cakes

1 cup fish cut in small pieces   2 cups potatoes cut small

Boil together for twenty-five minutes, then drain off water and mash. Allow to cool. Add one tablespoon of butter, pepper, and one egg. Make into patties. Fry in deep fat or sauté in pork fat. Serve with chili sauce.

Codfish Balls

1 cup codfish
½ tablespoon butter
2 cups diced potatoes
⅛ teaspoon pepper
1 egg

Wash the codfish in cold water and tear into shreds. Cover potatoes and fish with boiling water and cook until potatoes are soft. Drain. Mash thoroughly in the dish in which they were cooked, adding butter, pepper, and well-beaten egg. Form into cakes and roll in flour. Fry in deep fat until brown.

Baked Haddock, No. 1

Wipe fish clean. Put into greased baking dish. Season with salt and pepper. Cover with bread dressing. Add one cup water. Bake in moderate oven (350° F.) fifty minutes.

Baked Haddock, No. 2

Wipe fish clean. Put into a greased baking dish. Season with salt and pepper. Cover with two tablespoons chopped onion, one green pepper chopped, two cups canned tomatoes. Bake fifty minutes in a moderate oven (350° F.).

Haddock with Cheese

3 or 4 pounds haddock (skinned and boned)
½ cup flour
2 teaspoons dry mustard
2 tablespoons butter
1 cup cheese

Lay the fish flat on a well-buttered baking pan. Then melt butter, add flour and mustard mixed. Add milk and cheese and cook until smooth and pour over fish. Bake in moderate oven for thirty-five minutes. Increase heat the last five minutes to brown. Halibut or any firm fish is good prepared in this way.

Fish Chowder

5 pounds haddock
¼ pound bacon
6 medium-sized onions (sliced)
1 quart milk
⅛ pound butter
Salt and pepper
6 medium-sized potatoes (diced not too small)

Cook haddock in boiling water for fifteen minutes. Cut bacon into small pieces. Fry, add sliced onions and cook in frying pan for about twenty minutes. Take fish out of water, and remove bones and skin. Put water in which fish was cooked back on stove. Add onions and potatoes. Add one quart milk, butter, and fish, and salt and pepper to taste. Cook thirty minutes.

Quahog Chowder

1 pint quahogs (chopped fine)	1 raw potato (diced)
½ cup chopped onion	½ tablespoon salt
1 quart scalded milk	4 tablespoons butter

Melt shortening, and add quahogs. Simmer five minutes. Add two cups boiling water, onion, and potato. Then cook thirty minutes. Add milk and cook ten minutes longer. Serve hot.

Scallop Chowder

1 pint scallops	1 potato (diced)
½ cup chopped onion	½ tablespoon salt
1 quart scalded milk	4 tablespoons butter

Melt the shortening. Add scallops and simmer five minutes. Add two cups boiling water, onion, and potatoes. Cook thirty minutes. Add milk and cook ten minutes longer. Serve hot.

Clam Chowder

1 pint clams (chopped fine)	1 raw potato (diced)
½ cup chopped onion	½ tablespoon salt
1 quart scalded milk	4 tablespoons butter

Melt the shortening and add clams. Let simmer for five minutes. Add two cups boiling water, onions, and potato. Cook for thirty minutes. Add milk and cook for ten minutes more. Serve hot.

Lobster Bisque

1 cup lobster	1 tablespoon flour
2 pints boiling water	1 pint milk (scalded)
2 tablespoons butter	½ pint cream

Salt and paprika

Chop the lobster not too fine. Let simmer in boiling water for forty minutes. Add butter creamed with flour. Combine with the scalded milk and cream. Salt to taste.

To avoid curdling do not boil after the milk has been added. Serve at once, adding a dash of paprika and chopped parsley. Salmon may be substituted for the lobster.

Shrimps — Louisiana Style

2 tablespoons butter	Paprika
½ cup heavy cream	1 cup shrimp
3 tablespoons tomato purée	¼ teaspoon chopped celery
1 cup boiled rice	1 teaspoon chopped onion
1 chopped pimento	1 chopped green pepper

½ teaspoon salt

Cook butter with onions five minutes, stirring constantly. Add shrimps, rice, and cream. When thoroughly heated add rest of ingredients. Turn on hot serving dish and garnish with toast points and parsley.

Shrimp Wiggle on Toast

1 cup cooked shrimp	1 cup peas

1½ cups medium thick white sauce

Mix shrimp and peas with sauce. Beat thoroughly. Serve on toast. Garnish with paprika and parsley.

Shrimp in Aspic

2 tablespoons gelatine	1 cup cooked shrimp
½ cup cold water	1 cup chopped celery
¼ cup mayonnaise	1 green pepper (cut fine)
½ teaspoon salt	1 pimento (cut fine)
⅛ teaspoon paprika	1 tablespoon vinegar

Soak gelatine in cold water. Dissolve over hot water. Add mayonnaise, salt, paprika, and vinegar. Add the other ingredients to gelatine mixture. Put into mould. Chill. Serve on bed of lettuce leaves. Garnish with parsley and stuffed eggs.

Jellied Tuna Fish

2 tablespoons gelatine
½ cup cold water
¼ cup mayonnaise
½ teaspoon salt
⅛ teaspoon paprika
1 tablespoon vinegar

1 cup tuna fish (flaked)
1 cup chopped celery
1 cup chopped olives
½ cup chopped green pepper
3 tablespoons pimento (chopped)
Few grains cayenne

Soak gelatine in cold water five minutes. Dissolve over hot water and add mayonnaise, salt, paprika, vinegar, and cayenne. Mix together flaked tuna fish, celery, olives, green pepper, and pimento, and add to mayonnaise mixture. Put into fancy mould which has been dipped in cold water and chill until firm. When ready to serve, unmould on crisp lettuce and garnish with mayonnaise.

Tuna Fish Casserole

2 cups flaked tuna fish
4 cups medium white sauce

1 pimento (cut fine)

Mix the fish with the pimento and white sauce. Heat thoroughly. Put into a greased casserole. Top with baking powder biscuits. Bake twenty-five minutes in a moderate oven (350° F.). Biscuits should not be too thick or they will not cook sufficiently. Mushrooms may be added to this casserole if desired.

White Sauce, No. 1
(Thin)

2 tablespoons shortening
1 tablespoon flour

½ teaspoon salt
1 cup milk

Melt shortening, add flour, and blend smooth. Add milk gradually, stirring continually to prevent lumping. Cook until mixture thickens slightly. Egg yolk or paprika may be added to the mixture to color it.

White Sauce, No. 2
(Medium)

2 tablespoons shortening
2 tablespoons flour

½ teaspoon salt
1 cup milk

Melt shortening. Add flour and blend smooth. Add milk gradually, stirring continually to prevent lumping. Cook until mixture thickens. Egg yolk or paprika may be added to mixture to color it.

White Sauce, No. 3
(Thick)

2 tablespoons shortening
3 tablespoons flour

1 teaspoon salt
1 cup milk

Melt shortening. Add flour, and blend smooth. Gradually add the milk and stir constantly to prevent lumping. Cook until the mixture thickens. Egg yolk or paprika may be added to color it.

Hollandaise Sauce

1 cup sweet butter
1 tablespoon lemon juice

4 egg yolks
¼ teaspoon salt

Few grains cayenne

Divide butter into three parts. Put egg yolks, lemon juice, and one of the portions of butter in top of double boiler over boiling water. Beat constantly until butter is dissolved; add second piece of butter and continue beating until butter is melted; add third piece of butter with salt and pepper and beat until sauce is of the consistency of a thick mayonnaise. Remove from stove immediately. Serve at once.

Fish Sauce

Blend three tablespoons melted shortening with three tablespoons flour. Add one-fourth teaspoon salt and a dash of pepper. Add one and one-half cups scalded milk. Cook until thick. Add one-quarter cup capers. Paprika or egg yolk added to this sauce will pink it or yellow it as desired.

Tartar Sauce

To one cup mayonnaise add one-half cup chopped pickles and one tablespoon capers.

Cucumber and Pimento Sauce

Pare two large cucumbers; remove seeds, if large. Chop fine and squeeze dry. Add one chopped pimento and one tablespoon of parsley. Season with salt, vinegar, and paprika. Add one-half cup cream.

Anchovy Sauce

Mix one cup white sauce and two tablespoons anchovy paste; place in double boiler and allow to heat for about five minutes. Season with lemon juice.

Tomato Sauce

Brown one tablespoon butter with one minced onion, then add one tablespoon flour. When brown, stir in two cups tomatoes which have been cooked and strained, add one teaspoon of sugar, pinch of salt, pepper and paprika. Add one teaspoon vinegar and one tablespoon tomato catsup. Serve with fish.

Egg Sauce

¼ cup butter	2 tablespoons flour
¾ cup milk	½ teaspoon salt
⅛ teaspoon pepper	2 egg yolks
4 tablespoons lemon juice	Grated rind of ½ lemon

Melt the butter, add the flour, and blend to a smooth paste. Add the milk and stir until thick. Add salt, pepper, and egg yolks, and stir until smooth without allowing the sauce to boil. Add the lemon juice very gradually.

CUTS OF BEEF

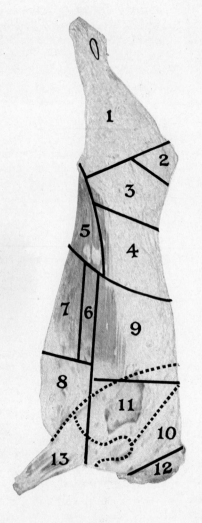

1	ROUND
2	RUMP BOTTOM
3 & 4	FULL LOIN
5	FLANK
6, 7 & 8	FULL PLATE
9	RIB
10, 11 & 12	CHUCK
13	FORE SHANK

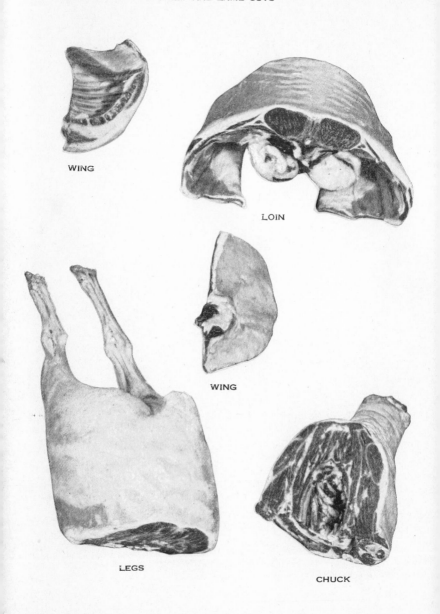

WING

LOIN

WING

LEGS

CHUCK

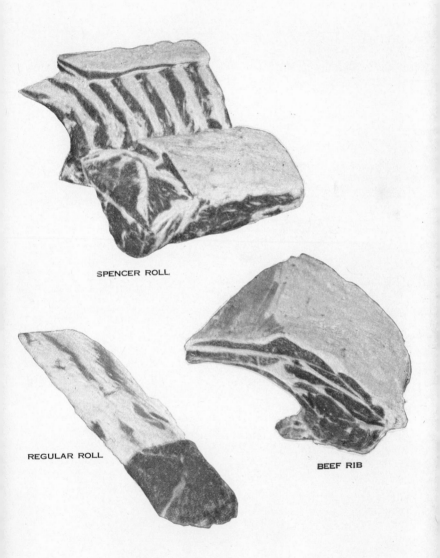

BEEF RIBS

SPENCER ROLL

REGULAR ROLL

BEEF RIB

CUTS OF BEEF

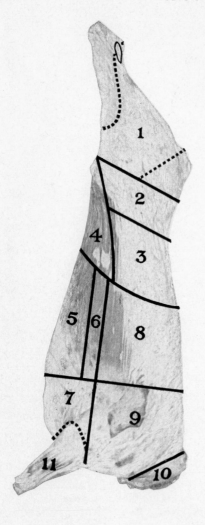

1	ROUND
2	LOIN END
3	SHORT LOIN PIN BONE
2 & 3	FULL LOIN
4	FLANK
5, 6 & 7	FULL PLATE
5 & 6	NAVEL END
6	SHORT RIBS
7	BRISKET
8	RIBS
9 & 10	CHUCKS
10	NECK
11	FORESHANK

CHAPTER XIX

Frozen Dishes

Vanilla Ice Cream, No. 1

1 quart cream
2 teaspoons vanilla

1 cup sugar
⅛ teaspoon salt

Mix cream, sugar, vanilla, and salt. Freeze.

Vanilla Ice Cream, No. 2

1 pint cream
1 cup sugar

4 eggs
1 tablespoon vanilla

1 pint milk (scalded)

Beat eggs, add sugar, then the scalded milk. Mix well. Cook to custard stage and chill. Add vanilla and freeze.

Neapolitan Ice Cream

1 cup sugar
2 quarts thin cream
3 egg yolks

1 cup pecan meats
½ cup cherries
½ cup pineapple

Heat cream. Caramelize sugar and dissolve it in the cream. Add the beaten egg yolks. Cool and partly freeze. Add the cherries, pineapple, and nuts. Mix well. Finish the freezing.

Chocolate Ice Cream

1 quart thin cream
1 cup sugar

⅛ teaspoon salt
1½ square chocolate (melted)

1 tablespoon vanilla

Scald the cream and add melted chocolate while the cream is hot. Do not allow cream to boil, as it will curdle. Add other ingredients. Allow mixture to cool and freeze.

Peach or Apricot Ice Cream

1 cup peach or apricot purée
2 tablespoons lemon juice
⅛ teaspoon salt
½ cup sugar

2 tablespoons confectioners'
  sugar
¾ cup orange juice
½ pint heavy cream (chilled)

Drain fruit. Put fruit through a strainer. Add purée to the fruit syrup, the lemon juice, salt, and one-half cup sugar; then add the orange juice. Whip the heavy cream, add the confectioners' sugar, and add to the mixture. Mix thoroughly. Freeze slowly.

Banana Ice Cream

3 bananas
2 teaspoons lemon juice
⅛ teaspoon salt

2 tablespoons confectioners' sugar
½ cup sugar
½ pint heavy cream
¾ cup orange juice

Slice bananas and force through a coarse sieve. To the banana purée add the lemon juice, salt, one-half cup sugar and orange juice. Whip confectioners' sugar with the heavy cream and add the whipped cream to the banana mixture. Freeze.

Peanut Ice Cream

1 pint cream
1 cup sugar
4 eggs

1 pint milk (scalded)
1 cup peanut butter (or
  peanuts chopped fine)

1 teaspoon vanilla

Beat eggs, add sugar, and then the scalded milk. Mix with cream. Cook to custard stage. Add vanilla and peanuts or peanut butter. Freeze.

Tutti Frutti Ice Cream

1 cup sugar
2 quarts cream
½ cup figs

3 egg yolks
1 cup roasted nuts
½ cup dates

1 cup candied cherries

Heat cream. Caramelize sugar and dissolve in cream. Add egg yolks. Beat well. Freeze. When partly frozen, add nuts and fruit cut fine. Freeze.

Macaroon Ice Cream

1 cup macaroon crumbs	1 teaspoon almond extract
½ cup confectioners' sugar	1 quart cream

⅛ teaspoon salt

Mix sugar, salt, and macaroon crumbs with the cream. Add almond extract. Mix well. Freeze.

Strawberry Ice Cream, No. 1

3 pints thin cream   1 quart strawberries

2 cups sugar

Clean and wash berries; add sugar and put through coarse strainer. Freeze cream partially, then add fruit and continue freezing.

Strawberry Ice Cream, No. 2

2 cups strawberries	2 tablespoons confectioners' sugar
2 teaspoons lemon juice	½ cup sugar
⅛ teaspoon salt	1 pint cream

¾ cup orange juice

Crush the strawberries and press through coarse strainer. To the strawberry purée add the salt, lemon juice, one-half cup sugar and orange juice. Add confectioners' sugar to cream and combine mixtures. Freeze slowly.

Pineapple Ice Cream

1 cup crushed pineapple	2 tablespoons lemon juice
½ cup sugar	1 pint cream.

Mix sugar, pineapple, and lemon juice with cream. Freeze.

Frozen Pudding

1½ pints cream	¼ pound quartered marshmallows
6 tablespoons confectioners' sugar	2 teaspoons vanilla
	½ cup macaroons (broken fine)
¼ cup black coffee	½ cup maraschino cherries

3 egg whites

Beat cream until stiff, add sugar, vanilla, coffee, macaroons, and cherries (cut fine). Add quartered marshmallows. Fold in beaten whites of eggs. Mix thoroughly. Freeze.

Banana Mousse with Marshmallow

4 bananas
Juice of ½ lemon

¾ cup sugar
1½ cups cream

Mix mashed banana pulp with sugar and lemon. Combine with whipped cream. Turn into mould, filling it to overflowing. Spread paper over the top of the mixture and over this put the cover. Pack in equal parts of salt and crushed ice. Let stand three hours, repacking once. Unmould.

Toast one-half pound marshmallows. Decorate mousse with maraschino cherries and toasted marshmallows. Cut mousse into slices and serve. Serve cherry and marshmallow with each slice.

Fruit Mousse

1½ cups sugar
3 cups peaches or strawberries
   or any fresh fruit crushed

1 tablespoon gelatine
¼ cup cold water
2 cups cream

Add sugar to crushed fruit and let stand thirty minutes. Soak gelatine in cold water five minutes. Dissolve over hot water. Add dissolved gelatine to fruit. Let stand until mixture begins to thicken. Fold in whipped cream. Put mixture into covered mould which has been dipped in cold water. Put wax paper over top. Put cover on tight. Pack in mixture of equal quantities of ice and salt. Let stand four hours. If ice melts, pour off water and repack with equal parts ice and salt. Unmould when ready to serve.

Macaroon Mousse with Pecans

1 cup cream
½ cup macaroon crumbs

½ cup chocolate sauce
4 tablespoons chopped pecans

1 teaspoon vanilla

Whip cream, fold in crumbs and pecans. Add chocolate sauce. Add vanilla. Mix thoroughly. Pour into mould. Freeze.

Strawberry Mousse

3 cups crushed strawberries   1 tablespoon lemon juice
4 cups cream (whipped)   ¾ cup sugar (confectioners')

Cover the berries with sugar and let stand one hour. Mash berries and put through a strainer. Add to the whipped cream and flavor with lemon juice. Put into mould and freeze for three and one-half hours. Peaches or apricots may be substituted for the strawberries.

Frozen Chocolate

2 squares chocolate (bitter)   ⅛ teaspoon salt
1 cup sugar   1 cup boiling water
3 cups milk   1 teaspoon vanilla

Scald milk. Melt chocolate and add to hot milk. Mix sugar with salt and boiling water. Boil five minutes. Add to scalded milk. Add vanilla. Cool. Freeze. Garnish with whipped cream.

Frozen Custard

3 cups milk   1 teaspoon salt
3 eggs (beaten)   1 cup whipped cream
1 cup sugar   1 teaspoon vanilla

Scald milk and add sugar. Add slowly to beaten eggs. Cook in double boiler to custard stage. Cool, add cream, salt, and flavoring. Freeze.

Coffee Parfait

2 egg yolks   1 cup strong coffee
¾ cup sugar (confectioners')   2 cups heavy cream
½ teaspoon salt   1 teaspoon vanilla

Beat the egg yolks, add the salt and sugar. Mix. Add coffee. Cook in a double boiler to custard stage. Cool. Freeze. Fold whipped cream into mixture when partially frozen. Add vanilla with whipped cream.

Butterscotch Parfait

½ cup brown sugar
3 tablespoons butter
½ cup water
⅛ teaspoon salt

2 teaspoons vanilla
2 egg yolks
1 pint cream

Put the brown sugar and the butter in a sauce pan and stir until melted. Cook for one minute. Add water. Mix well. Boil five minutes. Beat the egg yolks until very light. Add syrup gradually. Beat and cook over hot water until very light. Chill. Beat the cream until stiff, add the salt and vanilla and fold into egg mixture. Freeze three hours.

Angel Parfait

1 cup sugar
¾ cup water
1 tablespoon vanilla

Whites 3 eggs
2 cups cream (whipped)

Make a syrup of sugar and water. Pour over beaten egg whites. Beat continually. Add vanilla. Fold into cream and freeze.

Angel Parfait with Candied Fruit

½ cup granulated sugar
½ cup water
Whites of 2 eggs
 (beaten dry)
3 tablespoons orange juice

2 tablespoons cold water
1½ cups cream (whipped)
1 teaspoon gelatine
½ cup candied cherries (cut fine)
½ cup candied pineapple (cut fine)

Soak the gelatine in cold water five minutes. Make a syrup of boiling water and sugar. Pour over the whites of eggs, beating constantly. Add the gelatine and stir until the mixture begins to set. Fold in the cream, fruit, orange juice, and flavoring. Turn into a mould. Freeze three hours.

Strawberry Parfait

1 cup sugar
¾ cup water
1 teaspoon vanilla
¼ cup confectioners' sugar

Whites 3 eggs
2 cups cream (whipped)
1 cup crushed strawberries

Mix strawberries with confectioners' sugar. Make syrup of sugar and water. Pour syrup over beaten egg whites slowly. Beat continually until mixture begins to set. Fold into whipped cream. Add vanilla and strawberries. Pour into mould. Freeze. Other fruit may be substituted for the strawberries if desired.

Pineapple Frappé

2 cups water
1 cup sugar
Juice 3 lemons

2 cups water
1 can grated pineapple
Juice 2 limes

Make a syrup by boiling two cups water and sugar. Boil fifteen minutes. Add pineapple and fruit juices. Cool, and add two cups water. Freeze partially. Serve at once.
Other fruit may be substituted for the pineapple if desired.

Cranberry Ice, No. 1

4 cups cranberries
2½ cups sugar
½ cup orange juice

3½ cups boiling water
⅛ teaspoon salt
¼ cup lemon juice

Pick over and wash the cranberries. Add sugar and water and cook ten minutes. Rub through a sieve, cool. Add fruit juice. Freeze.

Cranberry Ice, No. 2

4 cups water
2 cups sugar

2 tablespoons lemon juice
2 cups cranberry juice

Cook cranberries in water ten minutes. Press through strainer. Add sugar and dissolve well. Flavor with lemon juice and freeze. Currants may be added if desired.

Mint Ice

2 cups sugar
1 quart water

Juice 2 lemons
3 tablespoons dried mint leaves

Make a syrup of sugar and water and pour over crushed mint leaves. Allow to cool, then strain. Add lemon juice and a little green coloring if desired. Freeze. Serve with meat course of lamb or mutton.

Maraschino Ice

4 cups water (boiling)   2 cups orange juice
2 cups sugar   ¼ cup lemon juice
    1 cup maraschino cherries (chopped fine)

Make a syrup by boiling water and sugar. Add fruit juices, cool, and freeze partially. Add maraschino cherries and finish freezing.

Apricot Ice

2 cups water (boiling)   ½ cup sugar
1 cup apricot juice   2 tablespoons lemon juice

Make a syrup of boiling water and sugar. Add fruit juice and cool. Strain and freeze.

Grape Sherbet

1 cup grape juice   1 pint milk
½ cup sugar   1 teaspoon gelatine
    1 cup water (boiling)

Soak gelatine in cold water for five minutes. Make a syrup of boiling water and sugar. Add gelatine. Stir until dissolved. Cool. Add fruit juice and milk. Freeze.

Pineapple Sherbet

½ cup shredded pineapple   2 tablespoons lemon juice
½ cup sugar   2 cups milk
1 cup pineapple juice   ½ tablespoon gelatine

Soak gelatine in cold water. Make a syrup of sugar and water. Add gelatine, pineapple, milk, and fruit juice. Freeze.

Pineapple and Maraschino Sherbet

½ cup cherries (cut in quarters)   ½ cup sugar
½ cup pineapple (shredded)   2 tablespoons lemon juice
2 cups water   ½ tablespoon gelatine
    1 cup pineapple juice

Dissolve gelatine in cold water. Make a syrup of sugar and water. Add gelatine, pineapple, cherries, and fruit juice. Freeze.

CHAPTER XX

Fruit Cocktails, Breakfast Fruits, Cereals

Fruit Cocktail, No. 1

Pulp of 3 oranges
Pulp of 1 grapefruit

3 bananas (sliced)
1 cup maraschino cherries

Mix fruit with one-half cup confectioners' sugar and one cup of pineapple juice. Chill thoroughly. Serve cold.

Fruit Cocktail, No. 2

3 cups pineapple (cubed)
2 cups strawberries (halved)

½ cup confectioners' sugar
½ cup lemon juice.

Mix fruit with sugar and lemon juice. Chill thoroughly. Serve cold, garnished with mint leaves and whole strawberries.

Fruit Cocktail, No. 3

2 cups diced fresh pineapple
2 cups seedless green grapes

½ cup confectioners' sugar
½ cup orange juice

Mix fruit with sugar and fruit juice. Chill thoroughly. Serve cold. Serve with a garnish of fresh raspberries or blackberries around edge of cocktail glass.

Fruit Cocktail, No. 4

2 cups sliced peaches
1 cup sliced pears

2 bananas (sliced)
1 cup diced pineapple

Mix the fruit with three tablespoons confectioners' sugar and the juice of two limes. Chill thoroughly and serve cold.

Fruit Cocktail, No. 5

1 cup strawberries (halved)
2 cups pineapple (diced)

2 bananas (sliced)

Pulp of one grapefruit. Mix the fruit with one-half cup confectioners' sugar and one-quarter cup orange juice. Chill thoroughly. Serve cold. Garnish with cherry.

Avocado and Grapefruit Cocktail

2 avocado pears   3 grapefruits. (Peel and section pulp)

Peel avocado pears. Cut in quarters. Slice. Mix with sections of grapefruit. Add one-half cup confectioners' sugar, one-half cup pineapple juice, and the juice of one lemon. Mix thoroughly and chill. Serve cold. Garnish with mint leaves.

Watermelon and Cantaloupe Balls

2 cups watermelon balls   2 cups cantaloupe balls

Mix fruit with one-half cup confectioners' sugar and one-half cup orange juice. Chill thoroughly. Serve cold. Garnish with mint leaves.

Strawberries with Hulls

Select large, firm, ripe strawberries. Do not hull them. Wash berries carefully one at a time. Chill them thoroughly. Serve on a glass plate. Arrange berries around the edge of the plate and put mound of confectioners' sugar in the center.

Jellied Apple

Core, pare, and quarter eight apples. Make a syrup of one-quarter cup water and three-quarters cup sugar. Drop apples into hot syrup. Cook until tender. Remove carefully with a fork. Pour syrup over apples. Cool and chill. One-eighth teaspoon cinnamon may be used for flavoring if desired.

Baked Apple

Select medium-sized apples. Core apples. Fill center with seedless raisins. Arrange apples in buttered bake pan. Cover tops of apples with brown sugar. Dot with butter. Add enough water to cover bottom of pan. Bake forty minutes in a moderate oven (350° F.). Serve cold with or without cream.

The center of the apple may be filled with brown sugar, granulated sugar and cinnamon, or with caramel and brown sugar, instead of the raisins. Dates are also sometimes substituted for the raisins.

Stewed Rhubarb

Remove outer skin from two pounds rhubarb. Dice rhubarb. Add one-half cup water. Cook over a low flame until boiling point is reached. Simmer twenty minutes. Add two cups of sugar. Mix thoroughly. Cool. If rhubarb is young and tender, and has pink skin, do not peel before cooking.

Stewed Rhubarb and Strawberries

Select young tender rhubarb. Dice two pounds of rhubarb. Add one-half cup water. Cook over low flame until it boils. Add two cups strawberries. Simmer twenty minutes. Add three cups of sugar. Mix thoroughly. Cool.

Stewed Prunes

Wash one pound prunes. Cover with water and soak overnight. In the morning bring to a boil, and let simmer twenty minutes. Cool. Stick of cinnamon and one-half cup currant jelly added while prunes are stewing will increase their flavor.

Cream may be served with the prunes.

Baked Pears

Peel and halve firm pears. Remove core. Put pears into a greased baking pan with round side up. Sprinkle with brown sugar. Dot with butter. Add one-half cup cold water. Bake in a moderate oven (350° F.) forty minutes. Cool before serving.

Apple Sauce, No. 1

Do not pare apples. Quarter three pounds of apples. Remove the core. Add two cups of water. Cook until boiling point is reached. Simmer twenty minutes. Force apples through colander. Add two cups of sugar. Stir until sugar is dissolved. Cool before serving. Brown sugar or a mixture of sugar and cinnamon may be used instead of the granulated sugar.

Apple Sauce, No. 2

Core and pare three pounds of apples. Quarter the apples. Add two cups of water. Cook until boiling point is reached. Simmer twenty minutes. Add two cups of sugar. Stir until sugar is dissolved. Brown sugar or a mixture of sugar and cinnamon may be used instead of granulated sugar. Cool apple sauce before serving.

Oatmeal

1 cup rolled oats	2 cups water
½ teaspoon salt	

Bring water to a boil. Add rolled oats slowly. Add salt. Cook over low flame in double boiler. Cook forty-five minutes. Note: some brands of oatmeal cook more quickly than others.

Oatmeal with Dates

1 cup oats	2 cups water
½ teaspoon salt	1 cup dates (pitted and halved)

Bring water to a boil. Add salt. Add rolled oats slowly. Cook over low flame in a double boiler. Cook forty-five minutes. When done add the dates. Mix thoroughly. Serve with cream and sugar.

Hominy

1 cup hominy	4½ cups water
2 teaspoons salt	

Boil water, add salt and hominy. Cook slowly two hours. Serve hot.

Farina

½ cup Farina	½ teaspoon salt
2½ cups boiling water	

Add farina slowly to salted boiling water. Cook over low flame in double boiler from one-half to three-quarters of an hour. Serve hot.

Rice

Wash one-half cup rice thoroughly in a bowl of water. Drain. After rice has been washed, add one quart of boiling salted water and cook slowly twenty minutes. Drain. Pour boiling water over the rice to carry off any excess starch. This may be used as a cereal or as a vegetable. Serve hot.

Corn-meal Mush

1 cup yellow corn meal   ½ teaspoon salt
1 cup cold water

Mix ingredients smooth. Add this mixture to two cups of boiling water. Cook in double boiler from an hour to an hour and a half. Serve hot with cream and sugar.

Fried Corn-meal Mush, No. 1

Pour hot corn-meal mush into square tin. Allow it to cool and set. Turn out of tin.

Cut cold corn-meal mush into half-inch slices. Fry in hot shortening until nicely browned on both sides. Serve for breakfast with maple syrup.

Fried Corn-meal Mush, No. 2

1 cup yellow corn meal   ½ teaspoon salt
1 cup cold water

Mix ingredients until smooth. Add to this mixture two cups of boiling water. Cook slowly in double boiler from an hour to an hour and a half. Add one cup pork scraps fried crisp. Pour hot corn-meal mush into square tin. Allow it to cool and set. Cut cold mush into one-half-inch slices. Fry in hot shortening until nicely browned on both sides. Serve with maple syrup.

CHAPTER XXI

Meats and Meat Sauces

Baked Virginia Ham

Wash ham with brush and warm water. Put it into a deep pot and cover with cold water. Bring to the boiling point. Pour off the water, cover again with fresh water, and bring to a boil. Reduce heat and simmer three hours, or until tender when tested with a fork. Take from pot and remove the skin. Score the fat in squares with a knife, and stick a whole clove in each square. Cover with brown sugar. Put in roasting pan, fat side up. Add one cup of water. Brown in moderate oven (350° F.) twenty-five to thirty minutes. Serve hot or cold.

Ginger ale, pineapple juice, or grape juice may be used instead of the water. If fruit juice is used, baste the ham several times while browning.

Boiled Ham

Wash ham with brush and warm water. Let ham soak overnight in sufficient cold water to cover. Trim off hard skin near the bone, place in kettle, cover with cold water, bring to boiling point. Boil ten minutes. Simmer four hours or until tender when tested with a fork. As water boils down replenish with hot, not cold, water. When tender, set aside to cool in liquid. When cool, remove outside skin. Chill before slicing.

Boiled ham may be served hot if desired.

Broiled Ham

One slice ham one and one-half to two inches thick. Put in skillet and cover with cold water. Bring to a boil and cook ten minutes. Drain. Broil under low flame until nicely browned on both sides. Serve at once.

Baked Ham with Pineapple

Cut the ham two inches thick. Bring to boil in water. Cook ten minutes. Drain and cut into individual servings. Arrange sliced pineapple on the top of each. Cover to one-fourth inch thickness with medium brown sugar. Pour pineapple juice over ham. Bake one hour in a moderate oven (350° F.).

Just before removing ham from the oven top each slice with a marshmallow and cook until marshmallow browns. Serve at once. Garnish with parsley.

Ham Casserole, No. 1

One thick slice of ham, or scraps of ham from near the bone may be used. Trim off the fat. Cover ham with milk and leave overnight. In the morning place the ham and milk in a baker and cover with the fat, finely chopped, to which has been added one tablespoon brown sugar. Stick several whole cloves on top and bake two hours in moderate oven (350° F.). Serve hot.

Ham and Potato Casserole, No. 2

2 slices ham (cut ½ inch thick)   6 potatoes
                              1 onion

Cut ham into strips two inches wide. Pare potatoes. Dice potatoes. Fill a greased casserole with alternate layers of ham and potatoes. Have potatoes as top and bottom layers. Dot top layer with butter. Grate or chop the onion fine. Add onion to enough milk to fill casserole to top layer of potatoes. Cook in a moderate oven (350° F.) for one hour. Serve hot. Onion may be omitted if desired.

Ham Baked in Milk

1 slice ham (cut 2 inches thick)   1 onion
                           3 cups milk

Put ham into skillet. Cover with cold water. Bring to a boil. Cook ten minutes. Drain water from ham. Pour milk around ham. Chop onion fine. Cover top of ham with chopped onion. Bake in a moderate oven (350° F.) one hour. Garnish with parsley.

Ham Loaf

1 pound pork (ground)
1 pound ham (ground)
¼ teaspoon pepper

2 cups bread crumbs
½ teaspoon salt
1 egg

½ cup milk

Mix ground meat and seasonings together. Add the well-beaten egg, milk, and bread crumbs. Mix thoroughly, and mould into a loaf. Place in a greased baking pan. Bake one hour in a moderate oven (350° F.). Chopped green pepper may be added if desired.

Creamed Minced Ham

2 cups minced ham

3 cups medium white sauce

1 green pepper (chopped fine)

Add the ham and chopped pepper to white sauce. Heat thoroughly. Serve on toast. Garnish with paprika and parsley. Pepper may be omitted if desired.

Ham Mousse

1½ pounds finely ground ham
1 teaspoon prepared mustard
1 cup heavy cream
1 pimento (chopped)

2 tablespoons granulated gelatine
¼ cup cold water
½ cup hot water
1 green pepper (chopped)

Add the mustard to the ham and mix well. Soak gelatine in cold water. Dissolve in hot water and add to the ham mixture. Fold in cream beaten until stiff. Turn into mould. Chill. Remove from mould to cold serving dish. Garnish with parsley. Serve with horseradish sauce.

Country Sausage

1 pound ground shoulder pork
1 tablespoon sage

1 teaspoon salt
¼ teaspoon pepper

Mix thoroughly. Form small patties. Bake in shallow pan in moderate oven (350° F.) twenty to twenty-five minutes. Turn once while cooking to brown both sides. Serve hot garnished with parsley.

Sauce for Tongue

4 tablespoons flour   4 tablespoons butter

Add four cups water in which the tongue was boiled. Brown flour in butter. Season with salt and pepper. May use one and one-half cups tomato in place of part water.

Hamburg Steak en Casserole

1 pound Hamburg steak   1 cup soup stock
2 tablespoons butter   1 tablespoon chopped parsley
2 tablespoons flour   Croutons
1 chopped onion   Salt and pepper

Heat butter. Add onion, and fry until brown. Then add flour, stir well, add gradually the stock, and simmer for ten minutes. Add Hamburg steak moulded into patties and cook slowly for one-half hour. Baste occasionally. Season with salt, pepper, and chopped parsley. Turn once while cooking. Just before serving add a few nicely browned bread croutons.

Beefsteak Roll

One large slice round steak cut one-half inch thick. Season with salt and pepper. Cover meat with dressing made from the following:

1 cup bread crumbs   1 egg
1 tablespoon chopped parsley   1 teaspoon salt
¼ teaspoon pepper

Mix dressing thoroughly. Roll meat like jelly roll and tie securely. Sear in hot fat. Put into covered roaster. Add one can tomatoes. Cook one and one-half to two hours in moderate oven (350° F.).

Tomatoes may be omitted. Add two cups water or stock instead of tomatoes.

Roast Fillet of Beef with Onions

One whole tenderloin of beef larded. Put beef into a roaster, season with salt and pepper, and cover with thin slices of onion.

Over onion put two or three slices of bacon. Add enough water to cover bottom of roaster. Put in hot oven (450° F.). After fifteen minutes reduce heat to 400° F. Roast ten to fifteen minutes per pound for rare meat. Roast fifteen to twenty minutes per pound for well-done meat. Thicken gravy and serve with the meat. Sautéed mushrooms may be served with this.

Beef Fillet (Baked Whole)

Clean, remove fat, veins, and tendonous portion in middle. Fold and skewer into compact shape, folding thin end under. Season with salt and pepper. Bake on slices of fat salt pork. Baste frequently.

Put into hot oven (450° F.). After fifteen minutes reduce heat to 400° F. Roast ten to fifteen minutes per pound for rare meat. Roast fifteen to twenty minutes for well-done meat.

Beef Roast

Rub meat with salt and dredge with flour. Place in pan, skin side down. Sear in hot oven (450° F.), then reduce heat (400° F.) and baste often with drippings. A little water may be added if desired. After a time turn roast to brown the skin. Roast meat ten to fifteen minutes per pound for rare meat. Roast meat fifteen to twenty minutes per pound for well-done meat.

Pot Roast

4 pounds chuck	1 quart cold water
2 tablespoons flour	4 tablespoons shortening
¼ teaspoon pepper	3 teaspoons salt

Wipe off the meat and rub over the surface with flour. Sear on all sides in the hot shortening until brown. Season with salt and pepper. Add water and cook slowly until tender, three and one-half to four hours.

Two cups diced carrots, one onion chopped fine, and one cup of peas may be added to the gravy the last hour if desired.

Broiled Steak

Cut steak desired thickness. Put onto broiler under hot flame. Cook an inch-and-a-half-thick steak ten minutes for rare, fifteen minutes for medium, twenty minutes for well done. Turn once while broiling. Serve with salt, pepper, butter, and garnish with parsley.

Planked Steak with Vegetables

You will need a steak plank and a steak one and one-half inches thick. Broil the steak on a very hot broiler under a quick fire. Heat steak plank slightly and grease well. Put steak on plank and have mashed potatoes ready. Put these around steak through a pastry tube or with a spoon, making hollow nests of potato in which you can put two or more vegetables.

Buttered peas, baked stuffed tomatoes, diced buttered carrots, cooked string beans, small fried or baked onions make a satisfying garnish for this steak. Brush over the potato, tomato, and onions with beaten yolk of an egg, diluted with a little milk or water to make it glaze and brown easily. Place in a hot oven (400° F.) and cook six or eight minutes, or until potatoes brown and steak is finished. Serve at once, garnished with parsley.

Steak with Vegetables

4 pounds beef   1½ tablespoons salt
                        ½ cup flour

Wash meat in cold water. Rub in salt and pound flour into meat. Brown in hot fat. Cover and let simmer three hours. One-half hour before meat is removed from fire, add two cups cooked diced potatoes, one cup diced cooked carrots, one cup chopped celery, and one-half cup minced onions. Serve hot.

Swiss Steak, No. 1

3 pounds round steak
½ cup flour
2 teaspoons salt

3 tablespoons chopped onion
½ teaspoon pepper
3 tablespoons shortening

2 cups tomatoes

Mix flour, salt, and pepper together. Wipe off steak and pound flour into it. Heat the fat in a frying pan and brown the steak on both sides. Add tomatoes and chopped onions. Cover and let simmer slowly over the fire or bake in a moderate oven (350° F.) two and one-half hours.

Swiss Steak, No. 2

4 pounds beef (round steak or rump)
1½ teaspoons salt

½ cup flour

Wash meat in cold water. Rub in salt and pound flour into meat. Brown in hot fat. Cover with three cups water and let simmer three hours. Serve hot.

Beef and Tomatoes

2 pounds lean beef
1 bunch celery
4 onions
3 cups tomatoes

¼ pound elbow macaroni
½ pound grated cheese
1 teaspoon salt
¼ teaspoon pepper

1 tablespoon Worcestershire sauce

Cut the meat, celery, and onions into small pieces, and put into frying pan. Fry in hot fat until well browned. Remove from fire, and put into large casserole. Add the tomatoes, the cooked macaroni, grated cheese, sauce, salt, and pepper.

Simmer two hours and serve hot. Sprinkle with chopped parsley.

Beef and Sausages

1 pound round steak (cut thin)
4 tablespoons butter
Bread dressing
½ teaspoon salt

½ pound sausages
½ cup flour
1 tablespoon chopped parsley
¼ teaspoon pepper

Cut meat into pieces 3″ x 3″. Season flour with salt and pepper. Roll the meat in this. Fold each piece of meat into rolls, placing small portion of bread dressing in each. Prick and divide the sausages. Place a layer of sausage in a casserole, then beef rolls, and then sausage. Sprinkle in remaining flour and chopped parsley. Cover with water, cover. Cook slowly for two and one-half hours. Moderate oven (350° F.).

Braised Beef

3 pounds beef (rump or lower round)
Flour
1 teaspoon salt
2 slices salt pork (cut thin)
½ cup diced celery
½ teaspoon pepper
3 cups boiling water
½ cup diced carrots
¼ cup diced turnips
½ cup diced onions

Wipe meat and dredge with flour. Add salt and pepper. Try out the pork and brown the entire surface of the meat in the fat thus obtained. Place the meat in a baking dish and surround it with the diced vegetables. Add boiling water, cover the dish tightly and place in a slow oven. Bake for four hours (325° F.). Remove the meat to hot platter, strain the vegetables.

Surround meat with vegetables. Thicken the gravy. Serve with meat and vegetables.

Hamburg Steak, No. 1

2 pounds Hamburg steak
1 teaspoon salt
½ teaspoon pepper
1 onion (chopped fine)
1 egg

Mix all the ingredients well. Mould into patties. Fry, bake, or broil meat. Turn once while cooking. Serve hot.

Hamburg Steak, No. 2

2 pounds Hamburg steak
1 teaspoon salt
½ teaspoon pepper
1 green pepper (chopped fine)
1 onion (chopped fine)
1 egg
1 cup moist bread crumbs

Mix all the ingredients thoroughly. Mould into patties. Fry, bake, or broil meat. Turn once while cooking. Serve hot. Green pepper may be omitted if desired.

Hash

1 cup of left-over beef put through food grinder
6 cold boiled potatoes (riced) ¼ teaspoon pepper
1 small onion (chopped fine) 1 teaspoon salt

Mix these ingredients thoroughly. Put into greased baking pan and bake in a moderately hot oven (375° F.) until nicely browned. Serve hot, plain or with chili sauce.

Hash may be fried instead of baked if desired. Meat other than beef may be used in making hash.

Corned Beef Hash

1 cup corned beef (put through food grinder)
6 medium-sized potatoes (cold boiled and put through grinder or riced)
1 small onion (chopped fine) ¼ teaspoon pepper
1 teaspoon salt

Mix the ingredients thoroughly. Put into greased baking pan and bake in a moderately hot oven (375° F.) until nicely browned. Hash may be fried instead of baked if desired.

Creamed Dried Beef

1 cup shredded dry beef 2 cups medium thick white
2 tablespoons shortening sauce

Melt shortening, and add beef. Fry over a low flame five minutes. Add white sauce. Mix thoroughly and cook until very hot. Serve on toast. Garnish with parsley.

Meat Loaf with Chili Sauce

1 pound ground beef 1 onion (chopped fine)
½ pound ground pork 1 tablespoon salt
½ pound ground veal ¼ teaspoon pepper
4 slices bread (soaked in warm 2 eggs
water and drained)

Mix all ingredients thoroughly. Pat into greased baking pan to two-inch thickness. Cover with chili sauce to one-fourth inch thickness. Dot with butter, and add one-half cup water. Bake forty-five minutes in a moderate oven (350° F.).

Meat Loaf

2 cups bread crumbs	½ pound ground pork
2 tablespoons flour	¼ teaspoon paprika
2½ teaspoons salt	1½ cups milk
¾ teaspoon pepper	1 egg
1 small onion (chopped fine)	1 pound ground beef

½ pound ground veal

Mix meat, bread crumbs, flour, and seasoning together. Combine with salt. Combine the milk with beaten eggs. Add gradually to the meat mixture. Mix thoroughly. Mould into a loaf. Put into baking pan. Strips of bacon may be placed over top. Add one cup water. Bake two hours in moderate oven (350° F.). Garnish with parsley.

Beef Loaf

1½ pounds chopped beef	¼ teaspoon pepper
1½ pounds chopped pork	1 onion (chopped fine)
1 teaspoon salt	1 egg
1 tablespoon chopped parsley	⅓ cup soft bread crumbs

Mix ingredients well and shape into loaf. Rest on slices of bacon, and put two or three strips on top. Add one cup water. Bake in a slow oven (325° F.) forty minutes. Baste frequently while cooking. Veal may be substituted for the beef if veal loaf is desired.

Hungarian Goulash

1 pound lean veal	4 cups boiling water
½ pound lean beef	1 teaspoon paprika
3 tablespoons shortening	1 bay leaf
4 potatoes (diced)	1 clove
2 onions	4 tablespoons flour
6 carrots (diced)	1 chopped green pepper
6 turnips (diced)	2 teaspoons salt

Slice onion and brown it in fat. Remove onion and put in veal and beef cut into small pieces. Brown these thoroughly and remove meat and place it in casserole. Add onions. Add paprika and boiling water. Cover the dish and place it in moderate oven (350° F.).

Fry potatoes, carrots, and turnips. Add them to meat after it has simmered for one and one-half hours. After vegetables are added, add salt, bay leaf, clove, and flour mixed with a little cold water. Pour this into casserole and stir until mixture is slightly thickened. Add pepper. Cover and let simmer for another hour and a half. Serve from casserole.

Meat Pie

2 onions
1 cup celery (cut fine)
6 tablespoons meat drippings
2 pounds beef
2 teaspoons salt

½ teaspoon pepper
1 green pepper (cut fine)
3 tablespoons chopped parsley
2 cups cooked diced carrots
2 cups peas

5 tablespoons flour

A baking-powder-biscuit dough made of the following:

2 cups flour
3 tablespoons shortening

¾ cup milk
4 teaspoons baking powder

1 teaspoon salt

Dice and brown the onion and celery in two tablespoons drippings. Add the meat and sear well. Cover with water. Add salt and pepper and let simmer until tender, two hours. Remove meat from liquid and cut in small pieces. Add carrots and peas.

Combine four tablespoons drippings with five tablespoons flour. Mix to a paste. Add the liquid from the meat and cook ten minutes. Place meat and vegetable mixture in a buttered baking dish. Cover with gravy.

Make the baking-powder-biscuit dough, roll out, and cut with a biscuit cutter. Place biscuits on top of meat and gravy.

Bake twenty minutes in a hot oven (425° F.). Serve at once.

Shepherds' Pie

4 cups cooked meat
1 teaspoon salt

½ teaspoon pepper
1 onion (chopped fine)

2 tablespoons parsley (chopped)

Chop or cut meat fine. Add salt, pepper, onion, and parsley. Mix thoroughly. Line a greased baking dish — bottom and sides — with mashed potato or cooked rice. Fill dish with meat

mixture. Cover meat with layer of potato or rice. Dot with
butter. Bake in a moderate oven (350° F.) for one hour. Serve
hot. Garnish with parsley.

Veal Pie

Five-pound knuckle of veal. Cook in salted water until meat
drops from bone. Drain out meat and thicken gravy slightly.
Cut meat into small pieces. Put meat and part of gravy into
deep baking dish. Cover the top with baking-powder biscuits.
Bake for thirty minutes in a hot oven (400° F.). Serve hot.

Heat and serve remainder of gravy with the veal pie. Onions
may be added to the pie if desired.

Veal Roast

Use meat from leg of veal. Wash thoroughly. Put meat into
roasting pan. Season with salt and pepper. Cover top of meat
with a generous layer of chopped onions which have been fried
in drippings until a golden brown. Add enough water to cover
bottom of roaster. Put roast into a hot oven (450° F.). After
twenty-five minutes reduce heat to 400° F. Allow twenty to
twenty-five minutes per pound plus fifteen minutes. Thicken
gravy before serving.

Breaded Veal

Use veal chops or cut slices of meat from leg one-half inch
thick. Cut meat into individual servings. Dip meat into beaten
egg, then roll in bread crumbs. Fry in hot fat until a golden
brown on both sides. Cook meat slowly over a low flame for
ten minutes after it has been browned. Season with salt and
pepper. Serve hot. Garnish with parsley.

Veal Birds

2 pounds veal

Use slices of veal steak and pound until one-quarter inch
thick. Cut in rectangular pieces, two by four inches.

Bread Dressing:

1 egg	2 tablespoons butter
1 cup bread crumbs	½ teaspoon salt
2 tablespoons chopped parsley	¼ teaspoon pepper
1 onion (chopped)	

Chop trimmings of meat and add to the dressing. Mix thoroughly. Place one tablespoon dressing on each piece of meat. Roll up, skewer, or tie in shape. Sprinkle with salt and pepper. Dredge with flour. Fry brown in butter. When birds are brown, pour hot water, cream, or tomato sauce over them, and let simmer forty-five minutes.

Thicken gravy before serving. Serve hot. Garnish with parsley.

Mushroom and Veal Timbales

1 cup milk	4 eggs
1 teaspoon salt	1 cup chopped veal
1 chopped onion	1 teaspoon paprika
1 cup mushrooms (fried in butter)	

Beat eggs lightly, and add milk and seasoning. Then add the veal. Turn into buttered moulds, and bake or steam until firm. Top with the mushrooms and serve with white sauce. For ham timbales substitute ham for veal and omit the mushrooms.

Pork Turkey

Cut pork chops two and one-half inches thick. Cut slit in loin end of each chop. Open slit wide and fill opening with bread dressing. Skewer or tie chop securely. Brown chops in skillet. Add water to cover bottom of pan. Season with salt and pepper. Bake in a hot oven (400° F.) for one hour. Add more water while cooking if necessary.

Baked Pork Chop Casserole

Brown six pork chops in a skillet. Arrange chops in bottom of roaster. Add six whole onions, six pared potatoes, and six apples cored, but not peeled. Fill center of apples with raisins. Season meat and vegetables with salt and pepper. Add two cups water, and bake in a moderately hot oven (375°–400° F.) fifty to sixty minutes.

Roast of Pork

Select nice rib roast. Rub with salt and pepper. Sprinkle with sage, and place in a roaster. Add water to cover bottom of pan. Put into oven of 450° F. After thirty minutes reduce heat to 400° F. Allow twenty-five to thirty minutes per pound plus fifteen minutes. Thicken gravy before serving. Vegetables such as potatoes, onions, carrots, or turnips may be cooked with the meat. If vegetables are used, place them around the meat one hour before roast is done.

Crown Roast of Pork

Meat man will prepare roast for use. Cover the ends of the ribs securely with cubes or strips of salt pork. Season with salt and pepper. Put roast into baking pan. Fill center of roast with apple, raisin, or bread dressing. Add enough water to cover bottom of roaster. Put meat into a hot oven (450° F.) for thirty minutes, then reduce heat to 400° F. Allow twenty-five to thirty minutes per pound plus fifteen minutes. Add more water if necessary. Thicken gravy before serving. Garnish roast with cooked vegetables and parsley.

Leg of Mutton Roast

Cut ligaments loose, skin, push flesh back from bone with knife until bone gradually comes out. Meat cutter will bone roast if desired. Wipe meat with wet cloth. Sprinkle with salt and pepper. Dredge with flour. Place on a slice of salt pork in a roasting pan. Put in hot oven (450° F.). Reduce heat to 400° F. after thirty minutes and cook, allowing twenty-five minutes per pound plus fifteen minutes. Thicken gravy before serving. The bone may be left in the meat if desired. Sliced onions added to the roast before cooking add flavor and may be used occasionally.

Roast Leg of Lamb

Wash meat. Put into roaster on strips of bacon or pieces of salt pork. Season with salt and pepper. Cover top of meat with strips of bacon. Add enough water to cover bottom of roaster. Put into hot oven (450° F.). Reduce heat to 400° F. after thirty minutes. Allow twenty to twenty-five minutes per pound plus fifteen minutes. Thicken gravy before serving. Vegetables may be cooked with the roast if desired. When vegetables are used they are added to the meat one hour before the roast is done. Garnish leg of lamb with parsley before serving. Bacon may be omitted if desired.

Crown Roast of Lamb

Cover the ends of the ribs securely with cubes or strips of salt pork. Put into roaster. Add salt and pepper, and enough water to cover bottom of roaster. Press a cup into the center of the circle of meat to keep it in shape. Put into hot oven (450° F.).

Reduce heat to 400° F. after thirty minutes. Roast until done. Allow twenty to twenty-five minutes per pound plus fifteen minutes. Add more water if necessary while meat is roasting. Thicken gravy before serving. To serve crown roast fill center with green peas, glazed carrot balls, Saratoga or French fried potatoes of chestnut purée.

The center of the crown roast may be filled with a bread dressing before meat is roasted. Cooked vegetables are then used to garnish the meat when it is served. Top dressing with parsley.

Irish Stew

2 pounds lamb	½ teaspoon pepper
6 whole potatoes	6 carrots
2 tablespoons flour	6 onions
2 cups peas	1 tablespoon salt

Cut lamb into small pieces, and dredge each piece with flour. Brown in a frying pan. Put in kettle, cover with water, and cook slowly two hours.

After cooking thirty minutes add the vegetables which have been diced. Season with salt and pepper. Thicken with flour moistened in enough cold water to form a smooth paste. Serve with or without dumplings.

Beef Stew

2 pounds beef (round steak)	½ teaspoon pepper
4 potatoes	6 onions
2 cups peas	8 carrots
1 tablespoon salt	1 cup celery

1 turnip

Cut meat into small pieces. Dredge with flour. Fry until brown in hot shortening. Put into kettle and add water to cover. Add seasoning and cook slowly two and a half to three hours. Dice vegetables. Add to meat one hour after meat starts cooking. Serve with or without dumplings. Add more water to meat during cooking if necessary. Thicken gravy if desired.

American Chop Suey

¼ pound lean pork (cut fine)	1 bunch celery (cut into strips)
1 onion (sliced)	½ tablespoon salt
2 cups soup stock	1 green pepper (cut into strips)
½ cup uncooked rice	1 cup mushrooms

Cut fat from meat. Put in pan and cook pork in this fat together with the onion until brown. When brown, add celery, green pepper, uncooked rice, salt, and stock. Cover and cook slowly. Time, forty minutes.

Serve hot with chopped parsley garnish. Coarsely chopped salted almonds are a delicious addition.

Corned Beef

Wipe the meat and tie securely in shape, if not already done at market. Put in kettle, cover with cold water, and bring slowly to boiling point. Boil five minutes, remove scum, and cook at a low temperature until tender, four to six hours.

Pressed Corn Beef

After wiping meat, tie securely in shape. Put in a kettle and cover with cold water. Bring slowly to boiling point. Boil for five minutes, remove scum, and cook at a low temperature until tender, four to six hours. Cool slightly in water in which it was cooked, remove to a dish, cover, and place on cover a weight, that meat may be well pressed. The lean meat and fat may be separated and put in alternate layers in a bread pan, then covered and pressed, if desired.

New England Boiled Dinner

Have corned beef tied in shape at market, wipe and place in a kettle, cover with water, and bring slowly to boiling point. Boil for five minutes, remove scum, and cook at a low temperature, until tender, four to six hours.

When meat has been boiling four hours, add cabbage, turnip, potatoes, and carrots. Vegetables require one hour to cook.

Parsnips, onions, and beets may be used with or in place of the other vegetables. If beets are used, they are cooked separately. Cabbage is cut into quarters for a New England boiled dinner. Other vegetables are left whole. To serve, put meat onto large platter and surround with vegetables.

German Meat Balls

2 pounds ground beef	1 cup bread crumbs
½ pound ground veal	1 tablespoon salt
½ pound ground pork	½ teaspoon pepper
2 tablespoons onion juice	2 eggs

Add bread crumbs, salt, pepper, onion juice, and eggs to meat. Mix thoroughly. Roll into small balls one inch in diameter. Roll in flour. Bring three quarts soup stock to boiling point. Add meat balls. Simmer slowly fifteen minutes. Mix four tablespoons flour with cold water to smooth paste. Thicken stock with this. Cook five minutes. Add six slices of lemon. Serve hot.

Scalloped Sweetbreads

Remove tubes and membranes from four pairs of sweetbreads and soak in cold water for one hour. Drain and put into boiling salted water to which two tablespoons vinegar have been added. Cook slowly twenty minutes. Plunge into cold water to harden and whiten. Line a greased baking dish with alternate layers of sweetbreads, cut fine, and medium white sauce. Cover with bread crumbs and dot with butter. Bake thirty minutes in a moderate oven (350° F.).

Creamed Sweetbreads

After removing tube and membranes, soak four pairs of sweetbreads in cold water for one hour. Put into boiling salted water to which two tablespoons vinegar have been added. Cook slowly twenty minutes. Plunge into cold water to harden. Cut sweetbreads into small pieces. Add two cups of medium white sauce and serve on toast or in patty shells. Garnish with parsley. Mushrooms may be added if desired.

Broiled Sweetbreads

Take four pairs of sweetbreads and remove tubes and membranes. Soak in cold water for one hour. Then put into boiling salted water to which two tablespoons vinegar have been added. Cook slowly twenty minutes. Plunge into cold water to harden. Brush whole sweetbread with melted shortening and put under low flame of broiler until brown. Garnish with parsley.

Sweetbreads on Ham

Cover rounds of buttered toast with circles of broiled ham. Put broiled sweetbreads on ham. Season with salt and pepper. Dot with butter. Garnish with parsley.

Baked Sweetbreads

Prepare sweetbreads and soak in cold water for one hour. Put into boiling salted water to which two tablespoons vinegar have been added. Cook slowly twenty minutes. Plunge into cold water to whiten and harden. Then roll in beaten egg and bread crumbs and put into greased baking dish. Bake in moderate oven until brown (350° F.). Garnish with parsley and crisp bacon.

Sautéed Sweetbreads

Take four pairs of sweetbreads and remove tubes and membranes. Allow to soak in cold water for one hour, then put into boiling water to which two tablespoons vinegar have been added. Cook slowly twenty minutes. Plunge into cold water to harden. Roll in beaten egg and crumbs and fry in skillet until brown. Garnish with parsley.

Calf's Heart

Wash a calf's heart, remove veins, arteries, and clotted blood. Fill with bread dressing. Season with salt and pepper, roll in flour. Brown in hot fat. Place in a small deep baking pan, half cover it with boiling water, cover, and bake slowly two hours in moderate oven (350° F.). Baste frequently. It may be necessary to add more water. Remove heart from pan, and thicken the gravy with flour mixed with a small quantity of cold water. Season with salt and pepper, and pour around the heart before serving. Garnish with parsley.

Calf's Liver, No. 1

Cut liver in slices one-half inch thick, and cover with boiling water. Let stand five minutes and wipe dry. Rub with bacon or other fat and broil under medium flame. Serve with crisp bacon.

Calf's Liver, No. 2

Cut liver in slices one-half inch thick. Roll in flour and sauté in bacon fat. Season with salt and pepper.

Calf's Liver, No. 3

Cut liver in one-half inch slices. Dip in egg and bread crumbs and fry in deep fat. Season with salt and pepper.

Calf's Liver, No. 4

Cut liver into thin slices. Prepare a bread-crumb dressing. Place two tablespoons dressing on each slice. Roll and skewer,

Lobster Salad and Popovers

or tie. Put into greased pan. Bake slowly in a moderate oven (350° F.) for forty-five minutes. Add enough water to prevent scorching.

Broiled Tripe

Fresh honeycomb tripe is best for broiling. Cook in boiling water ten minutes. Drain. Wipe tripe as dry as possible, dip in fine cracker dust and melted shortening, draining off all fat that is possible. Again dip in cracker dust. Place on a greased broiler and broil ten minutes under medium flame. Place on a hot platter, honeycomb side up, spread with butter, and season with salt and pepper. Garnish with parsley and lemon.

If fresh tripe cannot be obtained, pickled tripe may be used. Soak pickled tripe in cold water one hour before using.

Sautéed Tripe

Cook tripe in boiling water ten minutes. Drain. Cut into individual servings. Drop tripe in beaten egg and roll in bread crumbs. Fry in hot shortening until brown. Batter may be used instead of egg and crumbs. Garnish with lemon and parsley.

Béarnaise Sauce

3 tablespoons chopped onion	⅛ teaspoon cayenne
2 tablespoons vinegar	Yolks of three eggs
½ teaspoon salt	2 tablespoons chopped parsley
¼ teaspoon pepper	1 tablespoon chopped pickles

Cook onions in vinegar five minutes. Place in a double boiler and add egg yolks. Cook until creamy, then add seasoning. Serve.

Brown Sauce

2 tablespoons chopped onion	4 tablespoons flour
4 tablespoons chopped carrot	2 tablespoons butter
2 tablespoons parsley (cut fine)	1 teaspoon salt
2 cups stock	⅛ teaspoon pepper

Cook vegetables in butter until light brown. Add flour and brown well. Add stock and strain. Cook until thick.

Meat Gravy

1 tablespoon flour
1/4 teaspoon salt
1/8 teaspoon pepper
2 tablespoons water
1 cup stock or meat juice

Add flour to water and stir until smooth, then add stock slowly and cook for ten minutes, stirring constantly. Season with salt and pepper. Serve hot.

Béchamel Sauce

3 tablespoons butter
1/8 teaspoon pepper
1/4 teaspoon paprika
3/4 cup cream
1/2 teaspoon salt
3 tablespoons flour
1 cup stock

Melt butter, add flour, and blend thoroughly. Add stock. Stir constantly until mixture thickens, then add seasoning, and the cream. Beat until smooth. Serve with timbales.

Butter Sauce

6 tablespoons butter
2 tablespoons lemon juice
1/8 teaspoon pepper
2 tablespoons parsley (chopped fine)
1/8 teaspoon salt
1 tablespoon onion (chopped fine)

Cream butter. Add other ingredients and mix thoroughly. Serve with hot meats or vegetables.

Mint Sauce

1 cup mint (chopped)
3 tablespoons sugar
1/2 cup vinegar
1 tablespoon lemon juice
2 tablespoons water

Wash mint and pick leaves from stems. Chop fine. Add sugar. Mix well. Add lemon juice, water, and vinegar gradually. Let stand one hour.

Mushroom Sauce

Add one cup canned button mushrooms to two cups brown sauce. Heat thoroughly. Mushrooms may be sautéed and cut fine before adding to brown sauce if desired.

Sweetbreads and Almond Sauce

2 pairs sweetbreads   ½ cup blanched almonds
1 cup whipped cream   ¼ cup lemon juice
½ teaspoon salt   ½ tablespoon sugar

Remove membranes from sweetbreads. Cook twenty minutes in boiling water to which two tablespoons vinegar have been added. Plunge in cold water to harden. Drain and cool. Cut sweetbreads in slices. Cut almonds in half. Mix sweetbreads and almonds with cream, lemon juice, salt, and sugar. Mix thoroughly. Chill. Serve with cold boiled ham or veal.

Yorkshire Pudding

2 eggs   1¼ cups milk
1 cup flour   2 tablespoons juice of roast beef

Beat eggs. Add salt, milk, and flour, and beat thoroughly. Grease a quart baking dish or muffin tin thoroughly. Add the juice of beef. Then pour batter into dish until two-thirds full. Bake in a hot oven (450° F.) for fifteen minutes. Reduce heat to 350° F. and finish baking.

Have roast on rack over pudding, so that juice will drop through pudding while baking.

Dumplings

2 eggs   2 teaspoons baking powder
2 cups flour   ½ teaspoon salt

Mix dry ingredients thoroughly and add two-thirds cup milk and the beaten eggs, enough to make a soft dough. Drop by spoonful into stew or gravy. Cover tightly and cook fifteen minutes.

Dumplings may be cooked in salted water and then drained. Served as a potato substitute.

Mixed Sauce

To one-half cup of French dressing add two tablespoons horse-radish sauce, one tablespoon chopped chives, and one tablespoon chili sauce.

Cucumber Sauce

½ cup cream
¼ teaspoon salt
⅛ teaspoon pepper

1 tablespoon horseradish sauce
2 tablespoons vinegar
1 cup chopped cucumbers

Mix cream and seasoning together. Add two tablespoons vinegar very slowly. Add the chopped cucumbers. Mix well.

Egg Sauce

2 tablespoons flour
⅓ cup butter
¼ teaspoon salt

1 cup stock
1 green pepper (chopped)
Yolks of 3 hard-boiled eggs (riced)

Cook flour with butter and add stock. When thick, beat well. Add egg yolks and pepper, chopped fine. Mix thoroughly.

Hollandaise Sauce

¾ cup butter
3 egg yolks
¼ teaspoon salt

Cayenne (dash)
½ cup boiling water
Juice of ½ lemon

Cream the butter. Add the egg yolks one at a time, beating thoroughly, then add seasoning and water. Cook in a double boiler until thick, beating constantly. Add the lemon juice last. Serve at once.

Horseradish Sauce, No. 1

½ cup grated horseradish
¼ cup lemon juice

½ teaspoon salt
1 tablespoon sugar

1 cup whipped cream

Mix horseradish with salt, sugar, and lemon juice. Fold in the whipped cream. Garnish with chopped parsley and paprika.

Horseradish Sauce, No. 2

½ cup grated horseradish
⅓ cup vinegar

1 teaspoon salt
1 tablespoon sugar

Mix ingredients thoroughly and serve cold.

CHAPTER XXII
Meat Substitutes — Egg, Cheese, Macaroni

SUPPER DISHES

Macaroni and Cheese

½ pound macaroni
2 cups grated cheese
½ cup buttered bread crumbs

Salt and pepper
1 cup hot milk

Cook the macaroni in boiling salted water until tender. In a buttered baking dish place a layer of grated cheese, then a layer of macaroni. Alternate until the dish is filled. Season with salt and pepper. Pour hot milk over the mixture. Cover with buttered bread crumbs. Cover the dish and bake thirty minutes in a moderate oven (350° F.). Remove the cover and brown top. Spaghetti may be substituted for macaroni.

Macaroni and Fish Croquettes

2 cups flaked fish
2 cups cooked macaroni
¾ cup thick white sauce
1 small onion (chopped fine)

½ cup bread crumbs
2 eggs
1 teaspoon salt

Add the salmon, macaroni, and onion to white sauce. Let stand until firm. Shape into croquettes. Roll in the beaten egg and then in bread crumbs. Fry in deep fat.

Noodle Ring

1 pound wide noodles
1 cup brown bread crumbs

3 tablespoons butter

Boil noodles in salted water. Drain. Mix with butter and pour into a greased ring mould. Cover with the bread crumbs. Set in pan of hot water. Bake forty-five minutes in a moderate oven (350° F.). Turn out on hot serving dish when done.

Ham with Noodles

1 cup noodles
½ cup boiled ham
½ cup peas

½ teaspoon salt
1 cup milk
2 tablespoons butter

2 eggs

Boil noodles. Drain and mix with ham and peas. Add milk and seasonings. Add egg. Put in casserole, dot with butter. Bake twenty minutes in moderate oven (300° F.).

Macaroni Loaf

1 cup uncooked macaroni (elbow)
1½ cups milk (scalded)
1 cup soft bread crumbs
¼ cup butter
2 pimentos
  (chopped fine)

1 tablespoon chopped parsley
2 tablespoons chopped onion
1 teaspoon salt
1 cup grated cheese
3 eggs
2 green peppers (chopped fine)

Add four teaspoons of salt to two quarts of water. When boiling rapidly add macaroni. Boil until tender. Drain. Prepare sauce as follows:— Pour milk over bread crumbs. Add melted butter, pimento, green pepper, grated cheese, and seasonings. Lastly, add well-beaten eggs. Pour over macaroni. Place in buttered baking dish and set dish in pan of boiling water. Bake forty minutes in moderate oven (350° F.).

Serve plain or with mushroom sauce.

Chili Concarne

1 pound Hamburg steak
¼ pound elbow macaroni (cooked)
1 large can tomatoes
¼ teaspoon pepper

1 cup kidney beans
1 onion
½ tablespoon salt
1 tablespoon paprika

Fry onion and meat until brown. Add other ingredients and let simmer forty-five minutes. Serve hot in bowls.

Spaghetti Sauce

1 pound Hamburg steak
1 medium-sized onion

1 large can tomatoes

Cut onion small and fry in butter until brown, add meat and fry, stirring continually. Add tomatoes, let simmer for two or three hours. Mushrooms may be added if desired. Serve hot over spaghetti with Parmesan cheese.

Spaghetti, Italian Style

Drop the spaghetti into boiling water and cook until tender. Allow one tablespoon of salt to each quart of water. Drain. Put spaghetti on large platter. Add sauce made as follows:

½ pound ground round steak	½ pound fresh mushrooms
½ chopped sweet green pepper	1 can tomatoes
4 tablespoons butter	2 teaspoons salt
1 tablespoon chopped parsley	

Sauté steak for twenty minutes. Add parsley, salt, pepper, and mushrooms. Cover and cook slowly until mushrooms are lightly browned. Add tomatoes, cook slowly for one and one-half hours, stirring constantly. Pour over spaghetti and serve with Parmesan cheese. Garlic may be added to this.

Baked Spaghetti

½ pound spaghetti	4 tablespoons butter
4 tablespoons flour	2 cups milk
1 cup grated cheese	½ cup soft bread crumbs

Add the spaghetti slowly to boiling salted water. Cook until tender. Drain. Make a white sauce of butter, flour, and milk, and pour over the spaghetti. Mix well. Add one-half of cheese and pour into buttered baking dish. Cover top with remaining cheese and bread crumbs. Bake until brown in moderate oven (350° F.).

Spaghetti with Chicken Livers

½ pound spaghetti	¼ teaspoon pepper
2 tablespoons shortening	¼ pound Parmesan cheese
1 onion	½ pound fresh mushrooms
2 cups canned tomatoes	1 pound chicken livers
1 teaspoon salt	

Cook the spaghetti in boiling salted water until tender. Drain and rinse in cold water. Heat the fat and brown the finely cut onion in it. Add the spaghetti and cook gently. Add the tomatoes, grated cheese, salt, and pepper. Cook slowly until well blended. Serve in a casserole or on a platter garnished with whole mushrooms (sautéed) and the chicken livers (sautéed).

Spaghetti Baked with Oysters

½ pound spaghetti	1 teaspoon salt
1 quart oysters	1 green pepper (chopped)

Cook spaghetti in salted water until tender. Drain. Cook oysters in their own liquor until edges curl. Do not drain. Line a greased baking dish with alternate layers of spaghetti and oysters. Sprinkle each layer with chopped green pepper. Add milk to cover. Cover top layer with bread crumbs. Dot with butter. Bake forty-five minutes in a moderate oven (350° F.). Serve hot.

A Luncheon Dish

3 cold boiled potatoes	½ cup crumbs
6 hard-cooked eggs	¼ cup shortening
⅛ teaspoon salt	¼ cup flour
2 cups milk	¼ teaspoon pepper
1 onion	3 tablespoons butter

Cut potatoes and eggs in slices one-fourth inch thick. Melt shortening, add flour, and blend to a smooth paste. Add seasonings and milk. Heat to boiling point, stirring constantly. Place a layer of potatoes in buttered baking dish. Add a layer of eggs. Sprinkle with finely chopped onion. Cover with white sauce. Add more layers until the dish is full. Melt butter, add crumbs, and stir until well mixed.

Cover top layer with crumbs. Bake in moderate oven (350° F.) until brown.

Cheese and Rice

1 tablespoon butter	2 eggs
1 cup grated cheese	1 cup cooked rice
¼ teaspoon paprika	¼ teaspoon salt

⅔ cup milk

Separate yolks and whites. Beat yolks till thick. Add rice and seasonings, milk, melted butter, and cheese. Fold in the stiffly beaten whites. Pour into buttered baking dish and bake forty minutes in moderate oven (350° F.).

Welsh Rarebit

2 tablespoons butter	Dash of cayenne
¼ teaspoon salt	1 egg
½ pound cheese	½ teaspoon mustard
¼ teaspoon soda	½ cup thin cream

Melt butter in double boiler, add cheese, stir until melted, add beaten egg and seasoning, add soda and cream. Stir constantly, and when smooth and slightly thickened, pour over wafers or toast and serve at once. Garnish with broiled bacon and parsley.

Blushing Bunny

1½ pounds Young America cheese (cut into small pieces)	2 cups tomato purée ½ cup chopped stuffed olives

Heat tomato purée, add cheese, stir until cheese melts and is smooth. Add olives. Serve on crackers or on toast.

Spanish Woodcock

1 can tomato soup	1 can mushrooms (cut fine)
½ pound cheese (cut small)	

Heat tomato soup. Add cheese and stir until cheese is melted. Mixture should be smooth. Add mushrooms. Serve on toast. Garnish with parsley. One egg well beaten may be added before the mushrooms.

Bean Rarebit

1 cup baked beans (put through a sieve)	1 cup cheese (cut fine) 3 tablespoons butter
½ cup milk	

Melt butter, add one teaspoon salt, dash of cayenne, and the beans. Mix and add milk. When very hot, add cheese and stir until smooth. Add one teaspoon Worcestershire sauce. Serve on toast. Add more or less milk if beans are dry or juicy. Garnish with broiled bacon and parsley.

Tamale Pudding

2 eggs	2 cups corn
1 cup tomatoes	1 cup corn meal
1½ cups milk	1 chopped pepper
1 chopped onion	1 tablespoon shortening
½ teaspoon salt	Paprika
Cayenne	14 ripe olives

Beat egg, add milk. Add corn, and corn meal. Stir in the rest of the ingredients. Add olives last. Pour into a greased casserole and bake from fifty to sixty minutes in a moderate oven (350° F.). Serve hot.

Onion Pudding

1 cup chopped suet	1 cup onion
2 teaspoons baking powder	(put through chopper)
½ teaspoon salt	1½ cups flour
¼ cup water	

Mix the dry ingredients. Add onion and water. Add suet. Put into a greased mould and steam one hour. Delicious served with roast meats.

Mushroom Dream

4 slices bacon	8 medium mushrooms
½ can tomatoes	(quartered)
1 tablespoon Worcestershire Sauce	1 tablespoon sugar
½ teaspoon salt	⅛ teaspoon pepper

Fry bacon and remove from fat. Put in the mushrooms and add tomatoes, sugar, and sauce. Let simmer twenty minutes. Add salt and pepper. Serve on toast sprinkled with Parmesan cheese. Place a strip of bacon on top of each serving. Garnish with parsley.

Cheese Soufflé

4 slices bread (cut 1 inch thick)   1 quart milk
4 eggs   1 pound Young America cheese
½ tablespoon salt   (cut in not too small pieces)

Cut bread into cubes. Line a greased baking dish with alternate layers of bread and cheese. Beat the egg, milk, salt together and pour over the bread and cheese. Bake forty-five minutes in a moderate oven.

Egg in Bacon Nest

Line muffin tins with strips of bacon. Drop raw egg into each nest. Cook from five to ten minutes in a moderate oven (350° F.). Remove with fork and garnish with parsley.

Scrambled Eggs

Allow two eggs per person. Add two tablespoons milk, one-eighth teaspoon salt, dash of pepper to each two eggs.

Beat thoroughly. Pour into skillet, the bottom of which is covered with hot shortening, stirring continually while cooking. Serve either plain or on toast garnished with parsley.

Poached Eggs

Fill skillet two-thirds full of water. Bring to a boil. Do not boil violently. Add one-half tablespoon salt, one tablespoon vinegar or lemon juice. Drop egg carefully into the hot water. Cook until egg congeals and remove with skimmer to slice of toast. Dot with butter. Garnish with paprika and parsley.

Soft-Cooked Eggs

Put eggs into boiling water. Let stand over low flame two, three, or four minutes, as desired. Serve at once.

Hard-Cooked Eggs

Cover eggs with cold water. Bring to boil. Cook fifteen to twenty minutes after water starts boiling. Put into cold water before shell is removed.

Plain Omelet

Three eggs, beaten separately. Add one tablespoon water and one-fourth teaspoon salt per egg to the yolk. Fold in stiffly beaten whites. Pour in greased omelet pan and cook slowly over low flame. May be browned in the oven if desired.

French Omelet

5 eggs	⅛ teaspoon pepper
½ teaspoon salt	5 tablespoons hot milk
3 tablespoons butter	

Beat the eggs until yolks and whites are blended. Add salt, pepper, and liquid. Melt the butter in the omelet pan or frying pan; when the butter sizzles pour in the egg mixture. Cook very slowly until the egg is all set and the omelet is a light brown underneath. Fold or roll and turn onto a hot platter. Serve at once. Garnish with broiled bacon and parsley.

Creole Omelet

Prepare a plain omelet, and when cooked pour over it the Creole dressing made as follows:

1 tablespoon butter	2 tablespoons bread crumbs
4 tablespoons finely chopped onion	1 tablespoon flour
2 tablespoons chopped parsley	2 cups tomatoes
2 tablespoons minced ham	1 teaspoon salt
	¼ teaspoon pepper

Melt the butter, add the onion, parsley, ham, bread crumbs, and flour. Fry until quite brown. Add tomatoes. Season with salt and pepper. Cook slowly about twenty minutes. Pour over omelet. Serve at once.

Spanish Omelet

4 eggs	1 teaspoon salt
1 onion (chopped fine)	2 teaspoons paprika
1 green pepper (chopped fine)	3 olives (chopped fine)
2 cups canned tomatoes	3 tablespoons butter
1 pimento	

Simmer the onion, olives, pimento, and green pepper in the butter. Add the tomatoes and seasoning, and cook slowly one-half hour. Put one-half the mixture between fold of plain omelet and pour the rest of the mixture over the top. Garnish with parsley.

Puffy Omelet

2 tablespoons bread crumbs   4 tablespoons milk
5 eggs   ½ teaspoon salt
⅛ teaspoon pepper   3 tablespoons butter

Soak the bread crumbs in the milk. Separate the eggs. Beat the yolks until thick and lemon colored. Add the crumbs and milk, the salt and pepper. Beat the egg whites until stiff. Gradually fold the egg-yolk mixture into the whites. Melt the butter in an omelet pan or frying pan and allow it to run around the sides of the pan. Pour mixture into the pan and cook slowly ten minutes, or until light brown underneath. Place the pan in a moderate oven (about 350° F.). Bake five or ten minutes until it is dry on top. Fold and turn onto a hot platter. Serve at once.

Eggs Benedict

Cover round of toast with slice of fried or broiled ham. Put dropped egg on ham. Cover with hollandaise sauce. Garnish with paprika and parsley. Truffles may be used as a garnish.

Eggs Golden Rod

6 hard-cooked eggs   1 cup medium thick white sauce
4 slices of buttered toast

Cut egg in half. Slice egg white into white sauce, and heat thoroughly. Pour over toast. Cover with egg yolk, which has been put through a ricer. Garnish with paprika and parsley.

Stuffed Eggs

Cut hard-cooked eggs in half. Be careful not to break the white. Mash the yolk thoroughly. Add salad dressing enough to moisten egg yolk. Refill egg white with this mixture. Garnish top with sprig of parsley and paprika. Chill before serving.

A little prepared mustard may be added to the yolk if desired. Chopped stuffed olives or nuts, cavair or anchovy paste may be added to the egg yolk if desired.

French Toast

⅓ cup milk   ¼ teaspoon salt

3 eggs

Beat eggs, and add milk and salt. Take slice of bread and dip in batter until entirely covered. Fry in butter. Brown both sides. Serve with confectioners' sugar, maple syrup, or jelly.

French toast may be fried in deep fat if desired.

Milk Toast, No. 1

6 slices of buttered toast   1 quart scalded milk

Use two slices of toast for each serving. Put toast into bowl which has been heated. Pour hot milk over toast. Season with salt, pepper, and paprika.

Milk Toast, No. 2

6 slices of buttered toast   1 quart thin white sauce

Use two slices of toast for each serving. Put toast into bowl which has been heated. Pour hot white sauce over toast. Season with salt, pepper, and paprika.

Melba Toast

Take wheat bread twenty-four hours old and slice thin as possible. Cut off crust. Cut in half from corner to corner. Place bread in rows in shallow baking dish. Bake in moderate oven (350° F.) until nicely browned.

Mushrooms on Toast

1 pound mushrooms   3 cups white sauce (medium thick)

Brush the mushrooms clean. Sauté in melted shortening until nice and brown. Add the white sauce and mix thoroughly. Serve on toast. Garnish with parsley.

CHAPTER XXIII

Pancakes, Waffles, Fritters, Timbales, and Doughnuts

Pancakes, No. 1

1 egg
2 teaspoons baking powder
1 cup flour

¼ teaspoon salt
1 cup milk
2 tablespoons shortening

Beat egg thoroughly. Add salt and milk. Mix baking powder with flour. Add to first mixture. Beat until smooth. Bake on hot griddle.

Pancakes, No. 2

1 egg
1 baking powder
¼ teaspoon salt

1 cup flour
1 cup sour milk
½ teaspoon soda

Beat the egg thoroughly. Add salt and milk. Mix soda and baking powder with the flour. Add to first mixture. Beat until smooth. Bake on a hot griddle.

Egg Pancakes

1 cup flour
¼ teaspoon salt

½ cup milk
½ cup water

3 eggs

Beat eggs until light. Add salt, milk, and water. Beat thoroughly. Add flour. Beat until smooth. Fry in hot lard one inch deep. Pour batter into lard slowly. Turn once.

French Pancakes

Sift the following:

¾ cup flour   ⅛ teaspoon salt   1 teaspoon baking powder

Add one-half cup milk slowly so as to avoid lumping. Beat until smooth. Cook on a hot griddle. Cover cakes with butter and jelly in equal quantities, creamed together. Roll quickly like a jelly roll. Dredge liberally with powdered sugar. With a red-hot poker, score the sugar. Serve at once.

Buckwheat Pancakes

½ cup bread crumbs	½ teaspoon salt
2½ cups scalded milk	½ yeast cake
2 cups buckwheat flour	2 tablespoons molasses

Add bread and salt to scalded milk. Cool. When lukewarm add yeast and stir until yeast is dissolved. Add buckwheat flour and stir smooth. Put in warm place overnight. In the morning add molasses, and one-fourth teaspoon soda mixed with a little lukewarm water. Beat smooth. Bake on hot griddle.

Bran Griddle Cakes

2½ cups flour	1 cup bran
3 teaspoons baking powder	2 cups milk
1 teaspoon salt	2 eggs
1 tablespoon sugar	3 tablespoons melted shortening

Mix and sift flour, baking powder, salt, and sugar together. Stir in the bran. Add the milk to the well-beaten eggs. Pour slowly into the dry ingredients. Mix thoroughly and add the melted shortening. Bake on a hot griddle.

Rice Griddle Cakes

1 cup boiled rice	2 tablespoons melted butter
1 cup milk	2 eggs
2 teaspoons baking powder	¾ cup flour
½ teaspoon salt	

Beat eggs thoroughly. Add salt and milk. Mix baking powder with flour. Add to first mixture. Add shortening and rice. Mix smooth. Bake on a hot griddle.

Blueberry Griddle Cakes

1 egg	1 cup flour
1 cup milk	¼ teaspoon salt
2 teaspoons baking powder	½ cup blueberries

Beat egg until light. Add salt and milk. Mix baking powder with flour. Stir into first mixture. Beat until smooth. Add blueberries. Bake on a hot griddle.

Flannel Griddle Cakes

2 cups bread crumbs
2 cups sour milk
½ teaspoon salt

1 teaspoon soda
1 cup flour
1 egg

Soak bread crumbs in one cup warm water. Add milk and flour. Let stand overnight. In the morning add the beaten egg, salt, and soda which has been dissolved in a little warm water. Mix thoroughly. Bake on a hot griddle.

Waffles

1¾ cups flour
3 teaspoons baking powder
½ teaspoon salt

3 tablespoons melted butter
1 cup milk
2 eggs (separated)

Mix and sift dry ingredients. Beat egg yolk with the milk. Add salt. Add to dry ingredients. Fold in stiffly beaten egg whites. Mix until smooth.

Nut Bars

2 cups flour
¼ teaspoon salt
½ cup sugar
1 egg

2 teaspoons baking powder
1 tablespoon butter
1 cup chopped nuts
1 cup milk

Mix the dry ingredients. Add nuts. Cut in the shortening. Add milk to egg and beat thoroughly. Combine mixtures. Toss onto floured board. Pat to one-half inch thickness. Cut into strips one-half inch by three inches. Fry in deep fat (375° F.). Drain on unglaced paper. Roll in sugar and cinnamon.

Vanities

3 eggs
¼ teaspoon salt

1 tablespoon cold water
1 tablespoon sugar

2¾ cups flour

Beat eggs. Add salt, sugar, and water. Add flour. Mix well. Dough will be very stiff. Roll thin as possible on floured board.

Cut into diamond shapes. Fry in deep fat (375°–380° F.). Drain. Dust with confectioners' sugar.

Timbale Cases or Rosettes

½ cup flour	½ cup water
¼ teaspoon salt	1 egg (slightly beaten)
1 tablespoon sugar	1 tablespoon melted shortening

Mix dry ingredients. Beat egg with water. Add shortening. Combine mixtures. Let stand two hours. Strain batter into a cup. Put timbale iron in deep saucepan and cover with fat. Heat to 380° F. Drain iron, dip in timbale mixture until two-thirds covered. Then immerse in hot fat (380° F.) and fry until crisp and a delicate brown. Drain cases on brown paper. A rosette iron may be used instead of a timbale iron, if desired.

Rosettes may be dusted with confectioners' sugar and served for afternoon tea.

Batter for Fritters

1½ cups flour	1 egg
2 teaspoons baking powder	¼ teaspoon salt
⅔ cup milk	

Mix and sift ingredients. Add milk gradually and egg well beaten. Mix until smooth. Drop with a teaspoon into hot fat (380° F.). Fry until brown. Drain. Serve hot. One-half cup finely cut pineapple or peaches may be added to this batter if desired. Berries may be substituted for the fruit. Raspberries and blueberries are delicious.

Corn Fritters

1 cup corn (fresh or canned)	1 egg
4 tablespoons milk	¾ cup flour
1 teaspoon baking powder	Salt and pepper to taste

Mix milk with eggs, add flour, and beat smooth. Add corn and seasoning. Mix well and drop by spoonfuls in hot fat (380° F.). Fry until golden brown. Serve with maple syrup. May be sautéed instead of fried if desired.

Orange Fritters

Peel oranges and separate into sections. Remove seeds. Dip sections into fritter batter and fry in deep fat (380° F.). Drain and sprinkle with powdered sugar. Serve hot with orange sauce. Slices of pineapple or apple may be substituted for the orange.

Orange Sauce

¼ cup flour	¼ cup orange juice
¼ cup sugar	Grated rind ½ orange and
2 tablespoons lemon juice	½ lemon
1 cup boiling water	

Pour boiling water slowly over flour and sugar which have been thoroughly mixed. Cook until thick. Add orange and lemon juice and grated rind. Serve immediately.

Doughnuts

4 cups flour	¼ teaspoon cinnamon
1 teaspoon salt	1 tablespoon melted shortening
1½ teaspoons soda	¾ cup sugar
1½ teaspoons cream of tartar	1 cup sour milk
1 egg	

Mix and sift dry ingredients. Beat egg with sour milk. Add dry ingredients and melted shortening to egg mixture. Mix smooth. Turn onto floured moulding board. Roll to one-fourth inch thickness. Cut with doughnut cutter. Fry in deep fat until brown (375°–380° F.). Turn once while cooking. Drain on unglazed paper. Dust with confectioners' sugar.

Sweet-Milk Doughnuts

2 eggs (beaten lightly)	½ teaspoon nutmeg
1 cup sugar	2 tablespoons melted shortening
1 cup milk	3 teaspoons baking powder
3½ cups flour	

Mix the dry ingredients. Beat egg with the milk. Add sugar and shortening. Add the dry ingredients. Mix thoroughly. Turn onto a floured moulding board. Roll to one-fourth inch thickness. Cut with doughnut cutter. Fry in deep fat (375°–380° F.).

CHAPTER XXIV
Pies and Tarts

Pie Crust

1½ cups flour
½ cup shortening

Ice water
1 teaspoon salt

1 teaspoon baking powder

Sift flour, baking powder, and salt together. Cut in shortening. Add enough ice water to form ball of dough. Toss on floured moulding board. Divide into halves. Roll out each half to fit pan.

Line ungreased pie tin with dough. Fold over and slit top crust several times before covering pie with it. This will allow the steam to escape. Bake in hot oven (500° F.) until crust colors. Then reduce heat to 350° F. This amount will make one double crust pie. This recipe is also used for pie and tart shells.

Hot-Water Pastry

¾ cup shortening
3 cups flour

1 teaspoon baking powder
½ cup boiling water

1 teaspoon salt

with fork until it becomes a smooth liquid *Pour over shortening - beat*

Pour boiling water over shortening. Add flour, baking powder, and salt. Mix thoroughly. Sprinkle board with flour. Put dough onto board. Roll out and fit to pie tins. Time to be governed according to filling used. Bake pie in hot oven (500° F.), lowering temperature to 350° F. as soon as coloring appears. This amount will make one two-crust pie or two one-crust pies.

Puff Paste

2 cups flour
⅔ cup shortening
Ice water

½ teaspoon salt
4 tablespoons butter
1 teaspoon baking powder

Sift together flour, baking powder, and salt. Cut in shortening. Moisten with enough water to form ball. Toss onto floured moulding board. Pat and roll out to one-fourth inch thickness. Dot with one tablespoon butter. Fold top and bottom edge to center, overlapping slightly. Fold right edge to center, then left edge to center, slightly overlapping. Pat lightly with rolling pin to one-fourth inch thickness. Repeat until four tablespoons butter have been used. Chill for two hours before rolling out.

This amount will make one double-crust pie or two single-crust pies.

French Pastry

1½ cups flour	½ cup shortening
1 teaspoon baking powder	4 tablespoons butter
1 teaspoon salt	Ice water

Mix flour with baking powder and salt. Cut in shortening. Add ice water to form ball. Turn onto floured moulding board. Roll to one-quarter inch thickness. Dot with one tablespoon butter. Fold top and bottom edge to center, overlapping slightly. Fold right edge to center, then left edge to center, slightly overlapping. Pat lightly with rolling pin to one-quarter inch thickness. Repeat until four tablespoons butter have been used. Chill for two hours. Roll out to one-half inch thickness. Cut into diamond-shaped pieces. Bake on ungreased cookie tins in hot oven (450° to 500° F.) until brown. Dust with confectioners' sugar or ice with confectioners' icing.

These French pastries may be decorated with candies or colored icings, chocolate shot, or nut meats.

Rich Tart Shells

1½ cups flour	1 tablespoon sugar
½ cup shortening	2 tablespoons chopped nuts
1 teaspoon salt	1 teaspoon baking powder
Ice water	

Sift the flour before measuring. Mix flour, salt, and baking powder. Cut in the shortening. Add sugar and nuts. Add enough ice water to form ball. Toss onto floured moulding board. Roll out dough. Cut into pieces three inches by three inches. Fit dough over inverted muffin tins. Bake in hot oven (450° F.). Cool and fill shells.

Apple Pie

6 sour apples	2 teaspoons butter
⅔ cup sugar	1 teaspoon lemon juice

⅛ teaspoon salt

Line pie tin with pie crust. Pare, core, and slice apples. Put pieces of apple in plate, in regular order, and work toward center until pan is filled. Pile slightly in center. Mix sugar, salt, lemon juice, and sprinkle over apples. Dot with butter. Cover with upper crust. Bake forty minutes. Hot oven (450° F.). Reduce heat to 350° F. last thirty minutes. Cinnamon may be added to flavor apples if desired.

Apricot Pie

4 cups sliced apricots	1 tablespoon butter

¾ cup sugar

Line pie tin with pie crust. After preparing crusts in the usual way fill with the apricots and sugar. Dot with butter. Bake for thirty minutes. Hot oven (450° F.). Reduce heat to 350° F. last fifteen minutes. Berry and fruit pies are all made according to this recipe.

Prune Pie

4 cups prunes (stew and remove stones)	1 tablespoon butter

Line pie tin with pie crust. Put prunes between crusts. Dot with butter. Bake in hot oven (450° F.) for thirty-five minutes. Reduce heat to 350° F. last fifteen minutes.

Cranberry and Raisin Pie

3½ cups cranberries (chopped with ½ cup raisins)	2 tablespoons flour
	1 tablespoon butter

1 cup sugar

Line pie tin with pie crust. Mix above ingredients thoroughly. Put this filling in pie crusts and bake for thirty minutes in hot oven (450° F.). Reduce heat to 350° F. last fifteen minutes.

Lemon Pie

1 cup sugar
¼ teaspoon salt
6 tablespoons flour
1½ cups water

6 tablespoons lemon juice
Grated rind of 1 lemon
1 tablespoon butter
2 eggs

Mix sugar, salt, and flour together. Add water and cook until clear. Add lemon juice, grated rind, and butter. Add the beaten egg yolks and cook two minutes. Pour into a baked pie shell. Make meringue of two egg whites, one-half cup sugar, one-half teaspoon baking powder. Top pie with meringue. Bake twenty minutes in slow oven (300° F.).

Lemon Sponge

1 cup sugar
3 eggs (yolks)
1 cup hot milk

¼ teaspoon salt
1 tablespoon flour
Juice and rind of 1 lemon

1 tablespoon butter

Mix sugar with salt and flour. Add the hot milk and egg yolks. Beat thoroughly. Add rind and juice of lemon. Add melted shortening. Cool. Fold in beaten egg whites. Pour into pastry-lined pie tin. Bake in a slow oven (325° F.) until firm. Increase heat to 350° F. last few minutes to brown.

Caramel Pie

3 tablespoons butter
4 tablespoons flour

1 cup brown sugar
1 cup milk

1 egg or 2 yolks

Cream butter, flour, and brown sugar. Beat eggs with milk and add to creamed mixture. Mix well. Cook in double boiler until thick. Fill baked pie shell with this mixture. Top with meringue or whipped cream. One teaspoon vanilla may be added if desired.

Chocolate Cream Pie

4 tablespoons flour
3 tablespoons butter
1 cup granulated sugar

1 cup milk
1 egg or 2 yolks
2 squares bitter chocolate

Cream butter, flour, and granulated sugar. Beat eggs and milk and add to creamed mixture. Cook in double boiler until thick. Fill baked pie shell with this mixture. Top with meringue or whipped cream. One teaspoon vanilla may be added if desired.

Custard Pie

¼ cup sugar   2 cups milk
⅛ teaspoon salt   ½ teaspoon vanilla
                3 eggs

Beat the eggs. Add the sugar, salt, milk, and flavoring. Mix well. Pour this mixture into a pastry-lined pie tin. Bake in a very hot oven for fifteen minutes (450° F.). Reduce the temperature to 325° F. and continue baking until done.

Custard pie is done when a knife inserted in the custard comes out clean. Custard pie may be sprinkled with nutmeg before baking if desired.

Cocoanut Custard

¼ cup sugar   2 cups milk
⅛ teaspoon salt   ½ teaspoon vanilla
3 eggs   ½ cup cocoanut

Beat the eggs. Add the sugar, salt, milk, and flavoring. Mix well. Pour this mixture into a pastry-lined pie tin. Sprinkle cocoanut over the top. Put into a hot oven (450° F.) for fifteen minutes. Reduce heat to 325° F. Bake until a knife inserted in the custard comes out clean.

Prune Cream Pie

Soak prunes in water over night. Stew. Mix one cup chopped prunes with:

2 cups sour cream   ½ teaspoon cloves
1 teaspoon cinnamon   4 egg yolks
                2 cups sugar

Mix thoroughly. Pour into a pastry-lined pie tin. Put into a hot oven (450° F.) for fifteen minutes. Reduce heat to 325° F. Bake thirty minutes more until firm. Top with meringue or whipped cream. Cool before serving.

Date Pie

Cover one package of dates with water. Soak two hours. Cook until soft. Put through colander. Add one egg and one and one-half cups milk. Line pie tin with pastry. Fill with date mixture.

Put into hot oven (450° F.) for fifteen minutes. Reduce heat to 325° F. Bake until firm or until a knife inserted in the custard comes out clean.

Mincemeat, No. 1

3 pounds beef
2 pounds suet
3 pounds brown sugar
3 pounds raisins (seedless)
2 pounds currants
2 tablespoons each of ground mace, ground nutmeg, ground cinnamon and ground cloves

12 large apples
2 pounds citron (cut fine)
5 lemons (juice and grated rind)
5 oranges (juice and grated rind)
1 quart liquid
3 cups cider

Cover meat with water. Add one tablespoon salt. Simmer until tender. Cool in water in which it has been cooked. Chop meat fine. Pare, core, and chop apples. Combine meat and apples. Add sugar, raisins, currants, citron, cider, fruit juices and rind, liquid, and meat stock. Simmer slowly two hours. Add one pound broken walnut meats. Pack in fruit jars or stone crock. Ripen before using. Liquid may be grape juice, wine, canned fruit juice, or water.

Mincemeat, No. 2

4 pounds beef round
3 pounds suet (chopped)
3 pounds citron (cut fine)
1½ pounds blanched almonds
1½ teaspoons mace
1½ teaspoons cinnamon

5 pounds raisins
5 pounds apples (pare and chop)
3 pounds currants
4 pounds light brown sugar
2 quarts cider
2 teaspoons ground cloves

Cover meat with boiling water and simmer until tender. Cool in the water in which cooked. Chop the meat fine. Add the raisins, suet, apples, citron, currants, and almonds. Add the sugar, spices, and cider. Simmer slowly one and a half hours, stirring frequently to prevent burning. Put away in fruit or stone jars to ripen before using.

Mince Pie

Line nine-inch pie shell with pastry. Add one-quarter cup chopped maraschino cherries and one-half cup grape juice to three cups mincemeat. Fill pastry shell with this mixture. Cover with top crust. Bake thirty-five minutes.

For the first ten minutes have oven 450° F., then reduce heat to 350° F.

Pumpkin Pie

1¼ cups mashed pumpkin
¼ cup brown sugar
½ teaspoon salt
1 cup milk

¼ teaspoon cinnamon
¼ teaspoon ginger
1 egg
1 teaspoon vanilla

Mix sugar, salt, vanilla, and spices. Add pumpkin and beaten egg. Add milk gradually. Mix well. Pour into pie tin lined with pastry. Bake in hot oven (450° F.). Reduce heat to 325° F. after ten minutes. Bake until knife inserted in pumpkin comes out clean. For squash pie substitute squash for pumpkin.

Banbury Tarts

½ cup raisins
½ cup currants
¼ cup water
4 tablespoons lemon juice

1 cup sugar
2 tablespoons flour
½ cup walnuts
Pastry

Mix together raisins, currants, water, lemon juice, sugar, and flour. Cook until thick. Remove from fire and add the walnuts. Roll pastry very thin. Cut in squares three inches by three inches. Put teaspoon of filling in center of each. Bring edges together to form a triangle. Seal edges. Bake fifteen minutes in a moderate oven (350° F.).

Marmalade Tarts

¼ pound butter   ¼ pound cream cheese
1 cup flour   1 teaspoon baking powder

Mix ingredients thoroughly. Let stand in ice box overnight. Roll thin and cut in two-inch squares. Put one-half teaspoon orange marmalade on one half, turn other half over, making a little turnover. Seal thoroughly. Bake on baking sheet in hot oven (400° F.). Jam or other marmalade may be used.

Strawberry Tarts

Bake pastry on inverted muffin tins. Into bottom of baked shell to one-fourth inch thickness put chilled cream filling. Over this put berries that have been glazed in rich sugar syrup. Boil down syrup until jellied. Chill and pour over berries. Serve cold. Top with whipped cream before serving.

Butterscotch Filling

1 cup milk   1 tablespoon butter
1 cup brown sugar   ¼ cup flour
1 egg   ⅛ teaspoon salt
              1 teaspoon vanilla

Mix ingredients thoroughly. Cook in a double boiler until thick. Cool. Fill tart shells with this mixture. Top with whipped cream or meringue. One teaspoon vanilla may be added if desired.

Chocolate Cream Filling

1 cup milk   ½ cup sugar
1 square bitter chocolate (melted) ⅛ teaspoon salt
6 marshmallows (quartered)   4 tablespoons flour
              1 tablespoon butter

Mix all ingredients thoroughly except the chocolate and marshmallows. Cook until thick. Add melted chocolate and marshmallows. Cool. Fill tart shells with this mixture. Top with whipped cream. One teaspoon vanilla may be added if desired.

CHAPTER XXV

Poultry and Poultry Dressings

Roast Turkey

Remove pin feathers and singe turkey. Wash thoroughly. Fill with dressing, either bread, oyster, or chestnut. Sew up the opening. Tie wings to body securely with string. Fold neck under body and tie it securely. Press legs to side of body and tie them securely. Put bird into roasting pan, onto slices of bacon. Cover with strips of bacon. Season with salt and pepper. Add enough water to cover bottom of pan. Cook in moderately hot oven (375° to 400° F.) until brown. Baste frequently while roasting. Allow twenty to twenty-five minutes per pound, plus one-half hour. Thicken gravy before serving. Bacon may be omitted if desired.

Roast Goose

Remove pin feathers and singe goose. Wash thoroughly. Fill with dressing, either bread, apple, or raisin. Sew up the opening. Tie wings to body securely with string. Fold neck under body and tie it securely. Press legs to side of body and tie them securely. Put goose on rack in roasting pan. Season with salt and pepper. Add enough water to cover bottom of pan. Cook in moderately hot oven (375° to 400° F.) until brown. Baste frequently while roasting. Allow twenty-five to thirty minutes per pound plus one-half hour. Pour grease off gravy before thickening it.

Roast Duck

Remove pin feathers and singe duck. Wash thoroughly. Fill with dressing, either bread, apple, or raisin. Sew up the opening. Tie wings to body securely with string. Fold neck under body and tie it securely. Press legs to side of body and tie them securely. Put duck in roasting pan. Season with salt and pepper. Add enough water to cover bottom of pan. Cook in moderately hot oven (375° to 400° F.) until brown. Baste frequently while roasting. Allow twenty minutes per pound plus one-half hour. Thicken gravy before serving. Currant jelly may be added to duck while roasting if desired.

Roast Wild Duck

Remove feathers. Singe well. Wash thoroughly. Cover duck with milk and soak twenty-four hours. Drain off milk. Fill with bread dressing. Sew up the opening. Put into roasting pan. Season with salt and pepper. Add enough water to cover bottom of pan. Cook in moderately hot oven (375° to 400° F.) until brown. Baste frequently while roasting. Allow twenty minutes per pound plus one-half hour. Thicken gravy before serving.

Roast Capon

Remove pin feathers and singe capon. Wash thoroughly. Fill with dressing, either bread, apple, raisin, or chestnut. Sew up the opening. Tie wings to body securely with string. Fold neck under body and tie securely. Press legs to side of body and tie them securely. Put capon into roasting pan onto slices of bacon. Cover with slices of bacon. Season with salt and pepper. Add enough water to cover bottom of pan. Cook in moderately hot oven (375° to 400° F.) until brown. Baste frequently while roasting. Allow twenty to twenty-five minutes per pound plus one-half hour. Thicken gravy before serving.

Roast Capon with Fruit Stuffing

5 cups bread crumbs	4 pears (cut fine)
½ cup walnut meats	4 peaches (cut fine)
½ cup apricots	½ cup fruit juice
¼ cup raisins	½ cup apple (cut fine)
½ cup stewed prunes	2 eggs

Mix the crumbs, eggs, and fruit juice with the fruit. Remove pin feathers from a six-pound capon. Singe and wash thoroughly. Fill capon with fruit dressing. Sew up the opening.

Tie wings to body securely with string. Fold neck under body and tie securely. Press legs to body and tie securely. Put capon into roasting pan. Season with salt and pepper. Cover with strips of bacon. Add enough water to cover bottom of the pan. Cook in a moderately hot oven (375° to 400° F.). Baste frequently while roasting. Allow twenty-five minutes per pound plus one-half hour. Thicken gravy before serving.

Roast Squab

Remove pin feathers from squab. Singe and wash thoroughly. Fill with bread or raisin dressing. Sew up opening. Put in roasting pan. Cover squab with strips of bacon. Season with salt and pepper. Add enough water to prevent burning. Roast in moderately hot oven (375° to 400° F.) for one hour. Thicken gravy before serving.

Squab Casserole

Remove pin feathers from squab. Singe and wash thoroughly. Fill with bread or raisin dressing. Put into casserole. Brown in melted shortening. Season with salt and pepper. Add enough water to prevent scorching. Cover. Simmer over low flame for one hour. Serve at once.

Roast Chicken

Remove pin feathers from chicken. Singe and wash thoroughly. Fill with dressing, either bread, oyster, raisin, or chestnut. Sew up the opening. Tie wings to body securely with string. Fold neck under body and tie securely. Press legs to side of body and tie securely. Put chicken into roasting pan onto strips of bacon. Cover with strips of bacon. Season with salt and pepper. Add enough water to cover bottom of pan. Cook in a moderately hot oven (375° to 400° F.) until brown. Baste frequently while roasting. Allow twenty to twenty-five minutes per pound plus one-half hour. Thicken gravy before serving. Sautéed mushrooms may be added to the gravy if desired. Bacon may be omitted if desired.

Fried Chicken, No. 1

Remove pin feathers from chicken. Singe and wash thoroughly. Cut leg from chicken. Separate leg from thigh and cut wing from body of chicken. Then cut the body into quarters. Dredge with flour. Fry in hot melted butter until brown. Season with salt and pepper. Cover and simmer for thirty minutes. Serve with broiled bacon. Garnish with parsley.

Fried Chicken, No. 2

Singe and dress a five-pound chicken. Cook in salted water until tender. Two hours. Cut the leg from chicken, and separate the thigh from the leg. Cut the wing from chicken. Then cut the breast meat in slices. Roll pieces of chicken in egg and cracker crumbs. Fry in butter until nicely brown. Serve at once. Chicken stock may be used for soup or jellied consommé.

Fried Chicken, No. 3

Remove pin feathers from chicken. Singe and wash thoroughly. Cut leg from body. Separate leg and thigh. Cut wing from body. Cut body into four pieces. Put chicken in saucepan. Add one onion cut fine and enough salted water to cover. Simmer one to one and a half hours. Drain chicken. Fry chicken in hot melted shortening until nicely browned. Strain stock. Heat. To each cup of stock add one tablespoon flour mixed with cold water until smooth. Cook until stock thickens. Serve with fried chicken and hot baking powder biscuits.

Broiled Chicken

Remove pin feathers from chicken. Singe. Wash chicken thoroughly. Cut in half. Put on broiler and cook under medium flame twenty to thirty minutes. Turn once. Serve hot with melted butter. Season with salt and pepper. Garnish with parsley. Broiled bacon may be served with broiled chicken.

Chicken à la Maryland

Cut chicken as for fricassée. Dredge with flour. Season with salt and pepper. Put into greased roaster. Dot with butter. Bake in oven, adding small amount of water. Baste frequently. Fifteen minutes before removing from oven, add two cups cream, and simmer gently. Remove chicken, and thicken liquid. Pour over chicken. Serve hot. Bake chicken two hours in moderate oven (350° F.).

Chicken Casserole

1 five-pound chicken (fowl may be used)	2 cups diced celery
1 cup diced carrots	½ pound mushrooms
2 cups peas	2 onions
	1 pimento (cut fine)

Remove pin feathers from chicken. Singe and wash chicken. Cut leg from body. Cut leg from thigh. Cut wing from body. Quarter the body. Brown chicken in hot melted shortening. Peel and slice the onions. Fry until nicely browned. Put onion into bottom of casserole. Add carrots, peas, pimento, and celery. Put fried chicken over vegetables. Top with mushrooms. Season with one-half tablespoon salt and one-quarter teaspoon pepper. Add three cups of water. Cook two and one-half hours in a moderate oven (350° F.). Serve hot garnished with parsley.

Fricassée Chicken

1 five-pound chicken

Dress and cut up chicken, then dredge with flour. Brown in hot salt pork drippings, or butter. Cover with boiling water. Add one tablespoon salt and one-quarter teaspoon pepper. Simmer slowly until tender. Two and one-half hours. Thicken gravy before serving. Serve with dumplings. Chopped onions, carrots, or peas may be cooked with this dish.

Colorful Sandwiches that Taste Good

Chicken Pie

6 cups cooked chicken
  (cut in pieces)
3 tablespoons shortening
1 teaspoon salt

3 cups chicken stock
2 cups peas
4 tablespoons flour
⅛ teaspoon pepper

Pastry

Heat chicken stock and thicken with flour which has been mixed to a smooth paste in a little cold water. Cook until thick, stirring constantly to prevent lumping. Add salt, pepper, peas, and chicken. Put into a large baking dish. Cover with a top crust of flaky pastry or baking powder biscuits. Bake in a hot oven (400° F.) ten minutes. Reduce heat to moderate oven (350° F.) and cook forty minutes longer.

Creamed Chicken

2 cups cooked chicken
  (cut into pieces)
1 pimento (cut fine)
1 green pepper (cut fine)

1 cup chicken stock
½ cup cream
½ teaspoon salt
2 tablespoons flour

Heat chicken stock. Add salt and flour which has been mixed to a smooth paste with a little cold water. Cook until mixture thickens. Add green pepper, pimento, and chicken. Heat thoroughly. Add cream. Mix well. Serve hot on toast, in timbale cases or ramekins. May be served plain or topped with buttered bread crumbs.

Chicken à la King

3 cups cooked chicken
  (cut into pieces)
1 pimento (cut fine)
1 cup mushrooms
  (cut in half)

1 cup asparagus tips (cut fine)
1 tablespoon parsley (cut fine)
2 cups chicken stock
4 tablespoons flour
1 teaspoon salt

¾ cup cream

Heat chicken stock. Add salt and flour which has been mixed to a smooth paste with cold water. Cook until mixture thickens. Add chicken, pimento, mushrooms, and asparagus. Cook until thoroughly heated. Add cream. Mix well. Serve hot on toast, in timbale cases, or ramekins. Sprinkle with chopped parsley before serving. If fresh mushrooms are used, sauté them before using. Chopped green pepper and sliced hard-cooked eggs may be added if desired.

Chicken Timbales

1 cup milk	4 eggs
1 teaspoon salt	1 cup chopped chicken
1 chopped onion	½ teaspoon paprika

⅛ teaspoon pepper

Beat eggs lightly, add milk and seasoning. Add chicken and onion. Turn into buttered timbale moulds. Bake or steam until firm. Serve with white sauce. Garnish with parsley.

Jellied Chicken

Wash, cut up, and cook a three-pound chicken in water to just cover. Cook until the meat separates easily from the bone. Strain stock from meat, reduce to three cups. Add one teaspoon salt.

Soak two and one-half tablespoons gelatine in one-quarter cup cold water for twenty minutes. Dissolve in hot chicken broth. Cool. Add chicken meat which has been cut fine. Mix thoroughly. Pour into mould. Let stand until cold and firm. Cover platter with bed of lettuce leaves. Unmould on platter. Garnish with parsley and radish roses. Serve with dressing made by mixing equal parts of boiled salad dressing and whipped cream.

Jellied chicken may be made in individual moulds if desired.

Jellied Chicken Loaf

Wash and cut up a three-pound chicken. Put in water to just cover and cook until the meat separates easily from the bone. Strain liquid from meat, and reduce to three cups. Salt to taste.

Soak two and one-half tablespoonfuls gelatine in one-fourth

cup cold water for twenty minutes. Then dissolve in hot stock, and cool.

Remove meat from bones, separating dark meat from white. Do not cut meat. Arrange white and dark meat in alternate layers in bread pan. Sprinkle each layer with one-quarter cup chopped celery. Add stock. Let stand until firm. Unmould on cold platter. Garnish with lettuce, parsley, and radish roses. Serve with dressing made by mixing equal parts of boiled dressing and whipped cream.

Bread Dressing

1 cup milk	1 onion (chopped)
2 cups bread crumbs	1 tablespoon sage
½ teaspoon salt	2 eggs
⅛ teaspoon pepper	1 stalk celery (chopped fine)

Soak bread crumbs in milk. Add other ingredients. Mix well, and use for stuffing fowl, turkey, duck, or goose.

Chestnut Dressing

2 cups cooked chestnuts (chopped fine)	½ teaspoon salt
½ cup milk	⅛ teaspoon pepper
1 cup bread crumbs	1 egg

Soak bread crumbs in the milk for thirty minutes. Add beaten egg, seasoning, and chestnuts. Mix well. Use as dressing for turkey or chicken.

Baked Dressing

½ pound Hamburg steak	2 cups bread crumbs
1 teaspoon salt	2 tablespoons melted butter
⅛ teaspoon pepper	1 onion (cut fine)

Mix together bread crumbs, steak, salt, onion, and pepper. Add melted butter. Mix well. Put into greased baking dish and bake in moderate oven (350° F.) until brown. Forty minutes. Serve with main course.

CHAPTER XXVI
Puddings and Sauces

Christmas Pudding

1 pound raisins
¼ pound orange peel (candied)
¼ pound citron
½ pound chopped suet
½ pound bread crumbs
¼ pound flour
¼ pound cherries (candied)
8 eggs

3 teaspoons baking powder
½ pound brown sugar
1 tablespoon cinnamon
1 teaspoon nutmeg
¼ teaspoon allspice
1 cup grape juice
1 pound currants
2 teaspoons salt

Cut citron and orange peel very fine. Rub currants and raisins clean. Mix all dry ingredients together. Beat eggs. Add dry ingredients, add liquid, and mix thoroughly. Put into greased moulds and steam six hours. Serve with hard sauce.

Delicious Plum Pudding

2 cups chopped suet
1 pound currants
2 cups dates
¼ pound citron
¼ pound orange peel (candied)
4 tablespoons molasses
1 teaspoon soda
½ cup bread crumbs
1½ teaspoons cinnamon
1 pound raisins
4 eggs

½ pound walnuts
¼ pound lemon peel (candied)
2 cups sugar
1 cup sour milk
1 cup flour
2 teaspoons baking powder
1 teaspoon salt
¼ teaspoon cloves
½ cup cherries (candied)
½ teaspoon nutmeg
½ cup pineapple (candied)

Cut fruits fine. Mix suet with fruit and chopped nut meats. Mix dry ingredients. Mix liquid ingredients. Combine all ingredients and mix thoroughly. Pour into greased mould and steam eight hours. Serve hot with hard sauce.

Mock Plum Pudding

1 cup chopped raw carrots	1 cup chopped raw potatoes
2 cups raisins (seedless)	1½ cups flour
½ cup warm water	1 cup suet (chopped)
½ teaspoon salt	½ teaspoon soda
2 teaspoons baking powder	1 teaspoon cinnamon
4 eggs	½ teaspoon nutmeg
1½ cups brown sugar	½ teaspoon mace

Mix chopped carrots and potatoes with suet and raisins. Mix dry ingredients. Beat eggs. Add water to eggs. Add dry and liquid ingredients alternately to the first mixture. Mix thoroughly. Pour into greased mould. Steam four hours. Serve hot with hard sauce.

Rhubarb and Strawberry Pudding

4 cups rhubarb	1 egg
3 cups sugar	¼ teaspoon salt
½ cup crushed strawberries	

Make a biscuit dough of the following:

2 cups flour	4 teaspoons baking powder
1 teaspoon salt	4 tablespoons shortening
1 tablespoon sugar	¾ cup milk

Cut the rhubarb in inch pieces. Cook until tender. Add strawberries. Add the sugar, salt, and slightly beaten egg. Pour into a buttered baking dish. Drop the biscuit dough by spoonfuls on top of the rhubarb. Bake twenty-five minutes in a moderately hot oven (375° F.).

Serve hot topped with whipped cream. Ice cream may be used instead of the whipped cream if desired. Strawberries may be omitted from this recipe if desired.

Indian Pudding

Scald one quart milk and add one-half cup corn meal. Add:

½ cup sugar	1 egg
½ cup molasses	½ teaspoon cinnamon

Cook until mixture begins to thicken. Cool. Add one quart of cold milk and one-quarter teaspoon salt. Mix thoroughly.

Pour into a greased baking dish. Dot with butter. Bake in a slow oven (325° F.) from three and one-half to four hours. Serve hot with whipped cream or ice cream.

Tapioca Indian Pudding

¼ cup pearl tapioca	⅔ cup molasses
1 quart milk	2 tablespoons butter
3 tablespoons corn meal	⅔ cup sugar
2 eggs	½ teaspoon salt

Cook tapioca in milk until clear. Add corn meal and cook fifteen minutes. Cool. Add molasses, sugar, salt, and beaten egg. Pour into greased baking dish. Dot with butter. Bake two hours in a moderate oven (350° F.). Serve hot with whipped cream.

Baked Tapioca and Apple Pudding

¼ cup tapioca	¼ cup sugar
¼ teaspoon salt	2 cups boiling water

Soak tapioca in one-half cup cold water for five minutes. Add one and one-half cups water. Cook in double boiler until transparent. Add sugar and salt. Mix well. Fill a greased baking dish one-third full of sliced apples. Cover with sugar and cinnamon. Pour tapioca over the fruit. Bake one hour in a moderate oven (350° F.). Serve with whipped cream.

Apple Pudding

2 cups flour	4 tablespoons shortening
4 teaspoons baking powder	¾ cup milk
½ teaspoon salt	4 apples

Mix and sift dry ingredients. Cut in shortening. Add milk gradually. Toss dough on floured board, pat and roll out to one-quarter inch thickness. Cut apples fine. Place in middle of dough; sprinkle with eight tablespoons sugar, mixed with one-quarter teaspoon cinnamon. Bring dough around apples and seal edges carefully. Put into buttered mould. Cover closely and steam one hour. Serve with hard sauce.

Blueberry Pudding

2 cups flour	4 tablespoons shortening
4 teaspoons baking powder	1 cup milk
½ teaspoon salt	1 cup blueberries

2 tablespoons sugar

Mix and sift dry ingredients. Cut in the shortening. Add the blueberries. Add the milk. Mix thoroughly. Pour into a greased mould. Steam two hours. Serve with hard sauce or whipped cream. Blueberry sauce may be served with this pudding. If sauce is used top with whipped cream.

Steamed Pudding

½ cup molasses	½ cup milk
1 cup flour	½ cup raisins
2 tablespoons butter	1 teaspoon soda

1 egg

Beat egg with molasses and milk. Add melted shortening and raisins. Mix soda with flour. Add the dry ingredients. Mix smooth. Turn into greased mould and steam one hour. Serve with whipped cream, hard sauce, or foamy sauce.

Steamed Chocolate Pudding

½ cup sugar	2 teaspoons melted butter
1 egg	½ cup milk
1 teaspoon baking powder	⅛ teaspoon salt
⅞ cup flour	1½ squares bitter chocolate

1 teaspoon vanilla

Beat egg until light. Add sugar and salt. Add melted butter. Mix baking powder with flour. Add dry ingredients and milk alternately to egg mixture. Add melted chocolate. Add vanilla. Mix thoroughly. Pour into greased mould and steam one and one-half hours. Serve hot with whipped cream, hard sauce, or foamy sauce.

Snow Pudding

1 tablespoon granulated gelatine   1 cup boiling water
¼ cup cold water   ½ cup sugar
¼ cup lemon juice   3 egg whites

Soak the gelatine in cold water. Make a syrup by boiling sugar and water. Remove from fire and add to soaked gelatine. Stir until gelatine is dissolved. Add lemon juice when mixture is cool. Stir occasionally until it begins to thicken, then beat with egg beater until frothy. Add beaten egg whites. Put bowl into pan of ice water and beat until stiff enough to hold its shape. Pour into mould and chill. Serve with custard sauce.

Hard Sauce, No. 1

¼ cup butter creamed   ¾ cup confectioners' sugar
⅛ teaspoon salt   1 teaspoon vanilla

Cream ingredients thoroughly and chill.

Hard Sauce, No. 2

⅓ cup butter   ½ teaspoon vanilla
⅛ teaspoon salt   1 egg yolk
                1 cup confectioners' sugar

Cream butter and add sugar gradually. Add salt and vanilla. Mix thoroughly. Add egg yolk. Mix well. Chill before serving.

Hard Sauce with Egg

1 cup confectioners' sugar   ⅓ cup butter
⅛ teaspoon salt   1 teaspoon vanilla
                1 egg

Cream butter. Add salt, sugar, and vanilla. Mix thoroughly. Add beaten egg. Mix well. Chill before serving.

Creamy Hard Sauce

½ cup butter   ½ cup cream
1 cup confectioners' sugar   1 teaspoon vanilla

Cream butter. Add sugar and mix until well blended. Add vanilla. Fold in whipped cream. Chill before serving.

Foamy Hard Sauce

½ cup butter
1 cup confectioners' sugar
⅛ teaspoon salt

1 cup cream
1 egg
1 teaspoon vanilla

Cream butter. Add sugar and salt. Mix well. Add vanilla and beaten egg. Mix thoroughly. Fold in whipped cream. Chill before serving.

Peach Hard Sauce

⅓ cup butter
¼ cup peach pulp

1 cup confectioners' sugar
½ teaspoon almond extract
⅛ teaspoon salt

Cream butter and add the sugar gradually. Add the peach pulp, salt, and extract. Mix thoroughly. Chill before serving. Apricot or prunes may be substituted for the peach.

Lemon Sauce, No. 1

3 tablespoons flour
⅛ teaspoon salt
1 cup water

½ cup sugar
2 tablespoons butter
1 lemon (juice and rind)

Mix flour with salt and sugar. Add water. Stir until smooth. Cook until thick. Add rind and juice of lemon. Stir until well mixed. Serve hot or cold. Orange may be substituted for lemon if desired.

Lemon Sauce, No. 2

2 tablespoons flour
⅛ teaspoon salt
1 cup water

½ cup sugar
1 tablespoon butter
1 egg

1 lemon (juice and rind)

Mix flour with salt and sugar. Add water. Stir until smooth. Cook until thick. Add rind and juice of lemon. Add beaten egg. Mix thoroughly. Serve hot or cold. Orange may be substituted for lemon if desired.

Hot Chocolate Sauce

¼ cup cream
⅛ teaspoon salt
1 square chocolate

1 tablespoon butter
½ cup sugar
½ teaspoon vanilla

Melt chocolate over hot water. Add the butter and the cream. Then add sugar. Stir until sugar is dissolved. Cook five minutes. Add vanilla. Serve at once.

Chocolate Sauce

1 square bitter chocolate
½ cup sugar

1 teaspoon vanilla
¼ cup heavy cream

⅛ teaspoon salt

Mix ingredients. Stir over flame until chocolate melts. Cook two minutes. Serve hot. Top sauce with nuts or whipped cream.

Fudge Sauce

1 cup sugar
½ cup cream
⅛ teaspoon salt

2 tablespoons butter
1 teaspoon vanilla
2 squares chocolate

Mix sugar, salt, cream, and chocolate. Cook over flame until chocolate melts. Simmer five minutes. Add butter and vanilla. Mix well. Serve hot. Top with salted nuts.

Butterscotch Sauce, No. 1

¾ pound vanilla caramels   ½ cup heavy cream
1 teaspoon vanilla

Melt caramels in top of double boiler. Add cream and vanilla. Mix thoroughly. Heat. Serve hot. One-quarter pound marshmallows quartered may be added if desired.

Butterscotch Sauce, No. 2

1½ cups brown sugar
1 cup syrup
¼ teaspoon salt

2 cups cream
¼ cup butter
1 teaspoon vanilla

Boil sugar, syrup, salt, and cream until the mixture forms a soft ball in cold water. Add butter. Cool and add vanilla. Serve either hot or cold.

CHAPTER XXVII
Salads and Salad Dressings

Frozen Vegetable Salad

3 cups of cooked vegetables (peas, lima beans, carrots, celery, and onion juice)
1 cup mayonnaise

2 teaspoons gelatine (soaked in 2 tablespoons cold water and melted over hot water)
1 cup whipped cream

Add melted gelatine to mayonnaise and whipped cream. Fold vegetables into dressing. Freeze three hours.

Vegetable Salad

Put bed of chilled lettuce leaves on salad plates. Use whole cooked peas, carrots, beets, and string beans. Arrange the vegetables separately on lettuce. Have vegetables contrasting in color come next to each other. Garnish with radishes, celery tips, or pickles. Serve with French dressing.

Cabbage Salad

Soak two pounds cabbage in cold water one hour. Shred fine. Mix with boiled dressing and serve on a lettuce leaf. Top with whipped cream. Garnish with paprika and parsley. Center of a cabbage is best for salad.

Green Bean Salad

Remove strings from one pound string beans. Slice lengthwise and cook in boiling salted water for forty-five minutes. Drain and cool. Add one onion, chopped fine, and French dressing. Serve garnished with parsley and paprika.

Red Beet and Onion Salad

On bed of lettuce leaves place alternately slices of red beets and slices of onion. Serve with a French dressing and garnish with parsley.

Turned Salad

2 heads of lettuce   ½ cup French dressing
1 clove of garlic

Separate lettuce. Wash and chill thoroughly. Leave lettuce leaves large. Put into large bowl. Add garlic to French dressing. Let stand thirty minutes. Remove garlic. Pour dressing over lettuce. Mix thoroughly with fork and spoon, turning lettuce in dressing. Serve as dinner salad.

One-half cup sliced radishes or three tablespoons finely cut chives may be added to this salad on occasion. Roquefort dressing may be used instead of French dressing.

Tomato and Cottage Cheese Salad

Select four firm tomatoes. Cut slice from stem end. With a spoon scoop out pulp. Mix one pound cottage cheese with two tablespoons chopped chives and one-quarter cup cream. Season with one-eighth teaspoon salt. Mix thoroughly. Fill tomatoes with mixture. Serve on bed of lettuce leaves. Garnish with parsley. Serve with French dressing.

Endive Salad

Wash endive and chill until crisp. Serve with a French dressing. Garnish with paprika and parsley.

Rings of green pepper may be served with this if desired.

Potato Salad

6 medium-size potatoes   1 pint salad dressing
1 onion   6 hard-cooked eggs
1 cup whipped cream   1 cucumber

Boil potatoes. When cool, dice the potatoes. Add onion grated, cucumber diced, and egg whites sliced. Mix with salad dressing to which whipped cream has been added. Serve on bed of lettuce leaves. Garnish with egg yolk which has been riced. Top with parsley. One cup of celery may be substituted for the cucumber.

Stuffed Green Pepper Salad

2 cream cheeses
2 tablespoons nut meats (chopped fine)
1 pimento (cut fine)
1 green pepper

Mix nuts and pimento with cheese. Add enough cream to mix smooth. Remove stem end and seeds from green pepper. Fill pepper with the cream cheese mixture. Chill pepper thoroughly. Then slice with a sharp knife into as thin slices as possible. Serve slices on lettuce leaves. Garnish with paprika and parsley. Mayonnaise or French dressing may be served with this salad.

Egg and Tomato Salad

On a bed of crisp lettuce leaves arrange alternate slices of hard-cooked egg and tomato. Garnish with parsley. Serve with French dressing to which chopped chives have been added.

Cole Slaw, No. 1

3 cups shredded cabbage
4 strips bacon (fried crisp and cut fine)
1 small onion (chopped)
1 pimento (chopped)
1 green pepper (chopped)

Shred cabbage and put into cold water. Drain. Mix with other ingredients. Serve with French dressing.

Cole Slaw, No. 2

3 cups cabbage (shredded fine)
1 tablespoon chopped onion
½ cup boiled dressing
½ cup whipped cream
1 green pepper (chopped)

Mix ingredients thoroughly and serve on bed of lettuce leaves. Garnish with paprika and parsley.

Tomato Aspic

4 cups canned tomatoes
1 onion (chopped)
2 tablespoons sugar
1½ teaspoons salt
1 bay leaf
6 whole peppers
½ teaspoon celery seed
1½ tablespoons gelatine
¼ cup cold water

Mix tomatoes, onion, and spices. Simmer for one-half hour. Rub through strainer. Add gelatine softened in cold water. Pour into mould. Let stand overnight. Turn out on bed of lettuce leaves. Garnish with parsley. Serve with Mayonnaise dressing.

Tomato Jelly

1 tablespoon gelatine	¼ teaspoon salt (or other seasoning)
¼ cup cold water	1 cup stewed and strained tomato

Soak gelatine in cold water until softened, add hot tomato and seasoning. Pour into small moulds and chill thoroughly. When ready to serve, turn out on lettuce leaves. Garnish with capers, or olives, hard-cooked eggs, or pickles. Serve with mayonnaise dressing.

Perfection Salad

2 tablespoons granulated gelatine	6 small pickles (chopped fine)
½ cup cold water	2 cups boiling water
½ cup vinegar	½ cup sugar
2 tablespoons lemon juice	1 teaspoon salt
1 cup diced celery	1 cup finely shredded cabbage
1 green pepper (cut fine)	2 pimentos (chopped fine)

Soak the gelatine in cold water for five minutes. Add vinegar, lemon juice, boiling water, sugar, and salt. Stir until dissolved and set in a cool place. When the mixture begins to set, add the remainder of ingredients.

Turn into moulds which have been rinsed with cold water. Chill until firm. Serve on lettuce leaves with mayonnaise dressing. Garnish with parsley.

Jellied Cheese Salad

1 pound American cheese (grated)	Salt and pepper
½ cup cold water	2 tablespoons gelatine
1½ cups boiling water	

Soak gelatine in cold water. Dissolve in boiling water. Pour into mould. When gelatine begins to set, beat with rotary beater. Mix thoroughly with one cup whipped cream. Add cheese. Pour into mould and allow to set. Serve with peaches or pears on bed of lettuce.

Cucumber Salad

Slice one cucumber fine, and let stand one-half hour in ice water. Then drain. To one-half cup heavy cream add two tablespoons lemon juice, one-eighth teaspoon salt, dash of pepper, and one teaspoon sugar. Mix this dressing with cucumber and serve on lettuce leaves. Garnish with paprika and parsley.

Cream Cheese Anchovy Salad

1 can pears	3 tablespoons top milk
1 cream cheese	½ cup celery (cut fine)
3 tablespoons anchovy paste	

Drain pears and arrange on bed of lettuce leaves with hollow sides up. Add top milk to cream cheese and anchovy paste and mix thoroughly. Add celery. Fill center of pears with mixture. Serve with a French dressing and garnish with paprika and parsley.

Cabbage Pineapple Salad

1 medium head cabbage (shredded)	1 can pineapple (diced)
¼ pound marshmallows (quartered)	

Put cabbage into cold water for half an hour. Drain. Add marshmallows and pineapple. Mix thoroughly with one cup boiled salad dressing and one cup whipped cream. Serve on a lettuce leaf garnished with paprika and parsley.

Apple Celery Salad

6 red apples (cut not too fine)	1 cup celery (cut not too fine)
1 cup walnut meats	

Mix these ingredients with boiled salad dressing. Turn on lettuce leaves, and top with whipped cream. Garnish with paprika and parsley.

Cranberry Salad

Cook one quart cranberries in three and one-half cups water for thirty minutes. Soak two tablespoons granulated gelatine in one-half cup cold water. Strain the cranberry mixture over it, and stir until dissolved. Let stand until cool. When cool, add one cup chopped nuts, one cup diced pineapple, and one cup seeded white grapes. Pour into wet moulds. Chill overnight. Serve on lettuce leaves with mayonnaise or boiled dressing. Garnish with parsley.

Cucumber and Grape in Aspic

½ cup cucumber (chopped fine)	½ cup lemon juice
½ cup seedless green grapes	½ cup orange juice
2 tablespoons gelatine	¼ cup cold water

1 cup boiling water

Soak gelatine in cold water. Add boiling water, and stir until dissolved. Add fruit juices, then cucumber and grapes. Pour into individual moulds. Let set until firm. Serve on lettuce leaf. Top with boiled or mayonnaise dressing. Garnish with parsley.

Ginger Ale Salad

4 tablespoons gelatine	1 cup sugar
2 cups ginger ale	Juice of 1 lemon
2 tablespoons pineapple juice	Juice of 1 orange
¼ cup grenadine	1 cup cherries
½ cup pineapple	¼ cup blanched almonds

Soak the gelatine in one-quarter cup of cold water. Pour over it one cup boiling water. Stir until the gelatine is dissolved. Add the ginger ale and fruit juices, then other ingredients. Pour into moulds and chill. Serve in hearts of lettuce with a mayonnaise dressing, or boiled dressing. Garnish with parsley.

Pistachio Salad

1 tablespoon gelatine	Juice of 1 orange
¼ cup cold water	Juice of ½ lemon
1 cup hot water	¼ teaspoon salt

Soak gelatine in cold water. Add hot water. Stir until gelatine dissolves. Add fruit juices. Tint a delicate green, and when it begins to set add one-quarter cup chopped pistachio nuts and one-half cup finely cut celery. Turn into mould and put in cool place to set. Serve on lettuce leaves and garnish with mayonnaise, parsley, and paprika.

Fruit Salad Aspic

2 tablespoons gelatine	1 lemon
½ cup cold water	1 grapefruit
2 cups hot water	½ cup grapes (green, seedless)
¼ cup sugar	3 peaches
2 oranges	3 pears

Soften the gelatine in cold water and dissolve in hot water. In place of the water canned fruit juice may be used. Add the sugar and stir until dissolved. Add the juice of the oranges and lemons. When the mixture begins to stiffen, add grapefruit sections, grapes, and sliced peaches and pears. Turn into a mould (preferably a ring mould). When firm unmould onto bed of lettuce leaves. Serve with mayonnaise dressing.

The fruit may be omitted in making this salad. Pour the clear fruit mixture into ring mould. When firm, unmould onto bed of lettuce. Fill center with fresh fruit. Serve with mayonnaise dressing. Top with paprika and parsley.

Vegetable Aspic Ring

2 cups tomato juice (strained)	1 onion (chopped)
½ cup lemon juice	1 green pepper (chopped)
3 tablespoons gelatine	¼ cup cold water

Soak gelatine in cold water. Heat tomato juice. Add gelatine and stir until dissolved. Add lemon juice and cool. Add chopped onion and green pepper. Pour into ring mould. Let set until firm. Chill. Serve on bed of lettuce leaves. Garnish with slices of cucumber and celery. Serve with Perfection salad dressing.

Jellied Asparagus Loaf

2 cups chicken stock
1 green pepper (cut fine)
½ cup celery (cut fine)

3 tablespoons gelatine
1 pimento (cut fine)

Soak gelatine in cold water. Add hot chicken stock. Stir until gelatine dissolves. Add pimento, green pepper, and celery. Fill mould with layers of asparagus tips. Pour gelatine mixture over asparagus. Let stand until it sets. Cool and unmould on bed of lettuce leaves. Garnish with parsley and radish roses. Serve with dressing made by mixing equal parts of boiled salad dressing and whipped cream.

Cheese and Nut Salad

1 cup cottage cheese
1 tablespoon melted butter
½ cup sweet cream

⅓ cup chopped nuts
⅓ cup chopped pimento
⅓ cup chopped olives

Mash the cheese, then moisten with cream and melted butter. Season with salt and cayenne, add chopped nuts, pimento, and olives. Press into a mould and let stand two hours in refrigerator. Unmould. Cut in slices and serve on lettuce leaf with mayonnaise dressing.

Stuffed Egg Salad

8 hard-cooked eggs

Salad dressing

Cut eggs in half and remove yolks. Mix yolks with salad dressing and return to the whites. Serve on bed of lettuce. Garnish with parsley and paprika. Serve with mayonnaise.

Fruit Salad, No. 1

6 slices pineapple
8 large red apples
12 maraschino cherries

⅔ cup sliced peaches
1 cup white grapes

Use one slice of pineapple for each serving. Core apples, but do not peel. Quarter, and divide each quarter into fourths,

cutting so that some of red peel remains on each piece. Skin
and seed the grapes. Place slices of pineapple on crisp lettuce
leaves. Combine other ingredients in order given and place
on the pineapple. Serve with French, mayonnaise, or Chantilly
dressing. Garnish with parsley.

Fruit Salad, No. 2

Cut one-quarter pound marshmallows in thin strips. Add
one-half can sliced pineapple, drained and diced. Add two and
three-quarters cups white cherries, pitted and cut in halves;
one-half cup English walnut meats, and two bananas sliced.
Mix with cream salad dressing. Serve on lettuce leaves. Garnish top of each salad with a strip of pimento and finely chopped
parsley.

Fruit Salad, No. 3

1 cup pineapple (diced)	¼ pound marshmallows (quartered)
1 orange (diced)	12 dates (pitted and halved)
1 apple (diced)	2 pears (diced)
2 bananas (sliced)	2 peaches (diced)
12 strawberries (in season)	

Mix the above ingredients with one cup salad dressing and
one cup whipped cream. Serve on bed of lettuce leaves. Garnish with paprika and parsley.

Frozen Fruit Salad

3 cups fruit (pineapple, bananas, oranges, sliced peaches)	1 cup mayonnaise
	2 teaspoons gelatine (soaked in 2 tablespoons cold water and melted over hot water)
Raspberries, black cherries, or strawberries for color	1 cup cream (whipped)

Add melted gelatine to mayonnaise and whipped cream. Fold
fruit into dressing. Freeze three hours.

Chicken Salad, No. 1

2 cups cooked chicken (cut in small pieces)
2 cups celery (cut in small pieces)
¼ cup capers
½ cup stuffed olives
1 cup cooked peas
Mayonnaise

Mix together chicken, celery, and peas and let stand in French dressing half an hour. Drain, add olives, and enough mayonnaise to moisten. Arrange in bowl, or on a platter on crisp lettuce leaves. Garnish with mayonnaise and sprinkle with capers and paprika. Top with sprig of parsley. Slices of hard-cooked egg may be added if desired.

Chicken Salad, No. 2

Cut cooked chicken into cubes and marinate. Add an equal quantity of crisp celery, cut fine. Just before serving, mix with mayonnaise. Serve on bed of lettuce. Top with paprika and parsley. Garnish with hearts of celery and slices of pickles.

Veal Salad

Cut three pounds cooked veal into cubes and marinate with French dressing. Allow to stand an hour or more to develop flavor. Add an equal amount of crisp celery, cut fine. Just before serving, mix with mayonnaise. Nuts or peas may be added, if desired. Serve on lettuce leaves. Garnish with hard-cooked eggs, curled celery, capers, or pickles. Top with paprika and parsley. Pork may be substituted for the veal in this rule.

Sunday Night Supper Salad

On center of plate, tea size, place in cupped lettuce leaves one whole tomato, stuffed with chicken salad. Radiating from this four thin slices of buttered bread. On first slice heap ground chives; on second, cream cheese; third, ground nuts; on fourth, ground cold meats. Place whole stuffed olives on side of plate. Garnish with parsley.

Tuna Fish Salad

1 cup tuna fish	1 cup peas
(broken not too fine)	1 cup celery
3 hard-cooked eggs (sliced)	

Mix with salad dressing and serve on lettuce leaves. Garnish with paprika and parsley. Top with capers. Salmon may be substituted for the tuna fish.

Tuna Fish and Apple

2 cups flaked tuna fish	2 tart red apples

Do not peel apples. Cut into quarters and remove core. Cut into thin slices and arrange on bed of lettuce leaves. Marinate fish with French dressing. Put fish over apples. Serve with boiled dressing. Garnish with parsley.

Fish and Potato Salad

Flake two cups of cold cooked fish. Marinate with French dressing.

Marinate two cups of diced cooked potatoes. Let stand in cool place one hour.

Slice six hard-boiled eggs. Mix fish, potatoes, eggs, and three tablespoons capers with mayonnaise. Serve on lettuce. Garnish with parsley.

Shrimp Salad

2 cups cooked shrimps	1 cup peas
3 hard-cooked eggs	1 cup celery
1 cup salad dressing	½ cup whipped cream

Add cream to salad dressing. Add other ingredients. Mix thoroughly. Serve on bed of lettuce leaves. Garnish with paprika and parsley.

Crabmeat Salad

2 cups crabmeat	1 green pepper (chopped)
1 cup celery (diced)	1 pimento (chopped)
½ cup salad dressing	¼ cup whipped cream

Add cream to salad dressing. Add pepper, pimento, celery, and crabmeat. Mix well. Serve on bed of lettuce leaves. Garnish with hard-cooked egg and slices of tomato. Top with parsley.

Lobster Salad, No. 1

3 cups cooked lobster meat (diced)	½ cup whipped cream
1 cup celery (diced)	¾ cup salad dressing

Mix cream with salad dressing. Add celery and lobster. Mix thoroughly. Serve on bed of lettuce leaves. Sprinkle with capers. Garnish with paprika and parsley. Stuffed eggs may be served as a garnish for this salad.

Lobster Salad, No. 2

2 cups cooked lobster meat (diced)	1 cup peas
1 cup celery (diced)	1 cup salad dressing
3 hard-cooked eggs (sliced)	½ cup whipped cream

Mix dressing with whipped cream. Add celery, eggs, peas, and lobster. Mix thoroughly. Serve on bed of lettuce leaves. Garnish with paprika and parsley.

DRESSINGS

Best French Dressing

Fill a quart jar two-thirds full of oil and one-third full of vinegar. Add two tablespoons sugar, one tablespoon salt, and two tablespoons paprika. Will keep indefinitely in a cold place. Shake well before using. Chopped onion or garlic may be added.

French Dressing

1 clove	1 cup lemon juice
1 teaspoon salt	1½ cups oil (mixed with garlic
2 teaspoons sugar	and grated onion)
1 teaspoon mustard	Speck paprika
Few drops tabasco	1 teaspoon sauce

2 teaspoons catsup or chili sauce

Mix ingredients in order given. Beat well with egg beater. Bottle and shake well before using.

French Dressing with Pearl Onions

To one-half cup French dressing add one-quarter cup pearl onions. Serve on plain lettuce or endive.

French Dressing with Caviar

To one-half cup of French dressing add three tablespoons caviar. Serve on plain lettuce or tomato and lettuce salad.

Cucumber Dressing

½ cup French dressing   3 tablespoons chopped cucumber

2 tablespoons chopped onion

Mix well and chill before using.

Mayonnaise Dressing, No. 1

1 egg yolk	1 teaspoon paprika
1 tablespoon vinegar	1 cup oil
1½ teaspoons mustard	1 tablespoon lemon juice

½ teaspoon salt

Beat egg yolks thoroughly. Add cold oil drop by drop, beating continually until thick, then add vinegar and lemon until thin. Add more oil until thick, and then thin as before. Repeat until all ingredients are used. Whipped cream may be added if desired.

Mayonnaise Dressing, No. 2

1 egg (whole)
1 teaspoon salt
2 cups oil
3 tablespoons lemon juice
2 teaspoons dry mustard

Beat egg and add dry ingredients. Add oil drop by drop, beating all of the time until thick. Then add lemon juice and oil alternately. Pour into jars. Keep in cool place. Mix with cream before serving.

Thousand Island Dressing

To one cup mayonnaise dressing add:

2 tablespoons green pepper (chopped)
1 hard-cooked egg (chopped)
1 teaspoon sauce
¾ cup whipped cream
3 tablespoons chili sauce
2 tablespoons pimento (chopped)
1 tablespoon onion juice
1 tablespoon catsup

Mix thoroughly and chill.

Russian Dressing

To one cup mayonnaise dressing add:

1 hard-cooked egg (chopped fine)
2 sweet pickles (chopped)
½ cup chili sauce
1 small onion (chopped)
¼ cup capers
1 green pepper (chopped)
1 red pepper (chopped)

Mix well. Blend with cream before serving, if desired.

Perfection Salad Dressing

½ cup shortening
4 tablespoons flour
2 tablespoons sugar
2 tablespoons dry mustard
1 tablespoon salt
1 pint milk
4 eggs
1 cup vinegar

Melt shortening in top of double boiler. Add dry ingredients and blend smooth. Add milk and cook to soft custard stage. Beat eggs with vinegar. Put with first mixture and again cook to soft-custard stage. Pour into jars. Will make one quart dressing which will keep, in a cool place, for one season. Mix with whipped cream before using.

CHAPTER XXVIII

Sandwiches and Canapés

Toasted Cream Pimento Sandwich

1 pound American cheese	¾ cup milk
3 pimentos	1 teaspoon salt
¼ teaspoon paprika	¼ teaspoon mustard

Put cheese and pimento through food chopper. Put in double boiler and add milk, stirring until melted and creamy. Add salt and paprika and mustard.

For hot cheese sandwich, butter one slice of bread, spread the other slice with the cheese, and put together. Toast on both sides and cut diagonally. Serve at once. May be garnished with broiled bacon and sprig of parsley.

Mushroom Sandwiches

½ pound mushrooms	½ cup cream
3 tablespoons butter	1½ cups sugar
1 tablespoon flour	Yolks of 2 eggs
Salt	Paprika

Celery salt

Break off stems of mushrooms. Cut them in small pieces and simmer fifteen minutes in water. Peel mushrooms, put through food grinder, and cook in the butter five minutes. Add flour and stock from the stems (which are discarded). Add cream. Add seasonings. Cook five minutes. Add yolks the last minute of cooking. Cool. Make sandwiches with thin buttered triangular pieces of bread. Toast slightly under the broiler on both sides and serve immediately, very hot.

Open Sandwich

3 eggs	¾ teaspoon salt
½ teaspoon paprika	¾ pound bacon

¾ pound cheese

Beat eggs until light. Add grated cheese. Add other ingredients and mix well, then spread on eight slices of bread cut one-quarter inch thick. Cut bacon in very thin slices the length of the slice of bread. Cover cheese with bacon and bake ten minutes in hot oven (400° F.). Garnish with parsley.

Open Club Sandwich

Take two slices buttered toast, and cover both slices with lettuce. On one bed of lettuce arrange alternate slices of tomato and cucumber. On the other bed of lettuce put slices of breast of chicken. Garnish with parsley and strips of broiled bacon. Serve with mayonnaise dressing.

Club Sandwich

Four slices of toast, buttered. Cover bottom slice with lettuce and spread with mayonnaise, over which place three strips of bacon and a slice of white meat of chicken. Cover with second piece of toast on which is a lettuce leaf, spread with mayonnaise dressing, and sliced tomatoes. Cover with the next slice of toast. Spread with lettuce and mayonnaise dressing and white meat of chicken. Cover with fourth slice of toast. Cut in half diagonally. Garnish with olives and a sprig of parsley. Lobster, sweetbreads, or tuna fish may be used instead of chicken.

Cream Cheese and Celery Sandwich

1 cream cheese	2 tablespoons Anchovy paste
2 tablespoons cream	¼ cup finely chopped celery

Mix ingredients together and spread between thin, buttered slices of graham bread.

Cream Cheese and Date Sandwich

To one cream cheese add ten dates, cut fine, and one-half cup chopped nuts. Add mayonnaise dressing to spread. Put between slices of graham bread, cut thin and buttered.

Scrambled Egg and Pepper Sandwich

Chop one green pepper fine and cook in one tablespoon butter. When the pepper is hot, break an egg over it and scramble. Put between slices of buttered bread. Onion juice may be added if desired.

Egg and Olive Sandwich

Chop four hard-boiled eggs very fine. Chop twelve large stuffed olives and mix with the eggs. Moisten with mayonnaise dressing, season with salt and pepper. Mix thoroughly. Spread on slices of buttered bread.

Nut, Cheese, and Olive Sandwich

Mix one cream cheese with an equal amount of finely chopped pecan meats and olives. Moisten with mayonnaise dressing. Spread between thin slices of buttered bread.

Grated Cheese Sandwich

Grate American cheese fine and mix with melted butter. Spread between slices of unbuttered bread. Toast.

Swiss Cheese Sandwich

Cut rye bread very thin. Spread with butter. Between the slices place thin slices of Swiss cheese, spread with mustard.

Cheese Dream

Cut bread very thin. Spread with butter. Between the slices place thin slices of American cheese. Fry in butter. Turn once. Serve at once garnished with jelly.

Swiss Cheese and Ham Sandwich

Cut bread very thin. Spread with butter. Between the slices place a thin slice of ham. Cover ham with slice of Swiss cheese. Spread with mustard.

Shrimp Salad Sandwich

1 cup cold shrimp (chopped)   ½ cup celery (chopped fine)
¼ cup stuffed olives (chopped fine)

Mix ingredients with mayonnaise dressing. Spread between thin slices of buttered bread. Chicken, salmon, lobster, or tuna fish may be substituted instead of the shrimp.

Delicious Sandwich

Mix together equal parts of cream cheese and apricot pulp made by pressing through a sieve stewed or canned apricots which have been well drained. Add mayonnaise dressing to taste. Spread between thin buttered slices of bread. Nuts may be added if desired.

Cold Roast Beef Sandwich

2 cups cold roast beef   1 teaspoon vinegar
    (chopped fine)   Dash of pepper
1 tablespoon catsup   2 tablespoons melted butter
            Mayonnaise dressing to moisten

Mix well and spread between thin slices of buttered bread.

Corned Beef Sandwich

Slice beef very fine. Spread with mustard. Put on a lettuce leaf between thin slices of buttered bread. Rye bread is best

Appetizing Sandwich

Mash six slices of liver sausage with three hard-cooked eggs (chopped), one-half teaspoon mustard, one-half cup boiled ham (chopped), two sweet pickles (chopped). Mix ingredients with enough salad dressing to moisten. Spread between thin slices of buttered bread.

Vegetable Sandwich

6 tomatoes   1 medium-sized onion
                    1 green pepper

Chop onion and green pepper. Slice the tomatoes. Butter thin slices of bread. Cover with slices of tomato. Cover tomato with chopped mixture. Season with salt, pepper, and lemon juice. Cover with slices of buttered bread.

Tomato Sandwich

Cover a slice of buttered bread with slices of tomato and slices of onion. Season with salt and pepper. Top with another slice of buttered bread.

Tomato and Cucumber Sandwich

Spread thin slices of bread with salad dressing. Cover with lettuce. Put over the lettuce slices of tomato and slices of cucumber. Cover with slices of bread spread with salad dressing.

Hot Roast Beef Sandwich

Place one slice of hot, rare roast beef, cut not too thin, between slices of buttered bread. Cover with hot brown gravy and serve at once.

Veal, pork, lamb, and chicken may be used in the same manner.

Tongue Sandwich

Between thin slices of buttered bread lay a crisp lettuce leaf that has been spread with mayonnaise dressing, and slices of tongue. Cut in half diagonally. Garnish with parsley.

Celery Sandwich

1 cup celery (chopped fine)   ¼ cup stuffed olives (chopped fine)
½ cup cucumber (chopped fine)

Mix ingredients with salad dressing and spread between thin slices of buttered bread. Whole-wheat bread is best.

Peanut Butter and Strawberry Jam Sandwich

Spread two slices of graham bread with butter. Cover one with peanut butter and the other with strawberry jam. Fold together. Cut in half before serving.

Cream Cheese with Orange Marmalade

Spread two slices of whole-wheat bread with butter. Cover one with cream cheese and the other with orange marmalade. Fold together. Nut meats may be added. Halve before serving. Ginger marmalade may be used instead of orange marmalade.

Cream Cheese with Raspberry Jam

Spread two slices of whole-wheat bread with butter. Cover one slice with cream cheese and the other with raspberry jam. Cover jam with chopped black walnuts. Fold together. Halve before serving.

Cream Cheese and Pepper Relish

2 cream cheeses   ½ cup pepper relish

Mix cream cheese with pepper relish. Spread between thin slices of buttered bread. Halve before serving.

Dried Beef with Cream Cheese and Chives

To two cream cheeses, add one-third cup chopped chives and enough cream to mix smooth. Cover slices of buttered bread with dried beef. Put layer of cream cheese between beef-covered bread. Cut diagonally in half before serving.

Dried Beef with Pepper and Onion

To two cream cheeses add one green pepper cut fine and two tablespoons of onion cut very fine. Add enough cream to mix smooth. Cover slices of buttered bread with dried beef. Put layer of cream cheese mixture between beef-covered bread. Cut in half before serving.

Liver Sausage Sandwich

½ pound liver sausage

Mash the liver sausage thoroughly and add salad dressing to moisten. Spread between thin slices of buttered rye bread.

Picnic Sandwich

1 cup ham (chopped)   1 cup stuffed olives (chopped)
½ cup celery (chopped)   1 cup nuts (chopped)

Mix ingredients with salad dressing to spread. Put between thin slices of buttered bread. Halve sandwiches.

Bacon, Egg, and Onion Sandwich

5 slices crisp fried bacon   3 hard-cooked eggs
                      Small onion

Put above ingredients through food grinder. Mix with salad dressing. Spread on slices of buttered bread.

Supper Sandwich

1 cream cheese   ½ green pepper (cut fine)
½ pimento (cut fine)   2 hard-cooked eggs

Rice the eggs. Add the other ingredients. Mix with salad dressing to moisten. Spread between thin buttered slices of graham bread.

Lenten Sandwich

4 hard-cooked eggs (chopped)   3 sweet pickles (chopped)

Mix egg and pickles with mayonnaise dressing to spread. Put between thin buttered slices of bread. A leaf of lettuce added to this sandwich may be used occasionally for variation.

Sliced Chicken Sandwich

Spread thin slices of buttered bread with mayonnaise dressing. Cover each slice with leaf of lettuce. Cover lettuce with thin slices of breast of chicken. Garnish with paprika and parsley. May be served as an open or closed sandwich.

Sandwich Loaf

Remove crust from a loaf of bread. Slice bread lengthwise four times. Butter on both sides of all the slices except the top and bottom ones. Make filling as follows:

Red: Four slices ham (chopped), one pimento (chopped).

Yellow: Three hard-cooked eggs mixed with mayonnaise.

White: One-half package cream cheese softened with one-quarter cucumber (chopped) and one tablespoon onion juice.

Green: Four small sweet pickles, one-quarter cup chives (chopped).

Spread slices of buttered bread with the fillings in the order given. Mix three cream cheeses with sweet cream and spread on the outside of loaf. Keep in cold place several hours before slicing. Garnish for serving.

This loaf may be served for luncheon, supper, or tea. Arrange loaf on platter. Garnish with lettuce leaves, hearts of celery, stuffed eggs, slices of tomato, radishes, pickles, and olives.

Chicken salad and lobster salad fillings may be used instead of those given above.

Caviar Canapé

Slice bread thin. Cut into circles or diamond-shaped pieces and toast. Mix the following thoroughly: one-half cup caviar, juice of one-half lemon, one tablespoon chopped onion, and three tablespoons melted butter. Let cool and spread on the rounds of toast. Garnish with pearl onions and parsley. Hard-cooked egg may also be used as a garnish.

Smoked Salmon Canapé

Slice bread thin. Cut into circles and toast. Cover the rounds of toast with mayonnaise dressing. Cut smoked salmon into pieces the same size as toast. Cover the bread with salmon. Garnish with finely chopped, hard-cooked white of egg.

For Dessert in Hot Weather—Fruit Salad

CHAPTER XXIX

Soups

Corn Chowder

1 chopped onion
1 ounce salt pork
2 cans corn

1 potato (diced)
2 cups boiling water
1 quart milk

Salt and pepper

Cut salt pork fine. Fry the salt pork. Skim out the meat
and fry the onion in the fat. Simmer the corn in the two cups
of boiling water for about ten minutes. Add the milk and diced
potato, pork, onion, salt, and pepper. When well blended,
serve with crackers.

Vegetable Chowder

1 cup tomatoes
2 cups milk
½ teaspoon salt
⅛ teaspoon pepper
1 cup cooked potatoes (diced)

1 onion (chopped)
1 tablespoon butter
1 tablespoon flour
1 cup canned corn
4 slices bacon (cut fine)

Fry onion and bacon in butter until brown. Add flour and
cook two minutes. Add corn, potatoes, salt, pepper, and milk.
Let simmer forty-five minutes. Serve hot with crackers.

Chicken Soup

5-pound fowl
1 tablespoon salt

1 sliced onion
Rice or noodles

Clean and singe the fowl, and wash thoroughly. Put in kettle
and cover with boiling water. Add the sliced onion and salt.
Cook two to two and one-half hours. Remove fowl, then add
the rice or noodles to chicken stock. If there is an excess of fat,
soup may be cooled and fat removed before adding the rice or
noodles. Stock may be strained before adding rice or noodles.

Soup Stock

5 pounds beef (with bone)   ½ cup dried celery leaves
1 large onion (sliced)   2 carrots (diced)
            2 tablespoons salt

Put beef and vegetables into kettle and cover with boiling
water. Cook two to two and one-half hours. Rice or noodles
may be added. Stock may be strained before adding rice or
noodles.

Julienne Soup

2 cups mixed vegetables (celery,   2 quarts soup stock
    carrots, peas, potatoes, and   ½ teaspoon salt
    onions)   ¼ teaspoon pepper

Dice the vegetables. Mix all the ingredients and let simmer
one hour. Serve with chopped parsley and paprika.

Vegetable Soup

1 cup tomato   1 tablespoon salt
1 cup potato (diced)   1 cup carrots (diced)
1 cup string beans   1 cup celery (cut fine)
1 cup peas   1 cup corn
2 tablespoons parsley (chopped)   1 large onion (chopped fine)
            3 quarts boiling water

Mix all the vegetables together and add the boiling water.
Let simmer from one and one-half to two hours. A soup bone
may be added if stock flavoring is desired. Serve hot with
chopped parsley and dash of paprika.

Essence of Celery

One bunch of celery, stalks and leaves, cut fine. Cover with
two quarts cold water and one tablespoon salt. Bring to boiling point. Let simmer one hour. Add two cups soup stock.
Simmer one-half hour. Serve with chopped parsley and paprika.

Onion Soup

5 large onions   8 cups of soup stock

Cut onions fine. Fry in hot shortening until a golden brown.
Add the soup stock. Simmer forty-five minutes. Serve hot
with toast float. Toast may be covered with cheese if desired.

Consommé

3 pounds meat for soup   2 carrots (diced)
1 soup bone   1 onion (sliced)
½ cup celery leaves   1 tablespoon salt

Wash meat. Put in kettle, then add salt, vegetables, and
water to cover. Simmer two and one-half hours. Strain and
cool. When cold remove fat. Reheat and serve in bouillon
cups. Garnish with white of egg beaten stiff, paprika, and
finely cut parsley.

Mock Turtle Soup

5 pounds knuckle veal   ⅛ cup carrots (diced)
6 whole cloves   4 cups water
½ teaspoon pepper   ¼ cup butter
6 whole allspice   ½ cup flour
1 sliced onion   2 cups tomato purée
Juice of 1 lemon   1 tablespoon salt

Wash knuckle of veal and cover with water. Add salt. Cook
until meat falls from bone. Strain and add vegetables. Cook
until reduced one-half. Strain. Add one cup chopped veal.
Melt and brown butter, add flour, and stir until well browned,
then add stock. Add tomato and lemon juice. Simmer five
minutes. Serve hot, plain, or topped with whipped cream.

Tomato Soup, No. 1

2 tablespoons butter   1 onion (chopped fine)
3 cups tomatoes   2 tablespoons flour
½ teaspoon salt   ⅛ teaspoon soda
2 cups milk (scalded)   ⅛ teaspoon pepper

Melt the butter. Add the flour, stirring constantly to prevent lumping. Stir in the strained tomatoes and simmer for

thirty minutes. Add soda and seasonings. Add the milk last. Serve hot.

Tomato Soup, No. 2

4 cups cooked tomatoes
1 green pepper (chopped)
2 cups water
2 tablespoons butter
1 onion (chopped)

1 bay leaf
2 teaspoons sugar
1½ teaspoons salt
3 tablespoons flour
⅛ teaspoon pepper

Combine tomatoes with water, sugar, bay leaf, onion, and pepper. Simmer slowly for twenty minutes. Add salt and pepper, then strain. Make paste of the butter and flour. Pour the strained tomatoes into the paste. Cook five minutes, stirring constantly. Top with whipped cream.

Jellied Tomato Bouillon

3 cups canned tomatoes
2 onions
2 cups celery (diced)
1 tablespoon parsley (chopped)
1 bay leaf

½ teaspoon salt
1 teaspoon sugar
1 green pepper
(seeded and chopped fine)

Put tomatoes in saucepan and add other ingredients in the order given. Add two cups water, cover, and let simmer for twenty minutes. Then strain and add four tablespoons of gelatine, softened in one-half cup of cold water. Stir until the gelatine is dissolved, and pour into bouillon cups. Chill and serve.

Jellied Tomato Consommé

1 quart clear tomato soup (hot)   ½ cup cold water
3 tablespoons granulated gelatine

Soak gelatine in cold water. Add to hot soup and stir until dissolved. Pour into shallow cake tin. Let stand until firm. Chill. Cut in cubes one inch square. Fill bouillon cups with cubes. Serve garnished with finely chopped parsley.

CHAPTER XXX
Vegetables

Stuffed Peppers

6 green peppers	1 tablespoon parsley (cut fine)
2 cups chopped ham	1 teaspoon salt
1 onion (cut fine)	1 teaspoon butter
1 egg (beaten)	1/8 teaspoon pepper
1/2 cup bread crumbs	

Select broad, low peppers that will stand on end and are easy to serve. Cut slice from end of each pepper. Remove seeds and parboil fifteen minutes. Stuff with bread crumbs mixed with other ingredients. Bake slowly thirty minutes, basting frequently. Moderate oven (350° F.). Mushrooms, chicken, or meat other than ham may be used instead of the ham.

Stuffed Peppers Italian Style

1 dozen peppers	1 cup cracker crumbs
1/2 pound cheese (American)	4 tablespoons shortening
1 teaspoon salt	4 eggs
1/4 teaspoon pepper	

Beat eggs and melted shortening together. Add grated cheese and cracker crumbs. Mix thoroughly. Cut peppers in half. Remove stem end and seeds. Parboil fifteen minutes. Put peppers in greased baking pan. Fill with egg, cheese, and crumb mixture. Bake thirty minutes in moderate oven (350° F.). Put into broiler a minute before serving to brown top.

Corn Pudding

2 cups corn	1/8 teaspoon pepper
1/2 cup milk	2 eggs
1 tablespoon butter	1 tablespoon flour
1/2 teaspoon baking powder	1/2 teaspoon salt

Mix baking powder with flour. Stir milk, egg yolks, and flour into corn. Add seasoning. Add egg whites beaten stiff. Pour into greased baking dish. Dot with butter. Bake one-half hour in slow oven (325° F.). Serve at once.

Corn Pudding with Sausage

1 pound pork sausage	½ teaspoon salt
2 cups corn	2 eggs
½ cup milk	1 tablespoon flour
½ teaspoon baking powder	

Mix baking powder with flour. Stir milk, egg yolks, and flour into corn. Beat egg whites until stiff. Add to corn mixture. Put pork sausage into bottom of baking dish. Bake fifteen minutes in hot oven (400° F.). Pour corn mixture over sausage. Bake one-half hour in a slow oven (325° F.). Serve at once.

Scalloped Corn

2 cups corn	1 cup milk
½ cup bread crumbs	1 teaspoon salt
⅛ teaspoon pepper	1 tablespoon butter

Put layer of corn into bottom of buttered baking dish. Season with salt and pepper. Cover with layer of bread crumbs. Repeat with alternate layers of corn and crumbs until all used. Have crumbs as top layer. Dot with butter. Add milk. Bake in moderately hot oven (375° F.) forty-five minutes.

Squaw Corn

1 can corn	¼ pound bacon
(golden bantam)	(cut fine and fried crisp)

Add corn to hot bacon and heat thoroughly. Serve hot. One cup of tomato purée may be added to this recipe if desired.

Sautéed Corn with Peppers

3 tablespoons shortening	4 cups corn (golden bantam)
2 green peppers	½ teaspoon salt

Remove seeds from green peppers. Chop peppers fine. Cook in the shortening for five minutes. Add the corn and seasoning.

Cook until browned. Serve hot. Chopped pimento may be added.

Scalloped Cauliflower

Mix cooked cauliflower with one-half as much medium white sauce. Season with salt and pepper. Put mixture into a buttered baking dish. Cover with buttered bread crumbs. Bake in a moderate oven (350° F.) until hot and nicely browned. Grated cheese may be added if desired. Finely cut green peppers may be used for variation.

Baked Rice and Tomato

6 tomatoes	2 tablespoons butter
½ cup rice	3 tablespoons bread crumbs
1 small onion	1 tablespoon chopped parsley
1 cup soup stock	1 teaspoon salt
¼ teaspoon pepper	

Wash rice. Bring stock to boiling point. Add rice and cook until it has absorbed all the stock.

Butter baking dish. Peel and slice tomatoes. Arrange them in alternate layers with rice in dish. Sprinkle each layer with little salt, pepper, chopped parsley, and chopped onion. Put layer of buttered crumbs on top. Bake in a moderate oven (350° F.) for forty minutes,

Grilled Tomatoes

Select firm tomatoes. Cut in half. Cover with grated American cheese. Season with salt and pepper. Put under low flame of broiler until cheese melts and browns. Garnish with parsley.

Stuffed Tomatoes

6 tomatoes (large and firm)	Sprig parsley (chopped)
1 small onion	1 slice ham (chopped)
1 egg	½ cup bread crumbs

Cut slice from top of tomatoes. Scoop out pulp and liquid. Do not skin tomatoes. Put onion, ham, and parsley through a

meat grinder. Add bread crumbs. Add tomato pulp finely cut
and beaten egg. Season with salt and pepper. Mix together
thoroughly. Restuff tomatoes with this mixture. Dot with
butter before baking. Bake in a moderate oven (350° F.) for
thirty-five minutes.

Tomatoes Stuffed with Corn

Scoop out tomatoes and fill with canned corn which has been
drained and seasoned. Add one-half teaspoon shortening to top
of each tomato. Bake in a moderate oven (350° F.) for about
twenty-five minutes.

Baked Tomatoes

Scoop out the pulp of firm medium-sized tomatoes. Line
with American cheese. Drop raw egg into each one. Top with
cheese and bake in a moderate oven (350° F.) for ten minutes.

Parsnip Patties

Peel and wash parsnips well. Boil until tender. Drain and
mash. Season with salt, pepper, and butter. Cool. Make mixture into small cakes. Dip cakes in flour and sauté in pork fat
or butter, until brown.

Spanish Rice

1 cup rice (uncooked)	4 tablespoons butter
1 onion (chopped fine)	2 cups canned tomatoes
1 green pepper (chopped fine)	2 teaspoons salt
¼ cup celery (diced)	⅛ teaspoon pepper

Wash rice thoroughly. Cook in boiling water until tender.
Drain. Brown the onion, chopped pepper, and celery in the hot
butter. Add tomatoes, salt and pepper, and cook slowly fifteen
minutes. Add drained rice and cook five minutes longer. Serve
plain or with grated cheese. Garnish with parsley.

Mint Glazed Carrots with Peas

4 carrots	½ cup sugar
½ cup butter	1 tablespoon mint sauce
2 cups peas	1 teaspoon salt
	⅛ teaspoon pepper

Scrape carrots and cut in one-quarter inch slices. Cook in boiling water fifteen minutes and drain. Put in saucepan with butter, sugar, and mint sauce. Cook slowly until soft and glazed. Drain the peas and cook ten minutes in boiling water. Season with salt and pepper. Turn peas on hot serving dish and surround with carrots. Garnish with parsley.

Hungarian Carrots

1 quart carrots	¾ cup sugar
½ cup vinegar	1 tablespoon butter
1 teaspoon salt	1 tablespoon chopped parsley

Wash and scrape carrots. Cut into two-inch lengths. Place in saucepan. Add salt and hot water to cover. Cook until tender. Drain, and add butter, vinegar, and sugar. Cook slowly until transparent. Serve hot. Garnish with chopped parsley.

Harvard Beets

12 beets cut in cubes	½ tablespoon flour
½ cup vinegar	¾ cup sugar
1 teaspoon salt	1 tablespoon butter

Cook beets until tender. Remove skins. Cut beets in cubes. Add butter, vinegar, flour, and sugar, and return to fire. Cook slowly until transparent. Serve hot.

Scalloped Potatoes

Wash and pare potatoes. Slice and drain. Put layer of potatoes into bottom of greased baking dish. Season with salt and pepper. Sprinkle with flour or bread crumbs. Continue with layers of potato and other ingredients until dish is nearly full.

Add enough milk so that it can be seen between the potatoes. Finish top with crumbs and butter. Bake in a hot oven (400° F.)

one and one-quarter to one and one-half hours. Grated cheese may be added if desired.

Franconian Potatoes

Select medium- and uniform-sized potatoes. Wash and pare. Parboil for ten or fifteen minutes. Drain, arrange around meat and bake until browned. Allow thirty minutes for potatoes.

Baked Potatoes

Select medium-sized potatoes. Wash and prick potatoes with a fork. Bake forty-five minutes in moderately hot oven (375° F.).

Twice-Baked Potatoes

Six baked potatoes. Cut layer from top. Scoop out pulp from both top and bottom slices. Rice pulp. Add one teaspoon salt, one tablespoon butter, one egg, one-quarter cup hot milk, then mix and beat thoroughly. Refill large half of potato with this mixture. Sprinkle with grated cheese. Bake in moderate oven (350° F.) until potato heats and cheese melts and browns.

Potato Puffs

2 cups hot mashed potatoes   1 egg
¼ cup milk

Add egg and milk to mashed potatoes. Beat thoroughly. Drop with a tablespoon on greased baking dish, brush with melted shortening. Put under low flame of broiler until brown.

Buttered Potato Balls

With a ball cutter, cut out potato balls. Cook until tender in boiling salted water. Drain. Then pour over them a little melted butter and sprinkle with finely chopped parsley. Serve hot.

Duchess Potatoes

2 cups hot riced potatoes   2 tablespoons butter
½ teaspoon salt

Mix salt and butter with potatoes. Add enough hot milk to moisten. Beat thoroughly. Let mixture pass easily through forcing bag (pastry). Shape as desired on greased baking sheet and brush over with beaten egg diluted with milk. Brown in hot oven. Serve at once.

Saratoga Chips

Wash and pare potatoes, slice thin and soak in cold water one hour. Then drain and dry. Fry in deep fat (390° F.) until they curl and are delicately browned. Drain on unglazed paper. Sprinkle with salt.

French Fried Potatoes

Wash and pare the potatoes, cut into lengths about one-eighth inch thick, and soak in cold water. Drain and dry, then fry in deep fat (390° F.). When brown shake onto sheet of paper to absorb the fat and sprinkle with salt.

Lattice Potatoes

Peel potatoes and cut with lattice slicer. Soak thirty minutes in ice water. Drain and dry. Fry in deep fat (390° F.) until brown. Drain on unglazed paper. Sprinkle with salt. Serve hot.

Pan Fried Potatoes

Slice cold boiled potatoes very thin. Fry in hot shortening until brown. Turn carefully with spatula while cooking. Season with salt before serving. Finely chopped onion may be added to potatoes while frying if desired.

Potatoes au Gratin

6 cold boiled potatoes (diced)　　2 cups medium white sauce
½ cup grated cheese

Line a buttered baking dish with alternate layers of potatoes and white sauce. Sprinkle cheese over top layer. Bake twenty-five minutes in a moderate oven (350° F.). Serve hot.

Creamed Potatoes

6 cold boiled potatoes (diced)　　2 cups medium white sauce

Add potatoes to white sauce and heat thoroughly. Be careful to avoid scorching. Serve hot garnished with peas or chopped parsley and paprika.

Baked Sweet Potatoes

Wash potatoes thoroughly. Prick the potatoes with a fork. Bake forty-five minutes in a moderately hot oven (375° F.). Serve at once.

Candied Sweet Potatoes

Boil potatoes until tender. Cool. Peel and halve sweet potatoes. Arrange in buttered baking dish. Cover with brown sugar to one-fourth inch thickness. Dot with butter. Add enough water to prevent scorching. Bake forty-five minutes in a moderate oven (350° F.). Serve hot. Pour candied sauce over potatoes before serving.

Sweet Potato Puff

4 potatoes (boiled)　　　　　　½ cup milk
2 tablespoons butter　　　　　　2 eggs

Put the boiled potatoes through a ricer. Add the butter, egg yolk, and milk. Beat thoroughly. Fold in the beaten egg whites. Put into a greased baking dish and bake thirty minutes in a moderate oven (350° F.). Serve at once.

Scalloped Cabbage

½ head cabbage
2 tablespoons melted butter
2 tablespoons flour

1 teaspoon salt
1 cup milk
¾ cup buttered crumbs

Cut cabbage in quarters. Cook cabbage in boiling salted water until tender. Make a white sauce of the butter, flour, salt, and milk. Put cabbage in a buttered baking dish and pour the white sauce over it. Cover with buttered crumbs. Bake in a moderate oven (350° F.) until crumbs are brown.

Stuffed Eggplant

1 eggplant
1 cup crumbs
2 tablespoons butter

½ teaspoon pepper
½ tablespoon onion
1 egg

1 teaspoon salt

Cook eggplant fifteen minutes in enough boiling salted water to cover. Cut a slice from top and with a spoon remove pulp, taking care not to work too close to skin. Chop pulp and add bread crumbs. Melt butter, add finely chopped onion, and cook five minutes. Add to chopped pulp and bread. Season with pepper and salt, and, if necessary, moisten with a little water. Cook five minutes, cool slightly, and add one beaten egg. Refill shell with mixture and bake twenty-five minutes in a hot oven (400° F.).

Fried Eggplant

Peel eggplant. Cut in thin slices. Dip each slice in beaten egg then in bread crumbs. Fry in hot shortening until nicely browned on both sides.

Spinach Ring

Wash and cook three pounds of spinach. Drain. Chop spinach fine. Melt three tablespoons butter. Add two tablespoons flour. Blend smooth. Add one-half cup milk. Cook until thick. Add yolks of three eggs, one teaspoon salt, one-eighth teaspoon pepper. Add spinach. Stir well. Add beaten egg whites carefully. Pour into well-greased ring mould. Set mould in pan of hot water. Bake thirty minutes in moderate oven (350° F.). Loosen edges. Turn out on platter. Serve with white sauce or with mushroom sauce.

Pea Timbales

1 cup pea purée
2 eggs (beaten)
1 tablespoon onion juice
2 tablespoons white sauce
1 tablespoon melted butter
⅔ teaspoon salt
⅛ teaspoon pepper

To pea purée add the remaining ingredients. Mix thoroughly. Turn into buttered moulds and bake in a pan of hot water until firm. Moderate oven (350° F.). Serve with one cup white sauce to which is added one-third cup peas and one-third cup carrots which have been cut in fancy shapes. Garnish with parsley.

Vegetable Hash

1 cup carrots (cooked and diced fine)
2 cups potatoes (cooked and diced fine)
1 chopped onion
3 cooked beets (diced fine)

Mix vegetables thoroughly. Season with one-half teaspoon salt and one-quarter teaspoon pepper. Put in greased baking dish. Cover with bread crumbs. Dot with butter. Bake thirty to thirty-five minutes in a hot oven (400° F.).

Peas, celery, or other vegetables may be substituted for any of the vegetables given here.

Vegetable Loaf

1 cup cooked potatoes
1 onion
2 eggs
2 teaspoons salt
1 tablespoon drippings
1 cup bread crumbs
1 cup tomato purée
3½ cups diced mixed vegetables:
(1 cup carrots
1 cup peas
1 cup string beans
½ cup celery or cabbage)
2 tablespoons chopped green peppers
¼ teaspoon sage

Put all vegetables and bread crumbs through a food chopper. Add well-beaten eggs and tomato purée. Add salt, sage, and

drippings. Mix thoroughly. Put into a well-greased dish. Bake
thirty minutes in a moderate oven (350° F.).

Lentils, Spanish Style

1 cup lentils	1 green pepper (cut fine)
3 pimentoes	2 cups tomatoes
4 tablespoons butter	1 onion
¼ teaspoon pepper	1 teaspoon salt

Wash lentils, cover with cold water, and soak overnight.
Drain. Cook in boiling salted water one hour. When tender,
melt butter, add the onion and pimentoes chopped fine. Add
tomatoes, salt, and pepper. Drain lentils and add them. Cook
for half an hour without cover. Serve hot.

Baked Beans, No. 1

One quart beans soaked overnight. Parboil until skin cracks
when blown. Put into bean pot, and add two tablespoons
molasses; three-fourths pound salt pork, then cover with water.
Bake six hours in moderate oven (350° F.).

Baked Beans, No. 2

Soak one quart of beans overnight. Parboil thirty minutes.
Drain. Fill bean pot with alternate layers of beans and salt pork.
Cover with boiling water to which one-half cup brown sugar,
one teaspoon mustard, and one teaspoon ginger have been added.
Bake six hours in moderate oven (350° F.).

Grilled Onions

Peel large onions and cut into one-half-inch slices. Put into
greased baking dish. Season with salt, pepper, and dot with
butter. Add enough water to cover bottom of pan. Bake forty
minutes in moderate oven (350° F.). Put into broiler to brown
before serving.

Baked Stuffed Onions

Boil four large white onions for one-half hour in salted water. Drain, cool, and scoop out the centers. Mix together two tablespoons of chopped walnuts, one cup of celery cut fine, four tablespoons grated bread crumbs, and two tablespoons of melted butter.

Fill the onion cups, set in a baking pan and baste while cooking. Bake thirty minutes in moderate oven (350° F.).

Asparagus

Peel asparagus and cut off tough ends. Boil over low flame in salted water for twenty-five to thirty minutes. Drain and serve with drawn butter or hollandaise sauce.

Swiss Chard

Pick over and wash Swiss chard. Cook over low flame thirty minutes. Cook without water. Drain. Serve with vinegar, salt, and pepper. Swiss chard may be chopped after it has been drained, then seasoned and mixed with enough cream to moisten. Serve hot.

Pickled Beets

Slice eight cold cooked beets. Put into dish. Cover with sliced onion. Cook one-half cup vinegar with one cup water, one-quarter cup sugar, one-quarter teaspoon pepper, one tablespoon salt, and two bay leaves. Pour over beets. Cool before serving.

Baked Squash

Cut squash into pieces suitable for an individual serving. Put into baking pan and bake one hour in a moderately hot oven (375° F.). With a sharp knife cut slit in top of squash. Put small piece of butter into slit. Season with salt and pepper. Serve hot.

SECTION III
International Recipes

INTERNATIONAL RECIPES

Stuffed Squab

SOAK bread crumbs in a little broth. Press well to extract moisture; then place in a bowl with a quarter as much butter, a few egg yolks, and one whole egg. Mix thoroughly, season with salt, pepper, parsley, and chopped and blanched onions. Use this for filling the squabs. Then truss them for an entrée and run them on the spit to roast, basting occasionally with butter. Untie them, remove the larding pork covering the breast and lay them on a bed of sautéed tomatoes. Serve a brown sauce separately into which Worcestershire sauce, meat glacé, and chopped parsley have been added.

Chef ANTHONY ROTA, *The Mayflower*, Washington, D. C.

Chicken Sabaione

Put eight egg yolks into a high and narrow casserole. Dilute with one pint of chicken or game broth and place casserole in hot water. Stir over boiling water with a whip or wooden beater until the sabaione becomes thick and frothy. As soon as it is done, serve it very hot in cups. A little sherry added to each cup improves the dish.

Chef ANTHONY ROTA, *The Mayflower*, Washington, D. C.

Fillet of Beef, Henry IV

Place a trimmed fillet of beef in butter and cook in hot oven for eighteen minutes. Turn fillet over twice, placing on roast at first turn, cut onions, celery leaves, bay leaves, and a little thyme. Remove fillet from oven and place on fire. Make a sauce by adding to the pan Newburg sauce or salted sherry. Leave on fire for a few minutes, then strain and put in a bowl. Cover the fillet with brioche dough. Place in a pan and put in oven until dough is browned. Cut in slices, place them on a platter with a garnish around. At one side place several skinned baked tomatoes and mushrooms with asparagus tips; at the other side, potatoes cut in walnut form with small onions, carrots, and a little chicken broth. Sprinkle sauce around the fillet and serve.

Chef ANTHONY ROTA, *The Mayflower*, Washington, D. C.

Mayflower Salad

Take several fresh artichokes, clean well, then cook them in boiling water for about five minutes. When cooked, carefully remove the inside of each one, leaving the shape intact. Then fill each hollow with asparagus tips and sprinkle on top some fine julienne of truffles and celery. Serve with Russian dressing (mayonnaise, ketchup, and red and green peppers diced).

Chef ANTHONY ROTA, *The Mayflower*, Washington, D. C.

Delice of Clams Palmer House (For Six Covers)

36 cherry stone clams
4 ounces butter
3 ounces fresh mushrooms (chopped)
1 small onion (chopped)

1 spoon parsley (chopped)
2 raw yolks of eggs (diluted and well mixed with the juice of one whole lemon)

Fresh cherry stone clams are to be put in a stewing pan with one pint of water. Cover pan and let contents come to a boil as soon as clams begin to open. Drain on a colander, remove the meat from the shell, and cut off the hard part of the clam. Then cut in small dice. After this operation we are ready to proceed. Melt the butter in a saucepan, add onions and mushrooms. When these ingredients are smothered, add the chopped clams; when thoroughly heated, stir in one heaping tablespoon of flour, stirring constantly; then add two cups of the hot clam juice, boil for a few minutes, then stir in the lemon juice mixed with the yolks of eggs and the chopped parsley. Season to taste and do not let come to a boil any more after adding the eggs, otherwise, instead of binding, it would curdle the composition. Pour mixture into another dish and fill in your half shells of clams above the rim.

After this is done, place them in a small baking pan, sprinkle with a few bread crumbs and top with butter. Bake for five minutes in a moderate oven. Serve with parsley and lemon.

Chef ERNEST E. AMIET, *Palmer House*, Chicago, Ill.

Turban of Sole Prince de Galles

Fillet of sole well flattened and spread with a thin layer of fish farce made of smelts. Roll and lay into a buttered mould. As the rolls must hold together in turban style, it becomes necessary to cover the tops with the same farce which, when unmoulded, becomes the bottom of this preparation. Add a little reduced fish and mushroom bouillon. Cook in a water bath well covered. Cook in the oven. When cooked, the fillets and farce will hold together and be in the shape of a cork.

Carefully unmould fillets on a round platter. Reduce the juice left over from the cooking and incorporate same into a rich sauce well fed with butter.

Add a garnish of poached oysters, mushroom heads, and crawfish. Finish with a slice of truffle on top of each roll.

Chef ERNEST E. AMIET, *Palmer House*, Chicago, Ill.

Spring Chicken in Crust Chicago

Prepare a spring chicken, remove breast bones, season inside with salt and pepper. Add a filling made of sweet corn kernels creamed and chicken livers sautéed in butter with a liberal dash of paprika.

Lay out an oval mould with pattie paste and add the sautéed chicken, breast upwards. Cover with the same paste and make a round opening in middle; decorate nicely with paste leaves and tint with yellow of egg. Set this pie in a fairly warm oven until a nice golden color is obtained, then, if necessary, cover the preparation with a buttered paper so as to keep this golden color. Time of cooking one to one and a quarter hours, depending mostly on the size of spring chicken. This recipe is based on a two-pound spring chicken. Before sending to table, let it stand a few minutes and serve with a paprika cream sauce.

Chef ERNEST E. AMIET, *Palmer House,* Chicago, Ill.

Seafood Seales in Casserole Ernest

| ½ raw lobster | 3 raw medium-sized scallops |
| 3 raw shrimps | 3 raw little-neck clams in the shell |

These four items laid in an individual casserole.

Chop three branches of celery very fine, also the meat of two fresh-peeled tomatoes, a little chopped parsley, and one ounce of butter. Pour into casserole, seal the cover with pie dough, and cook in a medium oven for twenty-five minutes and serve.

Chef ERNEST E. AMIET, *Palmer House*, Chicago, Ill.

Tripe à la Mode

Scrape the tripe and wash it in several waters. Scald it in boiling water and put it to soak for twenty-four hours in cold water which must be changed several times. Line a brazing or baking dish with slices of carrots, onions, a little bacon, a bunch of herbs, whole cloves, one-quarter clove of garlic, pepper, one slice of beef cut in pieces. Drain the tripe and sprinkle it with salt and nutmeg; put the pieces in the dish with a ham bone in the center. Fill up to the top with white cooking wine and a little of the broth. Cover with strips of bacon. Close with a paste. Cover. Let bake in a moderate oven from six to seven hours. Serve hot on a platter with the gravy of the baking dish skimmed and thickened.

Chef ANGLADE, *Royal Hotel*, Deauville, France

Braised Shoulder of Veal

Take a shoulder of milk-fed veal with a few strips of salt pork, season with salt and pepper.

Place in a pan with a little dripping. Fry all around till well colored. Sprinkle with flour and fry a little more.

Take two nice green cabbages and blanch in salted water, drain, and place around the shoulder of veal. Add two onions, two carrots, and a pint of good stock. Cover and cook in oven for about two hours. Serve shoulder on a large platter with cabbages and gravy.

Chef LOUIS BALTERA, *Château Frontenac*, Quebec, Canada

Glazed Veal Chops

Take two veal chops, season, salt, and pepper. Roll in flour and fry in clarified butter. When cooked, put a little cooking wine over them and glaze in oven. Remove the chops from the oven. Put a little brown sauce in the pan, reduce a little, and pour over the chops. Garnish with rice croquettes, new peas, a little bouquet of cauliflower, new beans, and a couple of roasted potatoes.

Chef LOUIS BALTERA, *Château Frontenac*, Quebec, Canada

Celery Roots

Peel and slice celery roots very thin — if preferred cut them in julienne. They may be parboiled before seasoning. Season with oil, vinegar, salt, pepper, and mustard. Mix well and serve on lettuce leaves with a little tarragon.

Chef LOUIS BALTERA, *Château Frontenac*, Quebec, Canada

Stuffed Lobster

2 boiled lobsters	2 truffles
6 mushrooms	2 green peppers

Dice the lobster meat, add mushrooms, truffles, peppers. Mix well with cardinal sauce. Stuff the lobsters with the mixture, butter, and cover with bread crumbs. Bake ten minutes. Serve with a broth or stew made of onions, butter, rice, olive oil, over which chicken soup has been poured.

Chef JAN C. BORN, *S.S. Rotterdam*, Holland-America Line

Stuffed Pork Chop

Chop onions, mushrooms, parsley, and stuff the chop. Fry ten minutes and serve with any piquant sauce.

Chef JAN C. BORN, *S.S. Rotterdam*, Holland-America Line

Apple Pie

Slice six apples, add currants, raisins, cooking wine, and cinnamon. Line a pie dish with crust, add fruit, cover with pie crust. Bake thirty-five minutes. Serve hot.

Chef JAN C. BORN, *S.S. Rotterdam*, Holland-America Line

Saddle of Hare

Clean and lard two saddles of hare. Fry in one-half pound butter together with onions, carrots, one laurel leaf, two cloves, five pepper corns, until brown. Add one pint of sour cream and let it simmer for one-half hour in the oven. Pour sauce through a strainer and add a few drops of lemon. Add salt and season to taste.

Chef F. BOSCHEN, *S.S. Berlin*, North German Lloyd Line

Potato Dumplings

Cook four peeled potatoes, mash and cool. Add two tablespoons flour, three egg yolks, salt, pepper, and nutmeg, and mix the whole well. Take two rolls cut in small cubes, browned in butter. Now form dumplings, hollow the same and insert the cubes. Close dumplings and round them. Roll in flour, and let them draw in slowly cooking salt water for ten minutes, without cover, otherwise they will burst. Serve with cracker-meal browned in butter.

Chef F. BOSCHEN, *S.S. Berlin*, North German Lloyd Line

German Sauerbraten and Potato Pancake

Soak four pounds of shoulder beef for five days in half vinegar, half water with spices, onions, and carrots. Then roast until brown. Take two tablespoons flour, add to the mixture and let the whole smother for two hours. Season the thickened sauce with currants, cream, and sauce.

Chef F. BOSCHEN, *S.S. Berlin*, North German Lloyd Line

Queen Soup

Stew a fowl cut in pieces, and prepare a good broth with the usual seasoning. When the fowl is tender, take the meat from the breast and the rest of the white meat from the bones. After removing the skin, mince it very fine and put in a mortar. Pound fine with the yolks of three or four hard-boiled eggs. Strain the broth, add two white rolls cut in slices, which have first been browned lightly in the oven.   Then add the meat and egg yolks, put the whole through a fine sieve and serve the soup with toasted white rolls cut in cubes and browned in the pan.

Chef S. BORRA, *Hotel Tiberias*, Tiberias, Palestine

Roast Leg of Veal

The veal must not be pounded, or it will be stringy.   Put in a baking pan slices of pork, onions, carrots, and about one-quarter pound butter.   When the butter has become very hot, put in it the leg of veal.   When nicely browned add from time to time a little boiling water.   With the gravy made thus, baste frequently, turning the roast.   If the bone of the leg is left with the roast, it will add to its flavor.   Time for roasting two to three hours.

Chef S. BORRA, *Hotel Tiberias*, Tiberias, Palestine

Veal Cutlets

Cut the veal cutlets horizontally in two, leaving them attached to the bone.   Flatten the two halves and fill one of them entirely with very thin slices of truffle.   Place the two halves upon each other.   Beat them all around with the back of the knife.   Cover with egg, butter, and bread crumbs.   Fry slowly in butter on both sides and bake for five minutes in the oven.

Chef ALESSANDRO CEDRINI, *S.S. Conte Grande*,
Lloyd Sabaudo Line

Chicken Cutlets

Dip the pieces of chicken in butter, round off on top with mushroom purée, cover with egg and fresh bread.   Fry in butter. Arrange on half a tomato with sauce.   Sauce may be flavored with a cooking wine.

Chef ALESSANDRO CEDRINI, *S.S. Conte Grande*,
Lloyd Sabaudo Line

Sweetbreads

Braise one or more veal sweetbreads with butter, a little onion, or juniper. Soak in cooking wine, let boil gently till half the liquid is gone, bake in a baking dish, and pour sauce over it. Cut bananas in disks one inch thick, glaze, flour them, then dip in egg. Bake them with fresh butter. Place the bananas on the sweetbreads. Place platter in the oven for a moment and serve very hot.

Chef ALESSANDRO CEDRINI, *S.S. Conte Grande*,
Lloyd Sabaudo Line

Broth with Truffles

Cook a young turkey in salted water until tender. Strain. Add a little rice and cook thirty minutes. Add one yolk of egg beaten slightly and one cup of cream. Heat and serve in cups either hot or iced. Top with shreds of truffles.

Chef ENRICO COMOGLIO, *Grand Hotel*, Venice, Italy

Guinea Hen with Sauce

Dress a young guinea hen. Put into a baking dish with fresh mushrooms and butter. Add a little stock. Cook until hen is tender. Remove hen. Add some cooking wine to stock and cook until reduced one third. Add cream and butter. Pour hot sauce into dish. Add guinea hen. Cover hen with layer of truffles. Cover. Heat. Serve hot.

Chef ENRICO COMOGLIO, *Grand Hotel*, Venice, Italy

Capon with Truffles and Mushrooms

Take a fat pullet and stuff with one-half pound bread crumbs and one-half pound mashed goose liver. Cover with truffles and braise in an earthenware pot. When done, lay out on oval dish and surround with white truffles and fresh mushrooms. Reheat liquid and add a glassful of cooking wine. Reduce and add a little chicken stock (strain and thicken, if necessary). Pour over cooked capon.

Chef EUGENE CORDIER, *S.S. Rochambeau*, French Line

Fish with Vegetables

The fish generally used for the bouillabaisse are — whitings, mullet, and lobster. Cut large fish into slices and leave small ones whole. Mix in a casserole one-half pound small onions, one-quarter pound white part of leeks chopped, two good-sized tomatoes cut up, a mashed clove of garlic, one tablespoon parsley chopped fine, and a pinch of saffron, one glass of oil, one laurel leaf, and a little savory. A pinch of fennel may be added, also pepper. To this add fish, one-half tablespoon salt, and water to cover. Cook thirty minutes. Pour the broth on slices of bread arranged on a platter. Place the fish on another platter and surround with slices of lobster or with half-lobsters, according to the kind employed, and vegetables. Serve hot.

The fish, the flesh of which is tender like the mullet and the whiting, must be set aside and added to the bouillabaisse when the latter has cooked already seven to eight minutes.

Chef Gustave Coutant, *Restaurant des Ambassadeurs*,
Deauville, France

Poulet en Cocotte André

Stuff the chicken with foie gras and bake. Make a gravy with cooking wine and rum extract thickened with foie gras. Garnish with mushrooms and truffles.

Chef E. G. Dastugues, *Turnberry Hotel*, Ayrshire, Scotland

Fillet Ailsa

Fry the fillet until cooked, add cooking wine and cooking rum for sauce. Dress with asparagus tips in bunches, sliced foie gras, potatoes in half-moon shape, and gravy.

Chef E. G. Dastugues, *Turnberry Hotel*, Ayrshire, Scotland

Sea Bass, "My Recipe"

Clean a sea bass well, leaving the head on. Take the fillets, season with salt and pepper, make a little fish dressing: a mixture of onions sautéed in butter. Garnish with parsley. Place bass on platter or pan. Cover with a few chopped fresh mushrooms, pour on a little cooking wine, add a generous piece of butter, bake in a moderate oven for thirty-five minutes. Add a little lemon juice when done. Serve.

Chef GEORGE DHOYER, *S.S. Statendam*,
Holland-America Line

"Louisette" Poached Eggs

Use eight poached eggs, cooled. Make a stuffing of chopped chicken, bread crumbs, white celery hearts, and an apple. Season and thicken with cream. Take eight lettuce hearts, put a little stuffing in center, poached egg on top; on this pour mayonnaise. Place around the dish slices of peeled tomatoes, slice of truffle, and chopped parsley.

Chef GEORGE DHOYER, *S.S. Statendam*,
Holland-America Line

Capon, "Edith"

Take a very fine capon and separate the bone from the breast. Make a dressing of liver, fresh mushrooms, chopped parsley. Chop fine and season to taste. Then stuff the capon with this dressing. At bottom of the casserole put sliced carrots, onions, parsley sprigs, a good piece of butter. Place capon on top and bake in rather hot oven (400° F.) for fifty minutes in a covered casserole.

When done, take up capon, taking care to keep it hot. With a fork pierce the bottom of the casserole to loosen the vegetables, add a pint of heavy cream, boil down, strain. Add more butter, mix well. Pour the sauce over the capon and add a dash of paprika before serving.

Chef GEORGE DHOYER, *S.S. Statendam*,
Holland-America Line

Pheasant à la Perigueux

See that the pheasants are not too gamey. Break the breast bones and fill the empty breasts with forcemeat made with chickens' liver and truffles. Truss birds with legs inside and cover breasts with chopped bacon. Wrap each bird in buttered

paper, tied with string.   Cook for about forty-five minutes.
When cooked, take off papers and serve with sauce.

Chef HARRY DUKE, *S.S. President Madison*,
American Mail Line

Corned Potatoes

Take sufficient boiled potatoes for the number to be served.
Chop into small pieces similar size to lyonnaise or sauté potatoes.   Add fresh corn stripped from the cob.   Onions chopped
very small.   Mix well, adding a little chopped parsley.   Fry in
butter and serve in scallop dishes.   Serve very hot.

Chef HARRY DUKE, *S.S. President Madison*,
American Mail Line

Tsing Tao Cocktail

Preserved figs   Preserved pears

Chop the fruit into very small pieces as the base of the cocktail using about a dessert spoonful of the mixture to each cocktail.   Add lemon juice to taste.   Equal parts of each fruit juice
to fill the cocktail glass.   Serve very cold with chopped ice in
the underliner.

Chef HARRY DUKE, *S.S. President Madison*,
American Mail Line

Saddle of Hare

Cook a saddle of hare on a quick fire for twelve minutes.
Then remove saddle from pan and glaze the pan with tarragon
vinegar and serve the saddle with mashed chestnuts and cream.

Chef LOUIS DUPEROUX, *Adelphi Hotel*, Liverpool, England

Chicken Sauté Saucerre

Cut one good spring chicken into four pieces, salt and pepper
to taste and cook in butter for ten minutes, afterwards turning
over to cook for another ten minutes.   Glaze with a large glass
of cooking wine.   Add shallots and garnish with tomatoes.

Chef LOUIS DUPEROUX, *Adelphi Hotel*, Liverpool, England

River Trout

Salt and pepper on both sides one trout (about one pound) and put in a dish to cook with minced vegetables. Add one glass of cooking wine and a small quantity of butter. Cook very slowly for twenty minutes. Pour off the stock, add melted butter, and serve very hot.

Chef Louis Duperoux, *Adelphi Hotel*, Liverpool, England

Duck in Aspic

Arrange the finely hashed duck in a glass dish and place the browned breasts of duck on top. Cover with a jelly flavored with cooking port and garnish with orange cut in quarters.

Chef A. Eckert, *Hotel Bellevue*, Dresden, Germany

Puff-Paste Boats

Fill boats of puff paste with a forcemeat of lobster spread with a mixture of cheese and egg and bake in a quick oven.

Chef A. Eckert, *Hotel Bellevue*, Dresden, Germany

Breast of Chicken

Take the breast of chicken and brown in butter. Arrange in a circle on a dish. Garnish in the center with a mixture made of kidneys, mushroom buttons, and small truffle dumplings. Serve with an appetizing sauce.

Chef A. Eckert, *Hotel Bellevue*, Dresden, Germany

Savory Goose with Sauce

Take a fat goose and pluck it; draw it and singe it. Let it cook from three to four hours in salted water, to which has been added all the vegetables and seasoning used for stew; the time of cooking depends upon the age of the goose.

When the goose has been thoroughly cooked, take it off the fire and let it cool; then cut it in pieces of about four to five inches square. Dip these pieces in a well-beaten egg, then in bread crumbs. Then let them roast in fresh butter till nicely brown. In the meanwhile blend a tablespoon of flour with the same amount of butter, add one clove of garlic finely chopped, pepper, salt, and grated nutmeg and moisten with one and one-half cups of good sweet cream. Cook until thick. This gravy must be well mixed and tasty. Pour over the pieces of hot goose and serve.

Chef GASTON FERRAND, *Hôtel du Golf*, Deauville, France

Crab Meat Château

Chop one-half green pepper and fry in saucepan for a few minutes. Add crab meat and let sauté on a slow fire for ten minutes. Place in an au gratin dish. Cover with sauce.

Sauce: five tablespoons butter and one tablespoon flour. Warm this in pan for five minutes. Pour over it a little milk to thicken sauce, add one tablespoon Parmesan cheese, salt, pepper, and paprika. Pour this sauce over the crab meat, sprinkle with Parmesan cheese. Then bake in quick oven (400° F.) until brown.

Chef A. FRANCHI, *Château Laurier*, Ottawa, Canada

Fresh Haddock, Poor Man Style

Bone the haddock, cut in individual portions. Add a little salt and vinegar and let boil. Slice onions and fry in butter. Add a few drops of vinegar and pour browned butter over the fish and onions and serve.

Chef A. FRANCHI, *Château Laurier*, Ottawa, Canada

Château Laurier Salad

Take lettuce leaf, place on it julienne of celery, three sliced tomatoes, sliced pickles, and walnuts. Pour over salad mayonnaise dressing with paprika.

Chef A. FRANCHI, *Château Laurier*, Ottawa, Canada

Creamed Fried Lobster (Twelve Persons)

Halve six large live lobsters, and cook in oil. Mix one-quarter pound onion, one-quarter pound carrots, one-quarter pound red and green peppers (diced small), pinch of powdered thyme and bay leaves. Cook in butter and lay lobsters on top, adding five cups fish stock. Steam for fifteen minutes. Place lobsters on dish. Reduce stock to thick creamy consistency and add one-quarter cup heavy cream. Pour the sauce over the lobsters and serve very hot.

Chef PAUL GERMAIN, *S.S. Belgenland*, Red Star Line

Russian Soup (Six Persons)

Take two pounds white cabbage and slice small. Add one pound onions (chopped), one pound bacon (diced), one pound apples (sliced). Mix together, add one quart water, or stock, and braise. Add the juice of one pound red beetroot, one tablespoon vinegar, and one pound of cream. Serve very hot.

Chef PAUL GERMAIN, *S.S. Belgenland*, Red Star Line

Japanese Tenderloin Steak (Four Persons)

Cut one pound tenderloin in thick, narrow strips. Mix two pounds string beans, cabbage, carrots, onions (thick slices). Heat iron pan and add beef fat, cooking meat slightly first. Then add vegetables, pouring over all a little water. Add seasoning with salt and sauce. Cook until done through.

Hard-boiled eggs may be served with the meat and vegetables if desired.

Chef PAUL GERMAIN, *S.S. Belgenland*, Red Star Line

Sweetbread Suprême

Select a few calf sweetbreads and soak them in fresh water and blanch them. When cold, lay between two boards so as to press them gently, then lard them with bacon and truffles. Fry slowly in butter, add a glass of cooking wine, reduce the stock to half, then add some fresh cream, a little cayenne, truffles and mushrooms. When cooked, serve on toast around a timbale of asparagus tips and place the truffles and mushrooms around the whole.

Chef GUILLAUME GUILLOU, *Australia Hotel*, Sydney, Australia

A Pleasant Change from the Usual
A Vegetable Dinner

Quails Italian

Bone quails and stuff with chicken-liver forcemeat. Cook them in a succulent veal stock with addition of a glass of cooking sherry. When cold, coat them with a brown sauce prepared from the stock with which the quails have been cooked. Decorate the breast and sprinkle with aspic. Dress the quails around a timbale of salad.

Chef GUILLAUME GUILLOU, *Australia Hotel*, Sydney, Australia

Pigeon à la Mode Normandy

Fry a chopped onion in butter, add some chicken liver and bacon cut in dice and a little spice. Press all through a sieve. To this add a few raisins and bread crumbs and a glass of cooking wine. Stuff squabs with this preparation; cook gently for twenty-five minutes. Dress them on toasted bread spread with the first preparation and garnish with quartered apples fried in butter and braised chestnuts. Add sauce.

Chef GUILLAUME GUILLOU, *Australia Hotel*, Sydney, Australia

Poached Eggs, Spanish Style

Place poached eggs on a dish and garnish with one-half tomato broiled, braised green peppers, and one-half glass boiled rice. A garnish of small fried sausage may also be served.

Chef MAX GUTTERA, *Grand Hotel Elefant*, Graz, Austria

Ragout of Fish

Fry some finely chopped onions golden yellow. Add green peppers cut in dice and peeled tomatoes. Pour over them broth. Take boned raw fish cut in slices and thin slices of small mushrooms and let stew gently until done. Mix all ingredients together, add raw apples, stew for fifteen minutes and serve.

Chef MAX GUTTERA, *Grand Hotel Elefant*, Graz, Austria

Artichokes, Savory

Remove the outer leaves from the artichokes, cut off the tips and pull them apart. Put six tablespoons of oil in a dish, a handful of finely chopped green parsley, a clove of garlic, a handful of bread crumbs, salt, pepper. Mix all well together and fill the artichokes. Place them in a stewpan, one against the other, add water to the length of two fingers, and let them stew gently until the water has boiled away and only the oil remains. The artichokes may be allowed to catch a little on the bottom of the pot, as the light crust thus formed gives it a delicious taste.

Chef MAX GUTTERA, *Grand Hotel Elefant*, Graz, Austria

Braised Beef à la Mode

Lard five pounds of rump of beef with fresh larding pork. Season with salt and pepper and lay in earthen pot. Cover with half cooking claret, half water. Add one sliced onion, and one sliced carrot, and allow to stand for twenty-four hours. Put a tablespoon of melted butter in a casserole and when the casserole is hot, put in the piece of beef and fry brown on both sides. Remove beef to a platter. Add to the casserole two tablespoons butter and two tablespoons flour. Let this become brown, then add the cooking wine, water, and vegetables used in the earthen pot. Put the beef in it and simmer until tender. Place the beef on a platter and strain the sauce through a fine sieve. Garnish with carrots, onions, and peas.

Chef WILLIAM HAAG, *The Macdonald Hotel*, Edmonton, Canada

Chocolate Bavarian Cream

Mix the yolks of six eggs with four tablespoons granulated sugar and two ounces grated chocolate. Add one pint of milk. Set on fire in double boiler and cook over boiling water. Stir till the cream thickens. Dissolve in a little milk a package of gelatine. Add this to the cream and strain the mixture into a basin. Place on ice, stirring till the mixture begins to set. Then add one pint of whipped cream. Put a mould on the ice, pour in the cream, cover with ice. When quite set, turn it out and serve.

Chef WILLIAM HAAG, *The Macdonald Hotel*, Edmonton, Canada

Butterscotch Rice Pudding

1 tablespoon gelatine	3 cups milk
⅓ cup rice	1 cup brown sugar
2 tablespoons butter	½ teaspoon salt

½ cup cold water

Wash the rice and cook it until nearly done in a double boiler with two cups of scalded milk and the salt. Meanwhile cook together in a shallow pan the brown sugar and butter until it gets very dark brown, but not burnt. Add this to the rice and milk. Cook until the rice is tender and the caramel melted. Soften the gelatine in the cold water and then dissolve it in a cup of hot milk. Pour this into the cooked rice mixture and turn into a cold wet mould.

Chef WILLIAM HAAG, *The Macdonald Hotel*, Edmonton, Canada

Almond Pie

Make a paste of one pound brown sugar, one-half pound butter, and one and one-half pounds flour. Then cover the bottom and edge of a pie dish with it, about as thick as your little finger. Take one-half pound butter and mix with it one-half pound cut almonds, four eggs, and one ounce flour, and fill the pie with it. Cover with strips of the paste that is left over and bake slowly.

Chef DAVID DE HAAY, *S.S. Volendam*, Holland-America Line

Chicken Broth

Put a capon in cold water, enough to cover it, add a little salt and cook for about two hours. Then take out the capon and put in four ounces vermicelli and one piece of mace. Meanwhile bone the capon, cut in pieces and put back in the broth together with little balls of calves' meat.

Chef DAVID DE HAAY, *S.S. Volendam*, Holland-America Line

Apricot Dumplings

Cut in pieces eight ounces butter and mix with eight ounces flour. Add a little water and roll out a paste. Let it settle for about ten minutes. Repeat the process three times. Hollow out the apricots and fill with almond paste. Then cut the dough that is rolled out as thick as a silver dollar in square pieces so as to roll the whole apricot in it. Cover this with egg yolk, and let bake slowly in the oven. Serve with apricot sauce. Add a little cooking rum, if desired. The sauce should be poured over when warm.

Chef DAVID DE HAAY, S.S. Volendam, Holland-America Line

Braised Ox Tongue

Cook the tongue in water until tender, add one onion, one carrot, one sprig thyme, and a piece of whole mace. Stew separately one pound tomatoes and a little of the tongue stock together. When thoroughly stewed, rub through a sieve. Then bring the sauce to a boil, add a little arrowroot mixed with water, and let simmer until it has a thick, glazed appearance. Add salt, pepper, two tablespoons tomato ketchup, one tablespoon malt vinegar, and a pinch of sugar. Beat into the sauce one ounce butter, after removing from the stove. Cut the tongue in slices. Cook some fresh garden peas in water with a sprig of mint and a lump of sugar. Strain, place peas in the center of the dish, lay the slices of tongue around the base of the peas and pour the sauce over the sliced tongue. Serve with creamed mashed potatoes in a separate dish.

Chef WILLIAM H. HASEL, S.S. Adriatic, White Star Line.

Casserole Fish

Stew the fish in a cup of water and two cups of milk in a casserole dish. Add seasoning, finely chopped carrots, and onions, and stew slowly for three-quarters of an hour until the fish and vegetables are quite tender. Mix two tablespoons flour with a little cold milk into a smooth paste and pour into the dish, stirring constantly to prevent the liquid from becoming lumpy and melt into the contents one-half ounce butter and serve. Add grated cheese to the sauce.

Chef WILLIAM H. HASEL, S.S. Adriatic, White Star Line

Stuffed Shoulder of Lamb

Bone a shoulder of lamb. When boned rub the inside of the shoulder with garlic pod. Stuff with a forcemeat of minced half-cooked liver, chopped onions, three ounces sultanas, eight stoned chopped prunes, two ounces bread crumbs, pepper, salt, grated lemon rind, and a little chopped sage. Mix the ingredients of the forcemeat well. Put some dripping on the lamb and roast, basting it well. Serve with brown gravy, roast potatoes, garden peas, seasoned with a little chopped mint butter, and salt.

Chef WILLIAM H. HASEL, *S.S. Adriatic*, White Star Line

Pudding Tri-Color

Use strawberry flavoring for the red, powdered green tea for the blue, and chocolate for the black. Divide tapioca or egg pudding in three parts, using the above colors. Let harden in separate moulds and arrange in layers. Any other color scheme may be used.

Chef KYUTARO HISATOMI, *The Nara Hotel*, Nara, Japan

Lobster with Peony Sauce

Use Ise lobsters (known to be the best of their kind throughout the Empire, Japan). Cook lobster and remove the shells, leaving only the tails. After meat is diced place lobsters back in the shells. To decorate, cut the tail part in the shape of a peony, adding thereto a few leaves of the real plant.

Chef KYUTARO HISATOMI, *The Nara Hotel*, Nara, Japan

Fresh Pineapple, Hawaii

Cut off the top of the pineapple and about one-half inch of the bottom. Remove the meat without cutting the rind. Chop the pineapple meat fine and mix with fresh almonds, strawberry ice cream, and one-half pint whipped cream. Then place the mixture back in the pineapple rind and put back the top and bottom layers which were cut off in the beginning. Serve in glass bowl surrounded with chopped ice.

Chef ERNEST HUNZIKER, *S.S. Leviathan*, United States Lines

Lobster à la Newburg

Dice fresh lobster meat and place in sauté pan with butter seasoned with salt, pepper, and paprika. Braise the same for two minutes. Add one glass of thick fresh cream and heat until boiling. Then add yolks of two eggs mixed with one-quarter glass cream and one-quarter glass cooking sherry wine. Serve in chafing dish.

Chef ERNEST HUNZIKER, *S.S. Leviathan*, United States Lines

Oysters à la Casino

Place oyster in the deep half of shell, place one tablespoon oyster butter on oyster with one slice of bacon. Then place in a hot oven until baked. Serve with lemon.

Oyster butter: Mix fresh butter and red and green peppers, walnuts, mushrooms, and parsley together. Then add salt, pepper, paprika, one teaspoon sauce, and one tablespoon of cracker dust. Place in ice box to harden.

Chef ERNEST HUNZIKER, *S.S. Leviathan*, United States Lines

Homard Danincy

Remove the flesh from one-half lobster. Dry the shell and fill with sliced tomatoes, mushrooms, and lobster alternately. Cover with sauce, place under the grill until light brown.

Chef A. JAMMES, *Central Hotel*, Glasgow, Scotland

Noisette of Lamb

Fry lamb. Serve on heart-shaped pieces of fried bread, surmounted with slices of artichoke. Garnish with tomatoes baked with butter, and fried ball potatoes. Serve with truffle sauce.

Chef A. JAMMES, *Central Hotel*, Glasgow, Scotland

Hot Soufflé

Boil a fowl. Remove the fillets. Fill cavity with chicken stuffing. Decorate when cooked by placing the fillets on top the stuffing, also collops of foie gras, and button mushrooms. Garnish with tartlets filled with cucumbers fried in bread crumbs and cream sauce whipped with foie gras and the juice of the truffles.

Chef A. JAMMES, *Central Hotel*, Glasgow, Scotland

Stuffed Capon

Bake capon and stuff with one-half pound rice, one-quarter pound goose liver, one-quarter pound truffles cut in slices, cooked in chicken stock. When cooked make a sauce from the stock. Put this sauce over the capon and decorate with ox tongue. Garnish with mushrooms and lamb sweetbreads.

Chef KERN, *S.S. Empress of Australia*,
Canadian Pacific Railway Company

River Trout en Casserole

Roll a fresh trout in butter, mix with purée of fresh mushrooms, chopped parsley, purée of pistachio nuts, and white cooking wine. Roll up in oiled paper and bake in casserole in medium oven. Serve with browned butter and boiled potatoes.

Chef KERN, *S.S. Empress of Australia*,
Canadian Pacific Railway Company

Royal Hawaiian Chicken Fricassee

Take a well cleansed chicken of two or three pounds, cut off the wings and legs. Separate thighs from legs. Cut back in two. Leave breast whole. Retain all skin. Fill a saucepan with cold water. Soak the chicken in this for one hour. Drain. Add one quart of cold water to the chicken. Add two medium onions, three whole cloves, bunch of parsley, bay leaf, thyme, salt, and pepper. Cook the chicken slowly until tender. Mix one quarter pound butter with one-quarter pound flour. Cook until light brown. Add chicken stock and the liquid of two cocoanuts. Bring to a boil. Cook slowly one-half hour. Arrange chicken in casserole. Add three egg yolks to sauce. Heat. Pour over chicken. Garnish with cooked vegetables and sprinkle grated cocoanut over whole. Serve hot.

Chef EDGARD KINA, *Royal Hawaiian Hotel*, Honolulu, Hawaii

Veal Loaf

Grind three pounds of veal and three pounds of pork. Add one loaf of bread which has been soaked in milk, two onions, and one clove of garlic chopped fine (sauté onion and garlic in butter before adding to meat). Add salt, pepper, nutmeg, and three eggs. Mix thoroughly. Mould into two loaves. Put loaves into pan. Make hollow in top of each loaf. Fill hollow with butter. Bake slowly one hour in a moderate oven. Baste often while cooking. Serve with brown sauce and vegetables.

Chef EDGARD KINA, *Royal Hawaiian Hotel*, Honolulu, Hawaii

Loin of Pork Hawaiian

Take six cutlets from the back of a young pig. Remove the bones. The cutlets should weigh about four ounces each after being trimmed and boned. Put meat into a sautéing pan. Dot with butter. Sprinkle with chopped parsley, thyme, and bay leaves. Season with salt and pepper. Pour pineapple juice and cider over the meat. Cook in a moderately hot oven fifteen minutes. Turn cutlets and cook until tender. When done drain off stock. Add one-half pint brown sauce and simmer a few minutes. Strain. Add butter and a little lemon juice. Pour sauce over meat. Serve with purée of hot alligator pear, candied sweet potatoes, and diced pineapple. Sauce may be served in a separate dish if desired.

Chef EDGARD KINA, *Royal Hawaiian Hotel*, Honolulu, Hawaii

Chicken Grenadine

Remove the skin and bones from the breasts of spring chickens. Split each breast without separating. Lay them open on a clean board. Place in a mortar veal forcemeat (two ounces finely chopped raw veal) with an egg yolk and pound to a paste. Rub through a sieve into a bowl and add salt, cayenne, grated nutmeg, and chopped truffle, adding gradually two tablespoons cream. Spread the forcemeat evenly in the breasts of chicken. Cook for five minutes sliced mushrooms in butter. Arrange the breasts in the mushroom pan, fry for four minutes, moisten with one-half cup cooking wine and cooking sherry. Cover the pan and let the mixture reduce to one-half its quantity, pour in cream, salt, cayenne. Shuffle the pan and cook. Prepare heart-shaped croutons, place breasts on top of croutons and keep warm. Serve.

Chef KINJIRO KOJIMA, *Fujiya Hotel*, Miyanoshita, Japan

Frogs Legs

6 frogs (each ¾ pounds)	2 tablespoons cooking sherry
6 mushrooms	2 tablespoons melted butter
1½ cups milk	2 tablespoons white cooking wine
Cayenne	2 yolks eggs
1½ cups fresh cream	6 pieces toast
Grated nutmeg	Salt to taste

Cut and separate fresh frogs legs. Melt butter, add the legs, season with a light sprinkling of salt and cayenne and cook for ten minutes. Pour in cooking sherry and white cooking wine and reduce. Add milk, cream, and grated nutmeg. Mix well and let boil slowly for ten minutes. Add two yolks, and a little fresh cream to the legs. Sauté mushrooms in butter and add to the frogs legs mixture. Pour over toast on the dish and sprinkle with parsley.

Chef KINJIRO KOJIMA, *Fujiya Hotel*, Miyanoshita, Japan

Greek Soup

Add to the broth of two fat pullets one-half pound of rice and let it boil for thirty minutes. Beat the yolks of eight eggs with the juice of four lemons and add to the broth. Serve hot.

Chef JEAN KRITICOS, *Hotel Grande Bretagne*, Athens, Greece

Pullet en Casserole

Cut five pullets in quarters. Chop an onion with one clove of garlic and one pound peeled tomatoes. Put the pullets in a casserole in plenty of butter and season. Pour over the pullets one cup of white wine and bake in a moderate oven one hour. Serve with baked potato and eggplant fried in oil.

Chef JEAN KRITICOS, *Hotel Grande Bretagne*, Athens, Greece

Breast of Chicken "Île de France"

Remove from the bones as many breasts of chicken as you have guests. Trim and keep in a cool place. Use the carcass of the chickens to make a rich stock.

Prepare the same number of oval pastry crusts as breasts of chicken, as many slices of fresh goose liver, and one fine truffle per guest. Set the oval crusts on a large round dish. Season the slices of goose liver with salt and pepper, dip in flour and fry till a golden color. Place the slices of liver on the crusts. Season with salt and pepper the breasts of chicken, dip them in flour and fry in butter. Put the breasts on the slices of liver. Arrange on the platter. Cover the dish and place in warm oven.

Heat in a saucepan a glass of cream, some of the chicken stock that has been reduced, and a glass of cooking wine. Simmer and pass through a fine sieve, and add a little butter after having removed it from the fire. Pour this sauce over the breasts of the chickens, and set in pyramid, in the center of the dish, the truffles.

Chef JACQUES LINDAUER, *S.S. Île de France*, French Line

Breast of Chicken "France"

Remove the meat carefully from the breast of a very tender chicken. Season with salt and paprika. Cook without browning. Reheat with a glass of cooking wine, cream, and meat stock. Lay the meat on slices of bread fried in butter. Garnish with stewed artichoke bottoms cut in quarters and cooked fresh truffles.

Chef GASTON MAGRIN, *S.S. France*, French Line

"France" Timbale

Cook a bun in a mould. Make an incision in the bun half an inch from the rim and hollow it out without touching the bottom.

Make a cover for the bun, and moisten the bun with a glass of cooking wine. Fill the cavity of the bun with fruit, put on the cover, and pour some apricot syrup over the bun. Decorate with candied fruit. Serve very cold.

Chef GASTON MAGRIN, *S.S. France*, French Line

Paté de Macaroni à la Turque

Line a baking dish with puff paste. Fill with macaroni cooked soft and a thick layer of white cheese. Then cover with puff paste and bake to a golden brown. When somewhat cool, cut in large square pieces.

Chef A. MALLE, *Pera Palace Hotel*, Constantinople, Turkey

Turkish Pilaff

Fry four small onions brown in butter. Add cup of cooked rice, fill with broth, and let boil for fifteen minutes. Vermicelli and currants may also be added. Fry in butter chicken liver, chicken, brains, or baked eggplant cut in small pieces. Any of these may be added to the rice. A little tomato purée adds piquancy.

Chef A. MALLE, *Pera Palace Hotel*, Constantinople, Turkey

"Sish Kebab"

To slices of lamb add onion, peppers chopped fine, and tomatoes. Place the slices on skewers and grill.

Chef A. MALLE, *Pera Palace Hotel*, Constantinople, Turkey

Salmon Suprême

Place the slice of salmon on herbs, soak in cooking wine twice its height. Braise gently and glaze at the last minute. Surround with forcemeat balls (small) heads of mushrooms, strips of truffles (breaded), and crabs. Serve with sauce.

Chef BAPTISTE MONNIER, *Grand Nouvel Hotel*, Lyon, France

Indian Curry

Cut up in pieces a shoulder of mutton. Let cook till half done with chopped onions, salt, and a pinch of curry powder. When the onions commence to change color, sprinkle the pieces with flour. Let this boil for a moment, then soak with one and one-half pints cocoanut milk and boil gently for one and one-half hours. Ten minutes before serving add apples. Arrange in timbales and serve at the same time a timbale of rice.

Chef BAPTISTE MONNIER, *Grand Nouvel Hotel*, Lyon, France

Fruit Cake (Grand Nouvel Hotel)

Mix in a pan two and one-half cups sugar with eighteen eggs. Heat slightly. When the paste gets thick, mix two and one-half cups flour, one and three-quarters cups butter, one-half cup powdered almonds, and the juice of two lemons. Put the mixture into buttered moulds, sprinkle with flour and bake in a moderate oven.

Cut the cake in three sheets and soak each sheet with cooking wine and fill with chopped pineapple; cover with apricots. Glaze the cake with rose fondant and place around it chopped toasted almonds. Make a decoration with slices of pineapple cut in lozenge form and candied black cherries and the inscription "Grand Nouvel Hotel."

Chef BAPTISTE MONNIER, *Grand Nouvel Hotel*, Lyon, France

Pullet with Sauce Suprême

Take a young fat pullet. Cut it up as for frying, and divide the legs in two pieces; season with salt and pepper, cook in butter without allowing it to change color and above all without letting the butter get "blackened." When the preparation is half done, sprinkle the pieces with a very finely chopped onion. When the onion has become slightly cooked, moisten with a small glass of rum extract and a good glass of white cooking wine. Let boil down to half and add two cups of fresh cream, allowing it to simmer for about fifteen minutes. Take the pieces of meat and put them on a serving platter, keeping them hot and covered. Have the following garnish prepared separately: small glazed onions, ripe mushrooms fried in butter. Potatoes in the form of large olives, which can be strewn on the chicken. Complete the sauce and cover the whole, very hot.

Finally garnish around the platter with fine crabs cooked, interspersing with small pieces of apples cut in the shape of hazel nuts and fried, just before serving, in butter. Sprinkle with a little tarragon and chopped chives then serve boiling hot.

Chef PIERRE MOREAU, *Hotel Normandy*, Deauville, France

Curried Codfish

2 slices of cod (or the remains of any cold fish)	1 tablespoon curry powder
	Salt and pepper to taste
3 ounces butter	1 cup white stock thickening
1 onion (sliced)	1 tablespoon flour
¼ pint milk	

Flake the fish and fry a nice brown color with the butter and onions. Put this into a stewpan, add the stock and thickening and let simmer for ten minutes. Stir the curry powder into the milk. Put it with the seasoning and add other ingredients. Boil for two minutes and serve with boiled rice. Serves six persons.

Chef JOHN McGUIRE, *Newfoundland Hotel*,
St. John's, Newfoundland

Asparagus Soup

2 pints of second stock or water	1 pound spinach
1 pint milk	1 ounce butter
50 asparagus heads	1 ounce flour
2 tablespoons cream	Salt and pepper to taste

Cut off the points of the asparagus and put them aside. Trim the stalks and cut them into small pieces. Wash and pick the spinach. Put the stock or water into a stewpan and when it boils add the asparagus and spinach and cook until tender (about forty minutes). Then rub through a fine sieve. Have ready a small saucepan of boiling water, put in a little salt and asparagus points and cook for ten or fifteen minutes. Melt the butter in the stewpan, sprinkle in the flour, add the milk, and stir until it boils. Then put in the stock and purée of asparagus and spinach, salt and pepper to taste and simmer gently for ten minutes. Place the asparagus points into the tureen, add the cream and necessary seasoning to the soup and serve.

Seasonable from March to July. Time of cooking one to one and one-half hours. Serves six persons.

Chef JOHN McGUIRE, *Newfoundland Hotel*,
St. John's, Newfoundland

Water Ice made from Jam

½ pound jam
2 ounces icing sugar

Juice of 1 lemon
Liquid coloring

1 pint water

Put all the ingredients together in a stewpan. Bring to a boil, skim well, and simmer gently for ten minutes. Rub through a fine sieve and add a few drops of coloring matter to brighten the color. When cold, freeze in the usual manner. Sufficient for one and one-half pints.

Chef JOHN McGUIRE, *Newfoundland Hotel*,
St. John's, Newfoundland

Rices à la Veneziana

Fry onions and ham, cook peas on a slow fire. Boil rice separately in good broth. Put the whole together and mix with butter and Parmesan cheese.

Chef ALBERTO MORA, *Hotel Vittoria*, Venice, Italy

Rice with Scallops

Sauté scallops, flavor with garlic. Boil rice separately in a good broth. Put everything together and mix with butter and Parmesan cheese.

Chef ALBERTO MORA, *Hotel Vittoria*, Venice, Italy

Macaroni with Sauce

In three quarts of boiling water cook four cups of macaroni. Boil twenty minutes. Drain. Add butter and cheese. Mix and put on a vegetable platter. Cover with sautéed chicken livers and mushrooms. Pour tomato purée over top. Serve with cheese.

Chef DON FRANCISCO MORENO, *Hotel Imperial*,
Guadalajara, Mexico

Trout Belle Meunière

First clean the trout and pass them through some flour. Then take a frying pan with a little butter. Color the trout on both sides and cook slowly. Finish with slices of tomatoes, mushroom heads, and chopped parsley.

Chef NEWHOUSE, *Gleneagles Hotel*, Perthshire, Scotland

Glazed Partridge

Truss the bird as for an entrée, roast with small glazed onions and cooked mushroom heads. Swill the pan with cooking wine, reduce, coat the partridges with the wine and gravy, cook eight minutes longer, until the game is glazed, and serve.

Chef NEWHOUSE, *Gleneagles Hotel*, Perthshire, Scotland

Pigeons à la Noël

Split in halves, flatten, fry in butter. Let cool. Coat with forcemeat and chopped truffles. Poach in oven and remove to a dish. Surround with veal sweetbreads dipped in egg, crumbed, and cooked in butter. Garnish with mushrooms and sliced fowls' livers tossed in butter with a little brown sauce added.

Chef NEWHOUSE, *Gleneagles Hotel*, Perthshire, Scotland

Grilled Chicken

Split squab chicken, broil, dress on toast, with a slice of broiled Virginia ham. Garnish with asparagus tips and soufflé potatoes. Serve with water cress and sauce.

Chef HENRI ODIAU, *Banff Springs Hotel*, Banff, Canada

Breast of Chicken with Truffles

Season the breast with paprika, sauté with slice of Virginia ham, fresh mushrooms, and butter. Moisten with heavy cream and let boil until the breast is cooked. Then remove from fire, cook down the sauce, dress the breast meat on croutons with ham and mushrooms. Serve with truffles and sauce.

Chef HENRI ODIAU, *Banff Springs Hotel*, Banff, Canada

Venison Medaillon

Take two small venison steaks and lard and season with salt and paprika. Then roast the same in butter with two slices of fresh goose liver, which has been seasoned with salt and pepper. When done place the steaks on a round platter and the goose liver on top. Top with a glazed truffle. Garnish with stewed green peppers cut in halves, the one half filled with cherries, the other half with green shell beans.

Chef JACOB PIES, *Coblenzer Hof Hotel*, Coblenz, Germany

Frascati Melon

Cut off the top of the melon and cut what is scooped out into thin slices. Soak these in cooking rum and sugar and add slices of oranges, bananas, pears, and halved peaches. Stuff the melon with this mixture, cover with a meringue mixture. Heat in the oven and serve with dry pasties.

Chef JACOB PIES, *Coblenzer Hof Hotel*, Coblenz, Germany

Rolled Fillet of Sole

Wash twenty large potatoes and bake in the oven. Cut off the top of each and hollow them out. Cut five one-half pound soles into fillets and fill the fillets with forcemeat, roll, and "poach." Then cut a pound of fresh mushrooms in slices and stew them. Mix with a spoonful of béchamel sauce and fill the potatoes with this mixture. Place the rolled soles on top. Cover the whole with sauce, which has been cooked with the béchamel and mushroom liquid. Shortly before serving, put the fish in the oven for ten minutes.

Chef JACOB PIES, *Coblenzer Hof Hotel*, Coblenz, Germany

Braised Cabbage

Wash cabbage and cook in boiling water with a little salt until tender. Then strain. Butter a small pie dish and cover the bottom with cabbage. Then add a layer of sausage meat and then another layer of cabbage. Lay small pieces of bacon on top. Sprinkle with a little butter and bake in an oven for twenty minutes.

Chef JOHN PEARSE, *S.S. Majestic*, White Star Line

Tomato, Baked

1 quart bread crumbs	1 ounce butter
4 boiled onions	1 pound sliced tomatoes
Salt and pepper to taste	½ pint milk
2 eggs	Other seasoning if desired

Mix ingredients together, place in buttered dish. Cover with bread crumbs, dot with a little melted butter, and bake.

Chef JOHN PEARSE, *S.S. Majestic*, White Star Line

Fillet of Sole Midland

Cook in sauce and cooking wine a fillet of sole. Add grilled grapes and nuts glazed. Garnish with slices of truffles and skinned grapes.

Chef JOSEPH ROELLI, *Midland Hotel*, Manchester, England

Coté of Veal

Sauté a veal cutlet. Reduce with thick brown sauce and cooking wine. Garnish with fried croquettes, banana fritters, grilled tomatoes, and straw potatoes.

Chef JOSEPH ROELLI, *Midland Hotel*, Manchester, England

Pear Délicieuse

Peel pears, remove the tips and poach in a vanilla syrup. Fill the interior with grated chocolate. Place pears on a sponge cake and cover with sauce flavored with rum extract. Decorate with sliced almonds.

Chef JOSEPH ROELLI, *Midland Hotel*, Manchester, England

Pullet Suprême

Take the best parts of the meat of three pullets. Dress them with truffles and stuff them with goose liver. Take the bodies of the pullets and put them in a stewpan and stew with butter. Moisten them with half a bottle of grape juice as well as with two and one-half cups of white stock. Add the skin of the mushrooms, a small bunch of herbs, one onion, and let boil one hour. Then with this stock prepare a smooth, velvety gravy. On the other hand, put the chicken meat in a saucepan with butter and stew. Reheat it with a glass of grape juice. Let boil down: fill up to half the height with the prepared stock; remove the meat when stewed. Arrange on a layer of finely chopped forcemeat (stuffing) of chicken prepared from the flesh of the leg. Reduce the dish with two glasses of thick cream and two glasses of cooking sherry. Add the smooth sauce which has been put on the fire to one-half pound fine butter. In the center of the chicken meat place a garnish composed of a fine forcemeat of mushrooms and truffles. In the center of the platter place a crust of bread. Cover with sauce and make a border around the platter of large flowers of puff paste.

Chef ROGET, *Hotel Imperial*, Boulogne-sur-Mer, France

Cheese Pastry

Prepare three sheets of puff paste very thin. Bake. Take the following preparation: one and one-quarter cups béchamel sauce, thin with one and one-quarter cups thick cream (whipped cream) until the same clings. Take off the fire and add three-quarter pound of good cheese, season with salt, cayenne pepper, and nutmeg; put a layer of this cheese-cream on the first sheet of puff paste, cover with the second, and put a new layer of cheese-cream on this, cover with the third sheet and put a layer of cream on top and round about. With the leavings of the puff paste make a quantity of crumbs for spreading over and around and serve very hot.

Chef ROGET, *Hotel Imperial*, Boulogne-sur-Mer, France

Fish Mignonettes

Remove the fillets from the fish and cut in six pieces. Fry in butter, season with salt and pepper. Serve on toasted bread and surround with the following garnish:

Stew a small, peeled tomato in butter. Add a layer of mushrooms and corn, then a small layer of artichokes and fresh peas in butter. Cover all with a little browned butter.

Chef ADOLPHE ROUQUIER, *Hotel Negresco*, Nice, France

Savory Soup

Fry one-quarter pound bacon in a stewpan. When very hot add two onions chopped fine. Let boil five minutes. Then add four tomatoes skinned. Add potatoes, carrots, turnips, green cabbage, fresh peas, fresh green beans. Soak in boiling water and season with salt. Let boil hard for one-half hour. Add two-thirds cup of spaghetti cut fine, and let boil twenty minutes. Add a handful of grated cheese to the soup, and serve.

Chef ADOLPHE ROUQUIER, *Hotel Negresco*, Nice, France

Rabbit Fricassée

Cut a good-sized rabbit into small pieces, season, put in a frying pan with two ounces butter, two chopped onions, and herbs, and let stew. Dust with two teaspoons flour. Put in the oven for a short time. Soak in the clear broth and let simmer for one hour. When serving, remove the pieces of rabbit, mix the gravy with four egg yolks and the juice of one lemon. Add a few whole small onions and boil. After the onions are soft, garnish with crisp slices of toast.

Chef ADOLPHE ROUQUIER, *Hotel Negresco*, Nice, France

Chicken Soup à la Turque

Brown in a saucepan a quarter of a raw chicken in one ounce butter. Add one ounce raw ham and one sliced onion. Moisten with one quart consommé and one-half pint tomato sauce. Add two tablespoons raw rice, one-half tablespoon salt, half a cut-up green pepper, and one teaspoon of diluted curry. Boil for thirty minutes and serve.

Chef A. SALKOWSKI, *S.S. Bremen*, North German Lloyd Line

Bordeaux Squabs in Compote

Singe, draw, and truss, with their legs thrust inside, six fat squabs. Lay them in a saucepan with one tablespoon butter, one onion sliced fine, and one carrot chopped fine. Season with salt, put the lid on the pan, and cook on a good fire for ten minutes. Put in a saucepan six small glazed onions, one medium-sized carrot, cut with a vegetable scoop, one ounce salt pork cut into small pieces, and six cut-up mushrooms. Moisten them with a pint of sauce, and let cook for thirty minutes. Transfer the squabs to this preparation, let cook again for five minutes. Dress the garnishing on a hot dish, arrange the squabs on top, and serve.

Chef A. SALKOWSKI, *S.S. Bremen*, North German Lloyd Line

Tenderloin of Beef à la Bernardi

Lard a four-pound piece of tenderloin with very thin pieces of fresh ham and truffles, all cut the same size. Put it in the oven to roast for thirty-five minutes, and then lay it on a dish, trimming the fillets carefully, the larded part being on the top. Pour over one-half pint of good hot madeira-flavored sauce. Garnish with the three artichoke bottoms, filled with hot macédoine, spinach, and game.

Chef A. SALKOWSKI, *S.S. Bremen*, North German Lloyd Line

Pineapple Frozen Sandwich

Cut sponge cake in triangle, slice in two, and between the slices place a layer of ice cream (vanilla or pineapple) and half a slice of preserved pineapple. Dot the surface with a little whipped cream, and powder with icing sugar.

Chef CARLO SCARABELLI, *Jasper Park Lodge*, Jasper, Canada

Beef Tenderloin Steak

Flat the beef tenderloin steak and on one side cut a cross (not too deep); fill this with finely chopped green onions, green peppers, horseradish, and butter. Season. Broil on one side and finish cooking under a salamander. Serve with potato chips.

Chef CARLO SCARABELLI, *Jasper Park Lodge*, Jasper, Canada

Vegetable Marrow

Peel and slice some young vegetable marrow. Sauté in butter, and when cooked, add some peeled and chopped tomatoes, chopped parsley, salt, and pepper. Place this stew in an "au gratin" pan, sprinkle with grated cheese, and bake.

Chef CARLO SCARABELLI, *Jasper Park Lodge*, Jasper, Canada

Orange Surprise

Cut a cover from the orange at three-quarters of its height, and scoop out the rind. Fill with orange ice and cover with meringue. Then place the oranges on cracked ice. Later put them for a second or two in a hot oven to color quickly. Place the covers on them and put on top of drawn sugar (threaded).

Chef KARL SCHNEIDER, *S.S. New York*,
Hamburg-American Line

Stephanie Omelette

Put an omelette soufflé mixture in buttered frying pan. Place in moderate oven, not hot enough to color omelette. Spread over the omelette fruit jelly, fold in omelette form, sprinkle with powdered sugar, and glaze quickly in hot oven. Do not let the mixture get too heavy.

Chef KARL SCHNEIDER, *S.S. New York*, Hamburg-American Line

Strawberries Romanoff

Crush the strawberries. Arrange them in a deep crystal dish on a layer of vanilla parfait. Decorate with bars of cream. Dot with candied violets. Serve with small cakes or cookies arranged in a sugar basket.

Chef KARL SCHNEIDER, *S.S. New York*, Hamburg-American Line

Nuts of Lamb

Fry small pieces of lamb in butter. Lay them on flat shells of puff paste mixed with goose liver. Arrange in a ring on a round platter. In the center place green asparagus tips. Cover the lamb nuts with their own broth and lay on each a slice of tomato.

Chef W. SCHULZE, *Hotel Atlantic*, Hamburg, Germany

Mutton Cutlets

Boil six potatoes in their skins and when done slice, not too thin. Fry olive rings in butter, mix with the potatoes, and form a ragout with sauce. Put this ragout in a casserole, arrange the cutlets on it after sautéeing well in butter. Pour over the cutlets the broth after reducing it one-half. Bake until done.

Chef W. SCHULZE, *Hotel Atlantic*, Hamburg, Germany

Rolls of Sole

Spread the fillets of sole out flat, fold them together, and fry in butter. Prepare a lobster American style, cut in pieces and make into a ragout with vegetables and sauce. Arrange fillets in the center of a platter and strew with cheese. Place portions of the lobster ragout about the fillets of sole and garnish with glazed potatoes.

Chef W. SCHULZE, *Hotel Atlantic*, Hamburg, Germany

Stuffed Lobster

Cook lobster. Season well with salt and paprika. Stew in cream, finish with egg yolk and glass of cooking sherry. Refill the shell with the mixture and cover with a thick sauce. Sprinkle with Parmesan cheese and glaze. Garnish when serving with slices of truffles.

Chef SIMON, *S.S. Empress of France,*
Canadian Pacific Railway Company

Salad Montclair

Remove the meat from one-half a grapefruit and fill shell with grapefruit and celery diced. Garnish with maraschino cherries. Serve with French or cream dressing.

Chef SIMON, *S.S. Empress of France,*
Canadian Pacific Railway Company

Artichokes à l'Italienne

Cut artichokes in twos or fours. Peel, remove the interior, and arrange in a stewpan with oil and half a clove of garlic. Let it stew, add two fresh tomatoes mashed and let the whole braise, until the sauce is well boiled down.

Chef A. TURC, *Hotel Excelsior*, Rome, Italy

Tomato and Rice

Take six tomatoes, cut them at the top to make a cover, scoop out the inside. Fill with rice which has been soaked in tomato juice, parsley, and garlic, and seasoned with salt and pepper. Put a good portion of this filling in each tomato, put on the cover and bake in the oven for three-quarters of an hour.

Chef A. TURC, *Hotel Excelsior*, Rome, Italy

Timbale Milanaise

Grease a charlotte mould well with butter. Cut small, rectangular pieces of bread from the inside of the loaf. Dip this in melted butter and arrange around the sides and the base of the mould. Meanwhile, cut up some apples and boil them with sugar, a little cinnamon, the rind of one-half lemon and raisins. Add a little apricot marmalade, not very juicy. Fill up the mould. Cover with a layer of the soft part of the bread. Bake three-quarters of an hour in a rather hot oven. Serve with apricot sauce.

Chef A. TURC, *Hotel Excelsior*, Rome, Italy

Tropical Salad

Place a slice of pineapple on a lettuce leaf and add a slice of tomato in the center. Around the salad arrange quarters of grapefruit and decorate with whipped cream and chopped walnuts. Serve Thousand Island dressing on the side.

Chef MAURICE VANE, *The Fort Garry Hotel*, Winnipeg, Canada

Cold Stuffed Lobster

Cut cooked lobster in the center lengthwise. Remove contents and wash the shell. Dice. Season lightly, add cocktail sauce, and refill the shell. Cover with round slices of lobster and alternate layers of red and green peppers. Garnish with lemon slices and halves of hard-boiled eggs. Fish jelly chopped fine may be used as an additional decoration.

Chef MAURICE VANE, *The Fort Garry Hotel*, Winnipeg, Canada

Soup of Veal Sweetbread

Put a veal sweetbread on the fire with one pint of water until it boils. Then let cool and cut in small dice. Steam in a casserole two small onions cut in dice, one celery cut likewise with two tablespoons fresh butter. Add to the cut sweetbread. Let the whole bake through from five to ten minutes. Pour over it three pints of broth or hot water. Cook two pounds veal bones with the above, and take the bones out after cooking one hour. Season with salt, pepper, and nutmeg. Stir two to three egg yolks with one cup sweet cream and add to the soup, stirring constantly. Serve with white bread cut in small strips and fried in butter. Serves five to ten persons.

Chef KARL VETTER, *Hotel Tyrol*, Innsbrück, Austria

Eggs with Cream Sauce

Boil hard ten eggs and let stand in cold water for eight minutes. Shell and put into hot salt water again before serving.

Cut with egg cutter in small pieces, spread in a deep dish, and pour over the following sauce:

Melt in a casserole three tablespoons butter and stir in three tablespoons flour; pour on this one pint boiling milk and cook five minutes. Season with salt and pepper and one-half pint sweet cream and one tablespoon butter, beaten while hot. Pour over the sliced eggs. Serves five or six persons.

Chef KARL VETTER, *Hotel Tyrol*, Innsbrück, Austria

Salmon and Mushrooms

Take two slices of salmon one and one-half inches thick, salt, and let stand for one-half hour. Then moisten them with a little milk, strew thickly with flour, and fry in melted butter with a little olive oil, until the backbone can be easily removed. Then prepare the following sauce:

Fifteen fresh mushrooms, clean and cut in fine pieces. Put in a pan one finely chopped onion, three tablespoons butter, and the mushrooms and fry them to a light yellow. Add one-quarter cup of sweet cream, salt, pepper, the juice of one lemon, and a little meat extract. Boil up and pour over the fish. Serves five or six persons.

Chef KARL VETTER, *Hotel Tyrol*, Innsbrück, Austria

Fried Duck

Fry slices of duck in butter. Add sauce with green peppers, chopped. Garnish with mushrooms and cucumbers.

Chef S. WEIL, *New Grand Hotel*, Yokohama, Japan

Timbales of Lobster

Cut the lobsters in pieces, parboil in butter, and add sliced mushrooms. Mix with sauce, fill timbales with the lobster, cover with bread crumbs, and bake.

Chef S. WEIL, *New Grand Hotel*, Yokohama, Japan

Suprême Salmon

Immerse the salmon in cooking wine, cover with sauce, and boil. Serve on rice, steamed and garnished with truffles. Surround with meat jelly.

Chef S. WEIL, *New Grand Hotel*, Yokohama, Japan

Fowl Sauté

Chop two onions fine. Fry in two tablespoons fat until nicely browned. Add garlic, pinch of red pepper. Cut a fowl into pieces and simmer it in the onion and garlic mixture. Add two tomatoes cut in pieces. Add one-half pint cream, to the strained gravy, and serve with boiled potatoes.

Chef JOHN ZAPPA, *Hotel Excelsior*, Belgrade, Jugoslavia

Eggplant Sauté

Cut five eggplants in pieces. Brush them in pancake paste and fry in hot oil. Chop an onion and let it take color in three tablespoons fat. Add one pound minced pork and one-quarter pound minced mutton, and season with salt and pepper.

Put in a pan first a row of eggplant and then a row of meat. Pour over it one quart milk and six egg yolks. Bake in the oven until it turns golden brown.

Chef JOHN ZAPPA, *Hotel Excelsior*, Belgrade, Jugoslavia

Roast Goose

Roast a middle-sized fat goose. Cut in pieces and put in kraut. Let it simmer slowly for an hour.

Kraut: Fry three onions in the fat of the goose and add three cabbages chopped fine. Season.

Instead of goose meat, that of turkey, a duck, or pork may be used.

Chef JOHN ZAPPA, *Hotel Excelsior*, Belgrade, Jugoslavia

SECTION IV

Cookery Technique

Containing Information On

How to Buy Food Food Equivalents

Methods of Cookery Temperatures

Weights and Measures Calories

SECTION IV

Cookery Technique

TO buy food well is a real achievement. The woman who knows how to buy economically, getting quality for her money, has solved more than half of her problem of feeding the family. Today we find that the buying of food is divided into two classes: the canned food in one and the perishable in the other. A well-run home should have a storeroom or call it stock room if you like, in which there are foods on hand at all times. This storeroom should be so arranged that the vegetables are in one place, fruit in another, and jams and jellies in a third. The jams and jellies should be labeled as to product and year made. They should be arranged so that all of one kind are together. It is well to separate the jams from the jellies.

The buying of canned fruits and vegetables for the family can be so arranged that it will be necessary to place orders for these only occasionally. A well-stocked storeroom should have in it a carefully chosen assortment of vegetables and fruit which may be used in either hot or cold combinations the whole year round. The home which has in it a storeroom full of canned foods need never worry about the unexpected. The Emergency Meal may be quickly prepared after carefully choosing foods from the shelves.

It is possible to buy sandwich fillings and cheese in cans, and these too should be stocked so as to be on hand for emergency use. A reliable grocer will gladly arrange with you to sell these canned goods in quantity lots. Cases with an assortment of fruits and vegetables may be obtained at a reasonable price.

The clever homemaker will be sure to keep her storeroom well filled, buying more of any food which needs re-stocking. When new foods are added to the storeroom, it is of vital importance that the new lot be put back of the old so that the food which has been on hand longest will be used first.

Tongue, ham, and other assorted meats may be purchased in cans to have on hand when the unexpected guest arrives.

We do not want to live on canned food alone. No matter how well stocked the storeroom in any home is, there is always a place for fresh vegetables in planning menus. With our markets today, we find it possible to feed our families fresh vegetables the year round. It is the skillful cook who will so combine her fresh foods and her canned that the family is well fed.

When purchasing foods it is advisable to buy supplies for more than one day at a time. The practical cook will plan meals for several days instead of just one. She can then easily buy all of the fresh foods that she wants on hand for these meals. It may be disastrous to buy too much perishable food at one time, unless the storage facilities in the home are excellent. Potatoes and winter vegetables, such as carrots, turnips, onions, and parsnips may be purchased in large quantities if you like, if the storage facilities for keeping these vegetables in the home are good. Spinach, lettuce, tomatoes, cauliflower, and other fresh vegetables should be purchased as needed. However, they may be kept for several days without deterioration.

Fruits should be given the same consideration as vegetables. It is possible to buy and keep apples, grape fruit, and oranges in a large quantity to have on hand when needed, but it is difficult to keep bananas and most fresh fruits and berries for longer than a few days.

Ordering groceries over the telephone may be the easiest way of doing it, but the careful cook and good homemaker does her own shopping. Markets today are so alluring that most every woman enjoys going to them to do the buying. It is this personal shopping that is of greatest value. The purchaser can see the quality of the food she is buying and then there is no cause for complaint later.

The buying of meats should be given the most careful consideration. It is possible to buy cheaper cuts occasionally and by careful cookery to serve a nourishing and appetizing meal. But whether we buy the cheaper cut or the more expensive it is necessary to give thought to the purchasing. Buying food for the family is an interesting task and is deserving of every woman's consideration.

Raw materials are made into tempting food for the family through the art of cookery. This art is a scientific one. It is a well-known fact that there is no longer any luck in cooking. Having better luck this week than last or the other way round was an excuse that was accepted at one time; but today we know so definitely the value of weight, careful measurements, and correct time for cooking that there is no longer any luck about it. If the same thing is done the same way every time, the finished product will be successful. Measuring cups, flour sifters, and measuring spoons all help in getting the quantities right. The oven control of oven thermometers checks the heat.

There is a satisfaction in knowing that food will come out right if we obey all of the rules laid down.

Garnishing, the Final Touch

Food must appeal to the appetite, and food that makes an attractive appearance is always the most tempting. Well-cooked food if served with an artistic garnish will be more easily digested and assimilated. The very simplest garnish will have a decided effect upon the appetite and is within the reach of every one. Parsley and paprika are probably the two garnishes most often used. They are contrasting colors, and the red and green always blend beautifully and fit into almost any color scheme employed. They are brilliant in color and can be eaten. Two of the chief considerations in selecting garnishes are high color and edibility. The following are excellent materials for the purpose of garnishing: parsley, paprika, chives, berries, pimentos, water cress, and radishes. Well-cooked food arranged on a platter garnished with vegetables and fruit of contrasting colors can achieve an effect lovely to look at. At heart most women are artists. Ingenious housewives will plan and serve meals that are beautiful to look at as well as nourishing and appetizing. They will discover ways of bringing out the inherent beauty of the materials at hand by combining new colors and textures.

On first thought it would seem as if there might be a lack of garnishing material during the winter months, but during the cold season parsley and chives may be grown in flower pots and kept within easy reach on the kitchen shelves. Garnishes supply flavor and relish to food. Whole cloves, slices of cucumber, capers, and highly colored canned grapes can be used in many ways and in many different combinations. Orange slices and apple rings are to be recommended as garnishings for roast meats, duck, or goose. Not only do they serve as a garnish, but they also find favor as a relish when served with the meat.

The merits of toast points, slices of tomato, slices of lemon, or whole or chopped nuts as garnishes are evident. A sprinkling of shot, either chocolate or colored, served with or without whipped cream, is a delightful garnish for salads or dessert. The final artistic touch may be given to a dish by putting a sprig of parsley on a pat of butter, or a bit of parsley on the roast and vegetables with a sprinkling of paprika on the potato and the salad.

Contrasting colors are essential in the process of garnishing. For this reason highly colored foods are best, if care is taken not to choose combinations which clash. Red and green or green and orange are effective. Some shades of red and yellow are excellent combinations. If the maxim be true that "we eat with our eyes," then in every home the garnishing of the food should be given careful attention. American homes of to-day are setting a standard of good cookery in an artistic setting and environment, so that the question of garnishing is not a matter for company meals only. This same standard of good cookery is the aim in the family meals recommended in this book. And so the plea is made that the housewife garnish every meal, even the simplest menu, for the results obtained are worth the effort.

Garnishes

The following suggestions will help in planning more elaborate garnishes than those previously mentioned:

1. Croutons in fancy shapes.
2. Cucumber rings stuffed with pimento.
3. Green pepper rings stuffed with cream cheese.
4. Radish roses.
5. Beet roses.
6. Slices of lemon rolled in chopped parsley.
7. Stuffed celery.
8. Curled celery.
9. Hearts of celery.
10. Pimento cut into fancy shapes.

11. Stuffed eggs.
12. Slices of hard-cooked egg.
13. Aspic cut in fancy shapes.
14. Pearl onions.
15. Olives (green, ripe, or stuffed).
16. Watercress.
17. Lobster claws and legs.
18. Small sweet gherkins.
19. Pickle slices.
20. Truffles.
21. Sautéed mushrooms.
22. Grated cheese.
23. Cream cheese balls rolled in ground nut meats, paprika, or topped with a half nut meat.
24. Stuffed dates or prunes.
25. Whole strawberries with the hull.
26. Whole fresh blackberries, raspberries, or seedless green grapes.
27. Maraschino cherries (red or green).
28. Marrons.
29. Jellies.
30. Sections of orange and grapefruit.
31. Pineapple rings.
32. Rolled anchovies.
33. Salted nuts.
34. Crystallized ginger.
35. Angelica.

Carving the Meat

There is a general consensus of opinion that a roast of meat or a fowl of any sort looks best if brought to the table as a whole. Although in some families the carving is done in the kitchen, the ideal host likes to carve at the table. A succulent roast, beautifully browned, a well-broiled steak or slice of fish, an artistic ham baked in brown sugar with clove covering, or a fowl done to a turn, merely by their presence on the table add to its beauty. The aroma whets the appetite and creates the proper atmosphere for the meal.

But whether the carving be done at the table or in the kitchen the knife used for the carving must be sharp. Practice makes perfect, but even the amateur may carve well if he has a knife that is sharp. Always ascertain the grain of the meat beforehand and slice against the grain. This principle holds for any kind of roast. With steak the cut is across the entire slice, so that each serving will have a part of the tenderloin included in it. Fish or a slice of ham is also cut crosswise in strips like the steak. If the serving is done at the table and the host is inexperienced in carving, it is recommended that the meat course be such that it can be served without carving. Veal birds, meat loaf, or beefsteak rolls are suggestions. If the ham is big as a whole, it is also cut in slices against the grain of the meat. A crown roast of lamb is cut between the ribs and some of the dressing from the center is then served with each cut of meat.

To carve a fowl, cut the whole leg from the body, then cut the thighs from the leg. Next cut the wings from the body. Then slice the breast against the grain. Poultry shears are a great aid in serving fowl.

When serving a fowl give each person some of the breast meat and some of the dark. Turkey is served in the same manner. Goose and duck have only dark meat.

If the meat is served from the kitchen, the slices should be so arranged on the platter that they can be easily managed in serving at the table. Garnish the meat artistically before carrying it to the table, arranging the slices conveniently on the platter for the host to serve. The slices should be not too large or unwieldy, or jagged or uneven in appearance. The host should put a sprig of parsley on each serving as a garnish for each plate. If a large platter is used for the meat, it is often convenient to have the potatoes and vegetables arranged around the slices of meat. The host may then easily serve everything and arrange the food and garnishing suitably on each plate before passing it to the guest.

Carving

These charts will be of help to you in following the recipes as to measurements and heat of cooking.

Table of Weights and Measures
Measurements should be level

2 cups	1 pint
2 pints	1 quart
4 quarts	1 gallon

16 ounces	1 pound
3 teaspoons	1 tablespoon
4 tablespoons	¼ cup
16 tablespoons	1 cup
4 cups flour	1 pound
2 cups butter	1 pound
2 cups granulated sugar	1 pound
3 cups corn meal	1 pound
3⅓ cups confectioners' sugar	1 pound
2⅔ cups brown sugar	1 pound
1 cup shelled nuts	¼ pound
16 squares chocolate	1 pound
2 cups rice	1 pound
5 cups coffee	1 pound
4 cups cocoa	1 pound
4 cups fresh grated cheese	1 pound
8 cups dry grated cheese	1 pound

1. Dry ingredients, such as flour and sugar, should be sifted before measuring.

2. Spices and soda should be crushed fine before measuring.

3. To measure one-half spoonful without measuring spoons, fill and level the spoon, divide into halves lengthwise; to measure quarter-spoonfuls divide the halves crosswise.

4. All dry ingredients are measured level but not shaken down. To get accurate portions, use a standard measuring cup with thirds and fourths indicated.

5. To measure small quantities of shortening, use a tablespoon.

6. When a recipe calls for melted shortening, measure after melting.

7. When a recipe calls for shortening melted, measure before melting.

8. Measuring spoons come in all sizes.

Oven Temperature

Degrees Fahrenheit

Very slow oven	250–300
Slow	300–350
Moderate	350
Moderately hot	375–400
Hot	400–450
Very hot	450–500

Deep-Fat Frying

Food	Temperature Degrees Fahrenheit	Time
Doughnuts	375–380	3 to 5 minutes
Fritters	375–380	3 to 5 minutes
Timbales	375	3 to 5 minutes
Vanities	375	3 to 5 minutes
Potatoes	390	5 to 8 minutes
Croquettes	375	2 minutes

In deep-fat frying the food is divided into two groups: first, uncooked, as doughnuts; second, cooked, as croquettes. In the first group, the frying should extend over a long enough period to thoroughly cook the ingredients. In the second group, the frying is intended to heat through and brown.

Puddings

Food	Temperature Degrees Fahrenheit	Time
Custards (cooked in pan of hot water)	300–325	30 to 60 minutes
Bread pudding	300–325	50 to 60 minutes
Rice pudding	300–325	50 to 60 minutes

Low temperature is required for egg cookery (custards) Cereals also require long slow cooking (rice pudding).

Soufflé

Food	Temperature Degrees Fahrenheit	Time
Cheese soufflé	325–350	60 minutes
Vanilla soufflé	325–350	60 minutes
Chocolate soufflé	325–350	60 minutes

Breads

Food	Temperature Degrees Fahrenheit	Time
Loaf of bread	425	40 to 60 minutes
Rolls	400–425	15 to 20 minutes
Baking powder biscuits	400–425	15 minutes
Nut bread	350–375	45 to 60 minutes
Baking powder muffins	375–400	20 to 25 minutes
Corn meal muffins	375–400	20 to 25 minutes
Popovers	500–550	35 to 40 minutes

Cakes

Food	Temperature Degrees Fahrenheit	Time
Angel cake	275–350	60 minutes
Sponge cake	275–350	60 minutes
Layer (yellow or white)	350	25 to 30 minutes
Layer (chocolate)	325–350	25 to 30 minutes
Loaf	275–350	60 to 80 minutes
Cup cakes	350	15 to 25 minutes
Brownies	350	25 to 30 minutes
Gingerbread	350	20 to 30 minutes
Cookies	375–400	10 to 15 minutes
Jelly roll	350	20 to 25 minutes

The most common cake failures can be attributed to baking at too high a temperature. The best results will be obtained by following the temperature chart closely, using the lower temperature rather than the higher.

Pastry

Food	Time Minutes	Degrees Fahrenheit Start	Increase to	Decrease to
Apple pie	50	450	...	350
Apple pan dowdy	45 to 50	450	...	325
Double crust	45	450	...	350
Single crust (custard)	50 to 60	450	...	300
Deep fruit pies (without bottom crust)	30	450	...	350

Pastry Making

1. The ingredients and utensils should be well chilled.
2. Have the proper proportions of fat to flour; three to one.
3. Cut in shortening not too fine.
4. Add water gradually until dough forms ball.
5. Roll lightly without adding too much flour.
6. Bake according to temperature given on chart.
7. Meringue for pies — 300 degrees Fahrenheit for 15 to 20 minutes.
8. Bake tart shells on inverted muffin tins.

Meats—Roasting

Food	Minutes per pound	Degrees Fahrenheit Start	Increase to	Decrease to
Meat, average	20	450	...	350
Sirloin or rib roast (rare)	10	450	...	400
(well done)	15–20	450	...	400
Leg of mutton (well done)	25	450	...	400
Lamb (well done)	20	450	...	400
Veal (well done)	20–25	450	...	400
Pork (well done)	25–30	450	...	400
Fowl	20	425	...	350
Turkey	20	425	...	350
Meat loaf	15	350	400	...
Pot roast	40–45	350	400	...
Ham (baked)	30–40	350	400	...
Fish	15–20	350	...	...

The juiciness of roasts and steaks depends on cooking. The natural juices of the meat must be kept in; therefore first sear the meat by intense heat. Lower the heat to finish cooking. The amount of time varies from 10 to 45 minutes per pound depending on the kind of meat and the size of the roast and whether or not it is to be served rare or well done. Mutton, veal, lamb, and pork should never be served underdone. They require long cooking.

Broiling is the process of cooking the meat under direct heat. The meat should be quickly seared over, reducing the heat after the meat has browned. Meat must be turned to brown both sides.

Broiling

Food	Time
Steak — 1 inch thick	4 to 10 minutes
Steak — 1½ inches thick (rare)	10 minutes
(medium done)	15 minutes
(well done)	20 minutes
Lamb or mutton chops	15 to 20 minutes
Chicken	20 minutes
Shad	18 to 20 minutes
Fish, slices	15 to 20 minutes
Bacon (low flame)	10 minutes
Lobster	20 minutes

Meats and Vegetables—Boiling

Food	Time of cooking
Asparagus	25 to 30 minutes
Beans (shell, string, or snap)	60 minutes
Beets, young	50 minutes
Beets, old	3 to 4 hours
Beet greens	40 to 45 minutes
Broccoli	45 to 50 minutes
Brussels sprouts	25 to 30 minutes
Cabbage	20 to 30 minutes
Carrots	60 minutes
Cauliflower	20 to 30 minutes
Celery	35 to 45 minutes
Corn	15 to 20 minutes
Chicken (5 pounds)	1 to 1¾ hours
Corned meats	4 to 6 hours
Dandelion greens	45 to 50 minutes
Ham — 12 to 14 pounds	4 to 5 hours
Lobster	20 to 25 minutes
Onions	50 to 60 minutes
Parsnips	15 to 20 minutes
Peas	15 to 20 minutes
Potatoes	20 to 25 minutes
Macaroni	25 to 30 minutes
Spaghetti	25 to 30 minutes
Tongue	3 to 4 hours
Rice	25 to 35 minutes
Sauerkraut	2 to 2¼ hours
Spinach	20 to 25 minutes
Squash	30 to 35 minutes
Swiss chard	30 to 35 minutes
Tomatoes (stewed)	15 to 20 minutes
Turnips	35 to 45 minutes

Eggs

Hard-cooked eggs	10 to 15 minutes
Soft-cooked eggs	2 to 4 minutes

Some Food Values and Measures

Food	Household Measure	Calories
Soda biscuit	1 biscuit	27
Bread	1 slice	84
Toast (dry)	1 slice	84

Muffins	*Household Measure*	*Calories*
Graham	1 muffin	130
Twin Mountain	1 muffin	150

Dairy Products

Butter	2 level tablespoons . .	225
Butter	1 level tablespoon . .	117
Butter	1 level teaspoon . . .	45
Cottage cheese	1 rounded tablespoon .	29
Cream cheese	little over ⅓ cheese .	131
Cream 20%	16 tablespoons or 1 cup	496
Skim milk	1 glass	89
Whole milk	1 glass	152
Buttermilk	1 glass	77.9
Egg (whole)	1 egg	78
Egg (scrambled)	1 egg (1 teaspoon butter)	123

Fish

Cod, haddock	1 large serving	72
Shad, salmon	1 large serving	192

Fruit

Apple 15%	1 large apple	100
Banana 20%	1 large banana	120
Grapefruit 5%	½ medium size	40
Peach 10%	1 medium size	50
Prunes 20%	5 large prunes	136

Meat

Bacon	6 crisp strips (thin) .	155
Chicken	medium serving . . .	118
Lean meat	medium serving . . .	154

Soups

Canned tomato soup (un-diluted — 10% vegetable)	½ cup	50
Plain broth	1 cup	10
Bouillon	1 cup	0
Vegetable soup (canned) .	1 cup	30

Vegetables

Potato	1 medium size	112
Vegetable 5%	1 sauce dish	20
Vegetable 10%	1 sauce dish	34

Carbohydrate content of Vegetables (fresh or canned)

5%		10%
Lettuce	Tomatoes	String beans
Cucumbers	Brussels sprouts	Pumpkin
Spinach	Water cress	Turnip
Asparagus	Sea kale	Kohl-rabi
Rhubarb	Okra	Squash
Endive	Cauliflower	Beets
Marrow	Egg plant	Carrots
Sorrel	Cabbage	Onions
Sauerkraut	Radishes	Green peas (very young)
Beet greens	Leeks	
Dandelions	String beans (very young)	
Swiss chard	Broccoli	
Celery	French artichokes	
Mushrooms		
	Peppers	
	Tomatoes	

Vegetables (fresh or canned)

15%	20%
Green peas	Potatoes
Jerusalem artichokes	Shell beans
Parsnips	Baked beans
Lima beans (very young)	Green corn
	Boiled rice
	Boiled macaroni

Fruits (fresh)

10%	15%	20%
Strawberries	Raspberries	Plums
Lemons	Currants	Bananas
Cranberries	Apricots	Prunes
Peaches	Pears	
Pineapple	Apples	
Blackberries	Blueberries	
Oranges	Cherries	

Helps in Cookery

1. Grease dish in which chocolate is to be melted.

2. Grease cup in which molasses is to be measured.

3. Two tablespoons of lemon juice added to 1 cup sweet milk will sour it immediately.

4. Celery leaves dried and added to soup will improve the flavor.

5. To skin tomatoes quickly hold over flame until skin cracks.

6. Parsley and chives may be had the year round for garnish by growing them in flower pots.

7. Scissors dipped in water or flour facilitates the cutting of marshmallows.

8. Cream butter before using it to spread sandwiches.

9. Bread twenty-four hours old will cut best for sandwiches.

10. Heat milk before adding it to mashed potatoes.

11. Cookie mixture, cheese wafers, and pastry are easier to work with and less flour will be needed to roll if chilled before rolling.

12. Too sweet a mixture will not freeze.

13. The coating of the spoon is the best test for boiled custard.

14. Keep on hand for home use quart jars of French dressing, mayonnaise dressing, and boiled dressing. Having these ready facilitates the serving of salads.

15. A clove of garlic added to French dressing adds a delicious flavor.

16. Remove the outer leaves from a head of lettuce. Cut out the core. Leave as a head, hold under cold water faucet, drain. Wrap in damp cloth or lettuce bag and keep on ice. Unpeel leaves from heart of lettuce as needed.

17. Prepare lettuce as given before. Put in covered glass or enamel dish if automatic refrigerator is used.

18. Break off long stems from parsley. Wash parsley. Drain. Put in damp cloth or bag and keep on ice.

19. Prepare parsley as given above. Put in covered glass or enamel dish if automatic refrigerator is used.

20. It is important that everything for salads be cold, clean, and crisp.

21. Do not mix salads until they are ready to serve.

22. An equal quantity of whipped cream added to salad dressing gives a smoother and better tasting product.

23. Keep milk and cream bottles capped all the time.

24. Keep butter in a covered dish.

25. Keep candles in a cold place until needed.

26. Save the paraffin from jelly and jam glasses. Wash and dry. This can be used again.

27. A little cornstarch or a few kernels of rice added to the salt in the shaker will keep it from getting too moist during damp weather.

28. Do not grease an angel food tin.

29. Do not grease a sponge cake tin.

30. All measurements should be level.

31. Keep a brush in the kitchen to clean the toaster with.

32. Rinse the pan with cold water before using it to scald milk. It will prevent milk from sticking.

33. Use a pastry cloth rather than a moulding board when making pastry.

34. Left-over bread dried and put through a meat grinder will furnish bread crumbs for all occasions.

35. A soap shaker will help use up odd ends of soap.

36. A soap shaker will prevent soap sticking to silver while it is being washed.

37. A scissors is necessary to complete kitchen equipment.

38. A food knife sharpener should be in every kitchen.

39. Canned foods should not be stored in a damp place.

40. A good can opener is an asset.

41. Parsley may be cut fine and dried, then saved for use during seasons when it is hard to obtain it.

42. Rinse mould with cold water before putting gelatine into it.

43. Chopped onion put into cold water several hours before using greatly improves the flavor.

44. Water should be boiling and salted before rice, noodles, macaroni, or sphagetti are added.

45. Baking powder biscuits may be made and prepared for the oven several hours before needed, if automatic refrigeration is used.

46. To test a baked custard insert knife. If it comes out clean, custard is done.

47. Dip knife in hot water before cutting meringue.

48. An oven thermometer will insure good results if the stove used has no automatic control.

49. A thermometer is invaluable in deep fat frying.

50. A double boiler is advocated when long, slow cooking is desired.

51. Beating cocoa with a rotary egg beater prevents scum from forming over the top.

52. Tea should never be boiled.

53. Coffee should never be boiled after it has been made.

54. A syrup made by boiling sugar with water is the best means of sweetening fruit punches, or frozen desserts.

55. Salad dressing may be used to spread the bread for sandwiches instead of butter if desired.

56. Butter should be kept in a covered refrigerator dish.

57. Left-over foods should be kept in covered refrigerator dishes.

58. Cucumber, sliced and put into ice water for an hour or two, will crisp nicely for salad use.

59. Do not cut foods for salads too fine.

60. Time and energy will be saved in preparing breakfast if fruit, such as orange juice, is prepared the day before.

61. Wipe apples before serving.

62. Fresh fruit should be washed before serving.

63. Nuts are best purchased in the shell.

64. Do not keep large quantities of perishable foods on hand.

65. Bananas, peaches, apples, or pears should not be peeled until ready to use. They will discolor if exposed to the air.

66. Do not cut cake until it cools.

67. Sponge, angel, and sunshine cakes should hang cold in the tin before removing carefully with a spatula.

SECTION V
Index

INDEX

(Continued on Page 379)